162

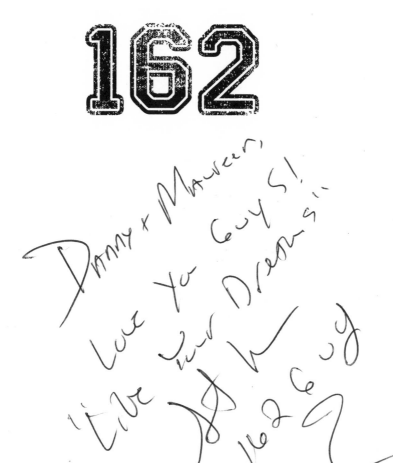

Danny + Maureen,
Love You Guy S!
"Live Your Dreams"
JW
162 Guy

162

The Almost Epic Journey of a Yankees Superfan

STEVE MELIA

With
PAUL BRAOUDAKIS

www.162yankeegames.com

Edited by Paul Braoudakis
Cover Design by Jayce Schmidt
Published by 162 Productions

ISBN

Printed in the United States of America.

I dedicate 162 to the memory of
Danny Taylor, Dan Eaton, and my dad, Daniel F. Melia

CONTENTS

Foreword i

Prologue iv

Introduction 1

The Wind-Up 9

Take Me Out to the Ball Game 17

The Law of the Inner Circle 33

You're an Idiot 47

Play Ball! 57

Have a Good Gay, Gays 73

Motor City Madness 95

The End of the World as We Know it 109

Go West, Young Man 131

Melia, Party of One 163

Halftime 187

You Can't Quit Now 213

Good Night, Buddy 243

Shut the Front Door 277

162! 309

The Dash 337

Epilogue 361

Acknowledgments 367

FOREWORD

There aren't a lot of fans who have been able to attend all 162 games in one season for a professional baseball team. For the New York Yankees, there are only five people I know of who have managed to accomplish this task. Four of them (including myself) did it as part of a reality show on the Yankees Entertainment and Sports (YES) Network in 2005. The other is Steve Melia.

For me, 162 games was a blast. As part of the cast for the Emmy-winning first season of YES's Ultimate Road Trip I enjoyed seeing new ballparks, meeting fans in different cities, and of course, all of the baseball. However, it's important to note, that all of the logistics for my trip were planned in production meetings. Every flight, rental car, hotel room, and game ticket was booked for us by the network. The cast of the show never needed to scalp a ticket or crash on a couch in a strange city.

Having been through the rigors of travel (let's face it, attending the games is the "easy" part of the task), I am in awe of Steve's dedication to attend all 162 games. Cross-country flights are not only draining on your wallet, but they take a physical toll as well. Sure, the players do it, but their travel is pampered and they have no other job than to be ready to play. For a "real life" person, all of the plane trips and car rides are an added hurdle.

Tickets to games in particular cities can be really tough to come by. For example, Opening Day in 2005 was at Fenway Park. Every Red Sox fan in the state of

i

Massachusetts wanted to attend that game. (Did I mention it was the first time since 1918 that the Sox were raising a World Championship banner in Fenway?) In the middle of Red Sox nation were four hard-core Yankees fans, definitely in the minority. At home, we had our own set of season tickets, so we never had to worry about ducats. For Steve, it was quite the opposite. As you will discover, finding tickets to premium games was not always easy. In fact, that is how the two of us came to meet. Steve was looking for a ticket one night to keep his streak alive, and a friendship was born. I was happy to always keep Steve in the loop when I had extra tickets because I was amazed at his dedication to hit all 162 games.

It's so easy to give up at so many points during the summer. Late flights, long car rides, and lack of food and sleep are all easy excuses to pack it in a miss a game. Heck, I was on a television show that covered all of that stuff for me and *I* considered giving up at one point! But we stuck through it, and now I look back on that year as a badge of honor.

Oh, you went to a Yankees game? That's great. I went to ALL of them!

It's takes a tremendous amount of time, money, patience, and dedication to accomplish an entire season of baseball, and I know there are thousands of fans who will live vicariously through this story.

Vinny Milano
aka. Bald Vinny

PROLOGUE

April 19, 1994
Tribeca, New York City

I am overlooking the Hudson River in my older brother's 1982 Pontiac. I'm 24 years old sitting in the passenger seat next to my oldest brother, Mike, who is 18 years my elder.

We have a lot in common. We are both broke and sick and tired of living that way. Mike has four kids and some serious college tuition staring him in the face. His marriage is such that we had to leave the loft just to have this meeting. Mike didn't want his wife, Judy, to get wind of the fact that we were starting a business.

I'm living in New Jersey with my sister, serving as her nanny and the neighborhood dog walker.

Mike and I can both be lazy, yet both of us also have an insatiable drive to succeed. We both feel like we are not living up to our potentials. My self-esteem has taken a huge hit.

I've heard some call it the *Day of Disgust*. I've heard others call it the day that you turns your life around. Whatever you call it, this is *our* day. We decide to change our circumstances and create some positive results.

We wrote a mission statement that day. If we are going to start a business, it had to satisfy three criteria: 1) Unlimited income potential 2) The ability to make a difference, and 3) It has to be fun.

Today, on a handshake, we outlined a plan that would do all three.

We became known as The Melia Brothers, and success followed fast and furious.

Fast Forward.

Seventeen years later, I'm sitting in a car once again. It's packed to the seams. Every square inch in the front and back seats is spoken for. The floors as well as the trunk were also filled to capacity. This resembled a scene straight out of *Sanford and Son*, the '70s hit TV show about a couple of junk yard haulers. Because of the large pieces of furniture in the back seat, as well as the mountain of personal junk on my passenger seat, the only functional mirror in my car was the exterior driver's side mirror. And I couldn't take my eyes off of it.

Perfectly centered, and growing smaller and smaller as my car inched forward, was the home I had shared with my wife, Kim, for the past nine years. It was a home filled with love, hope, promises, and some of the most exciting days of our lives.

And now I was leaving it for the last time.

Life has a funny way of teaching us what we can and cannot direct. Learning to discern the difference, and knowing when to seize a grander opportunity, can make all the difference between a life of regret and a life of experiential fulfillment. The way I see it, it always comes down to a personal choice: We can let the circumstances of our lives shape and define us, or we can shape and define *them*.

In that split second, I chose the latter. And it began one of the grandest adventures of my life.

As my home, my marriage, and all the dreams that went along with them grew smaller in the mirror, one dream was slowly fading.

But another was just starting to come to life.

INTRODUCTION

My mission was simple. I had a dream to attend every New York Yankees game in one season. This is the kind of dream that people often speak of but never actually realize. You can categorize it as more of a fantasy — something you'd love to do someday if all the planets lined up, but in all likelihood would end up in the scrap yard of dreams that most of us sadly drag into our graves. But I didn't want to be *that* guy. I knew this was within the realm of possibilities and if it were to happen, I — not the circumstances surrounding my life — would have to make it happen.

I tossed and turned in bed for weeks thinking about fulfilling this childhood dream. It had come to the point that this was all I thought about. It was less than two months before the start of the 2011 season. There were so many concerns and obstacles to identify and overcome.

I knew that my decision was not going to make everyone happy. My friend, mentor, and author of *The Slight Edge*, Jeff Olson, once shared with me a life-changing article about funerals. It stated that the average number of people who actually cry at a funeral is between 5-10. So many of us live our lives to please others. Chances are these will not be the ones crying or even in attendance during our life celebration. The article goes on to say that the biggest determining factor in whether someone goes to the burial is the weather. The weather! More than 50 percent will duck out of line if it is raining. Imagine that. We make thousands and thousands of decisions, often with the goal of pleasing others. And how do they honor us in return? Half of them head for the diner instead of the cemetery.

For several years I have been recommended to read the *New York Times* best-selling *The 4-Hour Workweek.* I picked it up in January of 2011 and was immediately blown away. The author, Timothy Ferris, had designed a lifestyle that was exciting, fulfilling, and most importantly, designed by him. He talked about the fact that most people plan and save to do things in the future when they retire. How does that usually end up? You find out that your body can't do the things it once did, you have a hard time traveling, your Social Security check isn't exactly funding the lifestyle of your dreams, and life snuck up on you just a little quicker than you thought. Ferris instructs his readers to design a way to do the things that matter to them *now*. He opens the book by recounting his ballroom dancing finals in Prague. He had never even attempted ballroom dancing two years prior. I knew that I was reading his book for a reason. The message I got was to enjoy life now. The problem with *someday* is that it usually never comes.

I also read that, on average, we live 28,000 days. I can attest that they go by fast. I hopefully have at least 14,000 left and plan on making them as meaningful and full of significant life experiences as possible. Every day counts. What is going to stop me? Only me.

CLEARING THE BASES

It is important to identify obstacles in advance.

The 2011 Yankees season would begin March 31 and would be over on September 28. I had identified five things that were really important to me between those dates. One was my niece Maryanne's wedding and four conventions for my business. I am an integral part of these events and have hundreds of my sales associates who attend. Normally these are non-negotiable events.

I also had a few major life situations percolating at the same time. I share these personal things because most people might use these as reasons *not* to do something that might ordinarily produce passion in them. There will always be temptation to let fear steal a dream.

Obstacle #1: The Breakup

In August of 2010, my wife Kim and I decided to separate after nine years of marriage. Like most, we never wanted to become a statistic. We had every intention of staying together the rest of our lives. I remember that day vividly as we sat on our couch and both admitted that we were not happy and cried our eyes out. As she cried that day, she thanked me for helping change her life and being where she is today. She also told me that it was bad enough losing a husband, she didn't want to lose her best friend. Those were two of the nicest things that anyone has ever said to me. It says a lot about her. Kim and I have been best friends since we met in 1998 and we both promised to stay that way. She's a very powerful business woman, motivational speaker, and yoga instructor, and she capably heads up our family foundation that raises money for underprivileged children all over the world. We have worked together as partners since we were married and decided that we would continue to be business partners. In September 2010, at age 40, I moved out and was able to get a six month lease on an apartment in downtown Wilmington, NC.

Obstacle #2: My Dad

The second major life situation centered around my father. I am the youngest of seven born in an Irish Catholic family in Long Island, New York. Our family is very tight. My dad was living down in Sebastian, Florida where he retired 33 years ago as a battalion chief in the New York Fire Department. At age 86, he had been on dialysis for six years. Naturally, he hated it. I think he was doing it more for us than for himself. We lost our mom six years prior, and I did my best to visit my dad as often as possible.

On New Year's Eve, he took a fall and for the first two months of 2011 he was in and out of the hospital and rehab. It had been very difficult for him. His will to live and keep fighting was fading as the grind of daily living was becoming more insurmountable.

My oldest brother and other business partner is Mike. He is 18 years older than me and my mom attended his high school graduation while she was pregnant with me. I was born the next day. He thinks that I've been upstaging him ever since. We have been business partners and best friends since April of 1994. He is a big part of my life.

Mike has lived down in Sebastian for five years taking on the role as primary caregiver. One of the reasons that Mike and I get along so well is that he's always been a bit of a rebel. In 1976, he opened up Rising Tide Natural Foods on the North Shore of Long Island. Along with his wife, Melanie, he turned a $5,000 investment into a business that still generates millions of dollars annually in revenues. He has had many ups and downs as an entrepreneur. My dad had always been a lot more conservative and traditional. For years, Mike had been the self-admitted black sheep of the family. Watching the two of them get along and develop into great friends had been amazing and is part of the great circle of life.

Obstacle #3: The Cost

Can I afford to attend all 162 games? I think so.

In 1994, Mike and I became business partners in his personal achievement seminar company and joined a network marketing company called The People's Network (TPN). The founder and CEO was the aforementioned Jeff Olson. Jeff is a stud in the industry and we eventually became two of his best students. We began to do well and focused all of our efforts in building a TPN business. Our product was personal development television over satellite. I was 24 and Mike was 42, and we became affectionately known as "the brothers."

By 1998 TPN was in financial trouble. It never saw its fourth birthday. Upon showing up to our convention in Dallas, we were informed that TPN had been purchased by some company called Pre-Paid Legal Services. Mike and I were very resistant to migrating over because of our love for our old company and what we were doing through it. We felt like we had lined up our purpose with our making a living. We liked being in the business of personal development and were not so quick to buy into some new company that came along and bought us out. We took a few days to calm down and look at the company with level heads.

What we found was a company with a strong product, a 27-year track record of success, and what seemed to be a lot ordinary folks earning extraordinary incomes. In a nutshell, PPL gave people all across North America access to the best law firms in the country for pennies on the dollar. For a nominal monthly fee, people could have access to legal help that had been typically reserved for high net worth individuals and companies. The Founder and CEO was a man named Harland Stonecipher, who had a reputation as a tough businessman with a huge heart. Stonecipher founded the company in 1972 and adopted the network marketing model in the mid-'80s.

Network marketing is one of the few industries that allows average people to start their own businesses with a modest startup fee and, with some sweat equity, build a very large income-producing business. It is also a very smart way to distribute a product, good, or service.

Network marketing is also a very misunderstood industry that is often referred to as a "pyramid" or "one of those things." For us it was *one of those things* that helped us achieve financial independence.

We have been able to generate well over $250,000 per year in commissions in each of our first 12 years. Our income is not based solely on what we do, but rather on the production of the team that we have built. This is what attracted us to the industry. We have figured out a way to gain leverage. As I consider the idea of attending 162 Yankees games, I know that our sales associates will continue to work and earn income, which, in turn, we would override. As long as I don't distract them, the cash flow is there.

One thing that Ferris points out in his book is that you do not have to be a millionaire to live like one. With or without me, our business will continue to produce. Ferris said that to live the life that you want now, you need a steady predictable income. I have mine.

NO JOKING MATTER

I remember sitting in front of *The Tonight Show* starring Johnny Carson when I was 12 years old laughing uncontrollably and I remember wanting to make people laugh like Johnny did. I first tried stand-up comedy after college for a few months. I loved the experience, but I had tremendous stage fright. At 23, I let fear stop me from doing something I loved. Although I went on to have a successful career in marketing and speaking, my failure in comedy was never far from my mind. Like many people, I would watch Comedy Central and mumble to myself that I was funnier than the featured comic.

As I became a speaker and trainer, I was able to use my humor as a tool to keep my audience's attention. I was often encouraged by audience members to get back into stand-up. Every New Year's Eve, quitting stand-up comedy was the one thing that would eat away at me.

In November of 2008, I fought through the fear and jumped back into the art that always fascinated me. When I approached Kim, she said, "Why don't you stop talking and do something about it?" I sought her blessing, but what I got was a challenge.

On November 15, 2008, I packed my living room with 25 family and friends. I busted out my karaoke machine that came complete with a microphone and an amp. I did about 12 minutes and my dream was alive again.

UNCHARTERED WATERS

In late January 2011, I stepped off a cruise ship in Miami in which 350 of our top sales associates cruised to the Bahamas. It was a long and exhausting weekend. I called the Pre-Paid Legal home office to check on some end of the month sales. Tiffany Layton, a good friend and loyal employee, answered.

"Steve, have you heard about the merger?"

"Nope," I mumbled, as I was still groggy from the three days of partying.

"Well, there was a press release issued this morning. You should go read it."

My heart sank as questions with no answers danced through my head. What did all of this mean? Were they going to change things? Were we all going to be "out of a job?" How was this going to change the substantial cash flow that we had so fastidiously worked on achieving for the past 12 years? Now what?

A few of my top producers were in the car with me, so I appeared to be confident and keep things together. Harland Stonecipher had recently retired. When we started, he was already in his 60s and a question that was always whispered behind closed doors was, "What is going to happen when Stonecipher retires?" He was the figurehead, the visionary, and most certainly the decision maker.

I didn't learn a lot that day except that MidOcean Partners, a $3 billion private equity firm out of New York City, was purchasing the company stock for a reported $651 million. They are serious players.

With the future of my marriage, my business, and my father all unknown, and with my passion for baseball and comedy at an all-time high, there was only one thing to do.

Get ready for the baseball season.

Chapter One

THE WIND -UP

NOTE: *From this point forward, the book's tone, or point of view, will shift to present tense, as I'd like the reader to experience the journey much as I lived it — as a day-to-day journaling adventure.*

Saturday, February 18, 2011

I am in downtown Wilmington, North Carolina, and there are less than five weeks until Opening Day of the 2011 MLB season. I feel like the days are slipping by. If I don't make a decision soon, I probably won't be doing this. It is a crisp Friday night and I am hanging out with another comic, actor, and budding film producer, Tim Boissey.

I met Tim at Nutt Street Comedy Club here in Wilmington. Tim has produced two independent short films, and making movies is his passion. He recently produced a short called "Firearm." It was my first job as an extra, where I got to see firsthand a movie being made. I don't think the movie will ever be a screaming success, but it allowed me to catch a glimpse of his ability to produce, work with a team, and have a front row to his undeniable work ethic.

Although I respect every comic that has the balls to get on stage, many comics are not very motivated. It sort of comes with the territory. Tim is the exception to the rule.

As I sit on Tim's couch sharing a couple of beers, I tell him that I have a crazy idea that I'd like to run by him. I have absolutely no intention of enlisting Tim in the project. I simply want to see what kind of equipment I might need to film this little adventure. Tim nods as I lay out my vision for the tour. The idea is to hit comedy clubs in the 15 major cities while attending 162 games and filming the entire experience. It is here on the couch that we construct the idea for *162: The Movie*. Within minutes, Tim is as excited as I am.

"Dude, this could be huge!"

"Let me know if you are interested."

"I'm in. I just need to talk to Rhonda." Rhonda and Tim are very recent newlyweds.

"Well, let's sleep on it."

Things are starting to come together. But I've talked about doing something like this for the past three seasons. How is this year going to be any different?

Monday, February 21

I am in a very high-spirited meeting with the executives of MidOcean Partners at The DFW Hyatt in Dallas, Texas. Today is about our future.

Kim and I are pre-occupied with our first public appearance as a "separated couple." We are both strong individuals, but this is tough. We have been separated now for almost six months, but this is the first time that we would be around our business colleagues. My dad was right when he observed, "People don't sit around and think about you as much as you think they do, if at all." He is right.

To be invited to this meeting, you had to be earning more than $250,000 per year. There are about 20 businesses represented. They are there thinking about *their* futures, not the future of my marriage.

Mike is there, too. And, clearly, his mind is on my dad who has recently taken a second spill and is in physical rehab again. Mike has been visiting him two to three times a day. He left my dad's hospital bed to be at this monumental meeting.

The MidOcean Partners have the floor as they share their vision and assure us that we will continue to be a huge part of the company. As independent associates, we all own our individual books of business. The Melia Family, as we're referred to, has been one of the top 10 money earners in PPL for a solid decade. Like everyone else in the room, we have a lot to lose … or if what MidOcean is telling us is true, a lot to *gain*.

One of the individuals seated in the back of the room is my friend and mentor Jeff Olson. Jeff serves as a member of the Corporate Marketing Team and is largely responsible for the company's growth in recent years. I've known him since 1994 and he is the reason that we are with PPL. We often say that whatever company Jeff is with is the one that we will be with. In recent years he has been primarily living a retired lifestyle and comes out to speak at company events once per month.

The Melias regard his perspective on MidOcean and the merger very seriously. We are continually, but subtlety, turning around to see his reactions to the meeting. He doesn't give us much.

The sales associates sit classroom-style. I sit in the middle with Kim on my right and Mike on my left. We think it is important to show our solidarity.

MidOcean announces that Rip Mason is the CEO-designate when the sale goes through in July. There is some tension in the air as the current CEO, Mark Brown is in the room. We have spoken with Rip on conference calls, but this is our first time meeting face to face. He certainly is smooth. He seems like he understands our concerns and he paints a bright future for our company. The underlying message is that they didn't invest $651 million to fail. They go over some numbers and speak of plans to run the company into the billions annually. In 2010, the company revenue was $450 million. Our income was a little over $500,000. We definitely have a lot to lose or gain.

Our goal is to always grow at the same rate as the company. If they rocket to $3 billion then our income should go to $3 million. These are all great things, but my mind can't stop thinking about the 162 idea. With all these big numbers on the table, my mind is drifting to "What will Fenway be like? Can I really do this? How many beers can I afford?"

I have been talking about doing all 162 games since I saw commercials for the YES Network's Ultimate Fan back in 2005. I only had the MLB package, not the YES Network, so I had never actually watched the show. My partners know that I really want to do this and they both know me better than anyone. I'm sure that they don't think I am crazy enough to pull this off. Whenever they speak of business plans for 2011, I try to point out that I may be at a game. They usually brush it off with a look that says, "Let's be serious and get back to work."

Towards the end of the meeting, the Q&A session begins. Rip Mason says something that flips the final switch in my mind. It is the very moment in the business meeting that I make a declarative statement to myself:

"I will be attending all 162 New York Yankees games in 2011."

He simply states that it is going to take them a good six or seven months to be ready to relaunch the new company. "Give us some time to get things right. We should be firing on all cylinders by our fall convention in September."

The light goes on for me. A baseball season lasts six months. My lease is up on my new apartment at the end of March. I make up my mind that day. I am jumping on the inside. Everyone leaves that meeting in Dallas with a renewed sense of enthusiasm. I, though, have an extra bounce in my step. My dream is going to come true.

I see Jeff's ex-wife, Renee Olson, after the meeting. She is friends with many of the top associates and is there to hang out as she lives in Dallas. Renee had spent hours and a lot of energy trying to talk me out of separating with Kim. I have always valued her friendship and opinion.

I pull Renee away from the group in the bar lobby. I ask her what she thinks of me attending all 162 games. She is more than encouraging. "Steve, if you don't do it now, when will you ever do it?"

Renee and I go back 17 years and I appreciate and welcome her advice. I ask her not to tell Jeff until I have a chance to tell him. Jeff is truly the one person whom I look up to in business and I want him to hear it directly from me. I am nervous that he will say that it is dumb or tell me to hold off and wait for a better time.

At the time I don't realize that maybe she had an ulterior motive.

Tuesday, Feb. 22

Tim Boissey and I are meeting at the Eat Spot, a restaurant in downtown Wilmington. We walk up to the street corner at exactly the same time. A good sign, I think. I always find people who are on time to be reliable.

We move to a table and I break out a notebook. My main objective is to find out if Tim is serious about coming with me. The waitress comes over and we order our drinks and tell her that we will be there for a while.

Before we even start talking logistics, Tim declares, "I talked to Rhonda. I'm in, we are both excited." Tim shares that he is in the middle of his final semester at Cape Fear Community College and he is scheduled to graduate in May. He is willing to put that off. He doesn't seem that concerned.

I walk through the rigorous 162-game schedule that spans 15 cities in six months and tell him a little bit about my cash-flow. Tim works at Front Street Brewery and doesn't need to replace a lot of income, but he does need to help Rhonda out with the rent. She is the head bartender at the brewery. We talk about living on a budget. He is on board and willing to endure any short term sacrifices for the project.

He is focused, alert, and excited. There is a buzz in the air.

His job will be to be in charge of all the production for our independent movie. We discuss everything from opening shots to a weekly show that we will produce from the road. We discuss what kind of cameras, audio, and other gear is needed. The waitress stops by three or four times before we even place our order. As we finally place our order, it dawns on me: *This is going to be expensive, paying for everything for six months!*

Tim has two main concerns. Being newly married he is going to need to see Rhonda from time to time. We talk about getting an apartment in New York where Rhonda could live with us. We look at the schedule and discuss a few possible visitations. The only two days off in a row are July 10-12 for the All-Star break.

Tim's second problem is helping Rhonda pay the rent if she stays in Wilmington.

"If I could just contribute $1,000 maybe $1,500, that is all she would need from me," Tim says. He goes on to tell me about one of his professors who is supposedly a millionaire and may like to invest in our new project. Our creative juices are flowing as we discuss sponsors, deadlines, and production ideas.

I even offer the house Kim and I lived in for Rhonda to live in. The house has five bedrooms and is 3,000 square feet. Kim and Rhonda have never met. I'm sure they'll like each other. I am being way too eager, maybe as an act of desperation. Now the doubt starts to settle in. I ask myself, "Are you kidding? A movie? Is the real purpose to find a friend to go to all of the games with me or to make a movie?"

One thing that sells me is that Tim is willing to do all this for making money on the back end. I get a guy who knows how to produce a movie and all I have to do is to pay his expenses for six months. How bad could it be?

We both agree that two comics hitting the road will make the story a hell of a lot more interesting. Tim talks about videotaping all of our sets, and how the movie will take on a life of its own.

The meeting lasts 2 ½ hours. We leave with to-do lists, a clear vision for our Academy Award-winner, and a new zest for life. I've got a lot to do.

It is official. I will be attending all 162 New York Yankees games this year with fellow comedian and friend Tim Boissey.

Chapter Two

TAKE ME OUT TO THE BALL GAME

Friday, February 25

Since my separation, I have been experiencing a lot of anger issues. I often lose my temper quickly and hate feeling out of control. I have decided to see a therapist. My first appointment was a few weeks earlier and it went very well. Dr. Tom is my therapist. He has helped me see things more clearly. He has given me some relaxation exercises that have helped me calm down in stressful situations.

It is my first time doing therapy, and I actually love it. Imagine that, sitting on someone's couch and sharing your problems. No judgment, no other motives. His job is to help me feel better. Dr. Tom went to high school with my brother Mike. Mike told me stories about how Dr. Tom played football and was an amazing tailback. They were hippies together and Dr. Tom still had a very peaceful and laid-back demeanor.

We had scheduled today's appointment a few weeks prior and I want to go more than I feel I need to go. As I look around the walls of his waiting room, I am bursting with enthusiasm. There are only four weeks to go before Opening Day.

"Come on in, Steve," welcomes Dr. Tom. He sits in his chair and I sit in my mine. Even the way he crosses his legs creates an environment of warmth. "How are things going?"

"They are actually going really well," I answer. "I've been happy and I haven't experienced much anger."

After a few minutes of small talk, I confess, "To tell you the truth, I'm doing great. I almost didn't keep the appointment, but I figured it couldn't hurt." I sit up a little straighter in my chair (I opt against the couch). "I have an idea. It might sound crazy."

On cue, in a very Bob Newhart-like fashion, he retorts, "I'll be the judge of that." We both laugh.

I think he must have been watching everything from my eyes to my body language. He listens, nods, and asks a few logistical questions. Once he realizes that finances aren't going to hold me back, he starts to get into it.

"What are your biggest concerns?" he asks.

"I sort of feel like I may be running away from my problems," I answer honestly. One thing that I like about Dr. Tom is that he never gives an answer immediately. You could almost watch him think it out as he pauses before responding.

He tells me that sometimes it's healthy to get away. He listens and seeks to understand my motivations. His next statement is another life-changing moment.

"Steve, I've met a lot of people who have a dream that cries out to them. People will often regret things that they never do. Rarely does someone regret living out a dream. I recommend you go for it."

Wow! I'm sure most therapists don't dole out advice so freely. I would expect them to just keep asking questions until you reach your own decision. Dr. Tom gives me the nod. Go for it.

I leave his office on top of the world. As I walk to the car, I want to jump up and down. I look at the calendar and continue to count down the days.

I later notice a quote later on Facebook from Lucille Ball: *I would rather regret things I've done than to regret the things that I never did.*

I'm getting advice from *I Love Lucy!*

The Law of Buy-In

I've learned in business and life that an important key in getting something done is the is the "law of buy-in." People will follow you or support you if they buy in in advance. I know that the journey of 162 will need to be staffed by a support team that buys in 100 percent. It is best to do this up front.

I am nervous dialing my brother, Mike. Since he and Kim are my business partners, they are the only two who can veto my trip of a lifetime. I bite the bullet and call him. I tell him all about my entire session with Dr. Tom, including my aspirations for the baseball season.

"Let me ask you a question," he interjects. "Are you 100 percent committed to this?"

"I am. I really want to do it."

"Well, as long as you stay connected to the business and carry your own weight, I don't have a problem."

A wave of relief and adrenaline shoots through my body. We have been partners since I was 24 and have been through a lot together. Getting Mike's buy-in is huge.

One partner down and one to go.

Here's how Mike summarized it in his own words:

"Kim and I have already talked about it. It is a tough time for her because they are going through the first year of separation. I think it would be good for her to be able to be at all the big events without Steve, so she would establish more of her own identity. I think that Steve is doing it now in part to give Kim the space to do just that."

Nutt Street Comedy

Fortunately for me, the launch of my stand-up career coincided with the opening of Wilmington's Nutt Street Comedy in June of 2009. The owner is Timmy Sherrill, a very funny Wilmington comic. I had performed with him around town at different bars and was ecstatic about his decision to start a full-time comedy room. Timmy had been doing stand-up a few years more than me and is highly respected and well liked.

The first thing he did was to start an open mic every Thursday. This gave the local comics a place to learn and practice their art. For the first few months it was mostly five or six comics telling each other jokes.

Today, Thursday nights are a hot ticket. We have 20-25 comics now perform for four to five minutes in front of packed rooms. I've found that the quality of most open mics is so poor it never gains momentum. This is the only one that I have been to that stands alone as a show every week.

Initially, Tim would bring in a national headliner for weekend shows once per month. He sank everything he had into Nutt Street and today it is considered one of the premiere rooms in the Southeast. He has used a mixture of word of mouth and local advertising to continually fill the room. He now has sold out shows every weekend. This gives the local comics a great opportunity to work great rooms and open for nationally touring headliners.

As a comedy club owner, Sherrill is a comic's dream. He is fair, honest, and willing to help others along the way. I don't know that I'd still be doing comedy if it wasn't for his willingness to keep the doors open.

Saturday, February 26

I am opening tonight along with another local comic, Steve Marcinowski (Marz). Steve and I met two years ago when we were both first starting.

We were doing an open mic at a place called The Brown Coat Theatre. This was the first place in Wilmington where I did stand-up and it was Steve's debut that particular night. I remember his family sitting in the front row rooting for the 25-year-old. They were all from Boston and it was funny listening to their accents.

On that particular night there was a "talent scout" who was looking for a few extra comics to be in a show. Out of the 12 comics performing that night, he invited only Steve and I to be in a paid show in Southport a month later. I was impressed that his first night out Steve was being offered a paying gig.

Over the next year-and-a-half we performed together a few times. Marcinowski works at Home Depot full-time, but his passion is comedy.

After my separation I am out and about a lot more. Steve and I often hit the bars after doing stand-up. Steve is a pretty cool guy who is also quite hilarious. He started to crash at my pad whenever he had too much to drink.

Steve and I are both coming through the ranks at

Nutt Street and are starting to host and open for touring headliners. Tonight we are opening for a veteran comic, Vic Henley.

Vic was great and hung out after the show. He has been doing stand-up for two decades and shares crazy stories about working with guys like Ron White, Jeff Foxworthy, and Lewis Black. The Nutt Street local comics always take out the headliner and show them a good time. This is a great chance to hang out with someone who's making it and an opportunity to get feedback on our sets.

Marcinowski, Vic Henley, Timmy Sherrill, and me

Tonight, Marcinowski and I have great sets and move the after-party to the infamous Blue Post.

Joining us is Tim Boissey and a few females from the show. The place is packed and we are jammed up against the bar. We keep having to move every time the waitress needs to squeeze by. Marz and I are still high on the adrenaline of our performances. I am constantly thinking and speaking of the 162 Tour. I notice that Tim isn't as enthusiastic as he was just days ago.

"There is something that we need to talk about," he said stoically.

Without hearing another word, I know what is coming next. I have run a sales organization long enough to know when someone is quitting. My stomach drops as my brain races with unanswered questions.

He proceeds to tell me that he and Rhonda have talked about it and she thinks it is foolish to throw out two years of community college. He goes on to say that he would like to join the tour in May, when school gets out. I'm not mad at him, but I am frustrated that my plans aren't working out. As he is telling me this, I can feel my own doubts creeping in. Our talk only lasts a few minutes. He had been trying to bring it up for the last few days. A week before, he sat there and fantasized what a killer movie this would make. I've never heard of a movie not being made because the producer has to finish up community college.

I don't tell anyone, but I am relieved. I feel like in my haste to make this work, I probably overcommitted to Boissey. It would be a big commitment to pay his rent as well as his expenses on the tour.

"What about Marcinowski?" Bossiey yells over the music and buzz of the Saturday night crowd.

We both turn around and look at him. He has a huge grin on his face and is trying to put the moves on a college co-ed. He looks over and flashes his smile at us.

"He doesn't even like sports," I reason. "And he's from Boston."

Again we both look at him in an evaluating sort of way. Marcinowski leans in. "You guys talking about me?"

We both smile back and say nothing at the same time.

Tim had already thought this out and said, "He does more comedy than I do and I can teach him to use all of the equipment. He also has a lot less obligations than I do."

I think about it as I stand at the bar. I really do like Steve. I hang out with him way more than I do with Tim. He is one of the funniest young comics around. He has been telling everyone that he is ready to break out of Wilmington and hit the road. Maybe this is his chance. The seed had been planted.

In goal achievement, I've learned that the plan you start with is rarely the plan that gets you there. The team you start with is rarely the team standing with you at the finish line. By the end of the night, the three of us are in conversation about Marcinowski replacing Boissey. I can tell by Marz's reaction that he is happy to be invited and is excited by the possibilities. His biggest concerns are his job at Home Depot and telling his parents.

Monday, February 28

I finally have "the talk" with Kim today about me going on the tour. She and Mike have already spoken in detail and she is very supportive. Her biggest concerns are that all of the bills are paid and kept current. I spend the day going over all of the business and our personal expenses. We develop a plan.

I start hitting my punch list:

- I call my rental place and give my 30-day notice.
- I call my accountant, Steve Cooper, and we strategize on how to run the finances while I'm on the road.
- I call my regional vice president in Pre-Paid Legal and let him know that I will be stepping down as Regional Manager.
- I call our graphic artist, Jayce Schmidt, and have her start working on a 162 theme.

Thursday, March 3

My friend and associate John Busch picks me up at the airport in Austin and proceeds to take me out for a killer Mexican lunch that is washed down with some Margaritas.

I am speaking tonight at a local hotel and he gets about 50 Pre-Paid Legal associates out. I deliver an electric talk as I focus on having a dream and going for it. It is all about having clearly defined goals and working a plan to achieve them.

One young lady, Kim Acosta, comes up to me after the seminar. Kim has been one of our top producers for several years and just experienced a tragedy that no parent ever wants. She lost her daughter who was in her late teens just a few months earlier. Meeting and talking with Kim is difficult, but inspiring at the same time. She has so much strength and faith.

In some ways, it makes my 162 Tour seem so trivial. It also reinforces the point that life is short and fragile. As empathetic as I am for Kim, I am even more committed to living a dream that existed in my heart. As the days and hours tick closer, my resolve grows stronger.

Friday, March 4

I start the day by going for a run by the water close to my hotel. To me there isn't a better way to think and get the endorphins going at the same time than to go for a run. There are tons of people out walking and jogging. At several points of my run, I find myself skipping because I am in such a great mood. There is something magical about creating, designing, and living the life that you want.

John has me doing seminars around the clock. We do a business lunch for local executives. My mind is on my long to-do list.

When the lunch is over, I call my Pre-Paid Legal provider attorney. I market legal services, and as they say in Hair Club For Men, "I am also a client." Within a few minutes, I am on the phone with my attorney and walking him through my project. One of my main questions is about the use of the word "Yankees" on my marketing materials and website. I describe my idea and he gives me the OK that I can use 162Yankeegames.com. He wishes me a successful season.

Later that evening, I am hanging out with an old friend, Rauly Williams. Rauly is a very talented musician and songwriter.

In his own words, here's what happened next:

> *I hadn't seen Steve in a couple of years, we were having a few beers and catching up on life. A lot has happened since we last had a chance to hang out. I am happy to hear that he's gotten back into doing stand-up comedy on a regular basis.*
>
> *Steve says, "Hey, check this out." He pulls out a piece of paper and writes "162" big enough to fill the page and says, "What does this make you think of?" My wheels start turning. I'm trying to think of something related to humor, but I come up with nothing. Steve is a master of self-improvement training, I guess something along those lines. I try sacred geometry, something mathematical. He says, "Dude, you're over-thinking this." I finally get it. "Games in a baseball season!"*
>
> *He proceeds to tell me his plan to attend all 162 Yankees games. It's brilliant. I think Steve hits the tipping point on this very night, because it was time to start putting up some hard American currency for flights and such. He says, "I'm gonna do it!" For the next couple of hours we talk about 162, toss around various ideas, make note of a few*

media contacts.

Back in the day, I had written some songs for Steve, Kim, and Mike and provided some musical entertainment at Pre-Paid Legal conventions. He asks me if I would be interested in doing some music for 162, and of course I say, "Hell, yeah!" (for the record, I don't think Steve knows any other musicians, but I was honored to be up for consideration). Of course, we start planning to go to a game when the Yankees come to Arlington, site of the Bombers' inglorious 2010 playoff exit and general Ranger spanking.

I know that the key to any endeavor is to surround yourself with a great supporting cast. Rauly is on board. His belief that this was a good idea is just further confirmation.

Sunday, March 6

I am flying back to Wilmington. It's go time. I have three weeks and two days until I leave for New York. Yikes. I have been tossing and turning at night, as I am running through hundreds of things that I need to get done.

I know that my trip of a lifetime is a race against the clock. I start to make lists of what I need to do. I have always said that 90 percent of everything gets done in the last 10 percent of time. I make a list of all my contacts that could help out in some way. I have an enormous network of people who would love to help. There are 15 cities. I make a list of all the contacts I have in each city.

The other list I made is all of the little things that I still need to do. I've never used a Day-Timer or any other type of time management system. I use notebooks. The kind a third-grader uses.

The Plan:
Create Website
Business Cards
Postcards
Social Media (Facebook page, Twitter, YouTube)
Press Release
Tickets for games
Apartment in New York/CraigsList
Give my 30-day notice to landlord
Teeth cleaned before I go
Final haircut
Travel — Go through 162-game schedule and map out transportation

One goal is to have half of my tickets comped. At this point I have no tickets and I do not know anyone who has season tickets. I have no place to stay and I have no transportation booked. Basically I'm at ground zero. I begin to run some numbers.

Game Tickets. This is purely a guesstimate:
162 games x 2 = 324. 324 x $50 = $16,800 for tickets. Broken down by month it is $2,620.
Let's talk about what costs I can eliminate:

Rent	$1,200
Electric	$100
Cable	$75
Gold's Gym	$20

Hmmm … not as much as I thought. $1,395 is what I'm saving. Over six months, that's $8,370 that I won't be spending in NC.

I have the schedule with me now at all times. Opening Day is March 31st at 1 p.m. I have broken down the cities that we will be driving to and the cities that will require a flight. There are 33 flights.

We will be leaving in my Ford Mustang on March 29th and arrive the next day in New York. We will not have to get on a flight until May 2nd. This gives us an entire month of not having to pay for flights. This will give me a chance to see if I can really do this and if I can afford to have Marcinowski along for the ride.

We will drive to Boston for the weekend of April 8-10. Then on April 17th, after the Sunday Night Game of the Week, we will drive eight hours to Toronto. Normally this would be nuts, but they are only playing two games there and there is a day off on both sides. Tuesday and Wednesday in Canada and then back to Baltimore for a three-game weekend series. Then we'll drive back to New York on April 25th for another week there.

Airfare

Let's see, 33 flights x 2 = 66. These will all need to be booked as one-ways for several reasons. Only twice is there a straight round-trip. Most road trips include two or three cities. For instance, on May 2nd we will fly to Detroit. On the 6th, we will be in Dallas. On Monday the 9th, we fly back to New York.

The second reason is that because of rain and weather, a game and or flight may need to be rescheduled. So If you have a round trip and miss one, the entire trip is unusable.

A quick calculation tells me that 66 flights x $200 per flight = $12,200. Again divided by 6 months = $2,333.33. Let's call it $2,500 per month.

Accommodations
Hotel and accommodations are a little harder to guesstimate. Here are the cities that we are traveling to:

Boston	9 games
Baltimore	9 games
Tampa	9 games
Toronto	9 games
Seattle	6 games
LA	6 games
Oakland	3 games
Texas	3 games
Detroit	4 games
Cleveland	3 games
Chicago	7 games
Kans. City	3 games
Minnesota	4 games
Cincinnati	3 games
NY Mets	3 games

So, 81 away games in 14 cities not counting the New York Mets games.

I'm hoping that we can stay with friends/associates half of the time.

So let's call it 45 x $100 = $4,500.

So, just for tickets, air and hotel, we're looking roughly at:

$16,800
$12,200
$4,500
$33,500.

Oh jeesh!

This isn't counting spending money, gas, food, beer, rental cars, other transportation needs, or anything else.

We do not have a place to live in New York. If we are able to get a sublet or apartment, it will run at least another $2,000 per month.

Well, this is the plan. I have to laugh to myself, because for most people this is not a plan at all. I have a lot of confidence that I can pull this off. It will not be easy.

One day at a time.

Chapter Three

THE LAW OF THE INNER CIRCLE

I need a few crucial things to happen before we hit the road. I believe that my story is worthy of media attention. I also do not expect anyone to pay attention for a few months. My job is to create a buzz. Just to be clear I have zero media contacts.

My sister Mary, however, owns her own advertising agency in New Jersey. She moved down to Wilmington two years ago and bought a house less than a mile from us. She is a powerful businesswoman and I have a tremendous amount of respect for her. She is also the oldest of the seven children. She has helped me in life as much as any other person. The year after I graduated from college I showed up on her doorstep and didn't leave for five years. I nannied for her son Matt during his formative years. Matt is now grown and has an apartment two blocks from me.

I am nervous to call her as I think that she might shoot down my idea. She does just the opposite. She loves the idea.

When Kim and I separated, Mary and Kim, who were already great friends, became even closer. This means a great deal to me. Mary thinks it would be great to get away for a while and wants to know what she can do to help. She agrees to do a press release announcing the tour. She works fast and bangs it out by evening.

On March 7, we begin to tell the world about 162.

March 7, 2011
PRESS RELEASE
Wilmington, NC

Comedians plan trip and documentary to 162 Major League Yankees games

Wilmington NC Stand-up Comics, Steve Melia and Steve Marcinowski are heading to all 162 New York Yankees games this season. They plan to make a movie of all their experiences as well as expand their comedy careers by booking themselves in comedy clubs across the nation and Canada, hopefully in up to 15 major cities, while attending the games. At this point, they will finance the trip themselves.

Steve Melia, originally from New York, is an avid Yankees fan and has been doing stand-up comedy for several years.

"I love the Yankees and comedy, so what could be a better combination? It seems like a crazy plan, but I am fulfilling a lifelong dream," says Melia. "The life of a stand-up comic on the road isn't always glamorous. We plan on capturing that as well as the grueling schedule of attending 162 games."

Steve Marcinowski, originally from Boston,

is part of the Nutt Street Improv Group. He has been doing stand-up comedy for two years, and hopes to expand his experiences while traveling over the next six months.

"The funny thing is I'm not even a big baseball fan, but it'll be great fun traveling with a fellow comedian. Steve Melia is such a crazy Yankees fan that I think the whole experience will be wild – if the Yankees fans don't kill me in the process!" says Marcinowski.

The two get on the road at the end of March, and will film and take photos of the entire experience. They are currently seeking sponsorship to help finance their expenses and the production equipment necessary to film their escapades. The two will also produce an ongoing webisode from each series. "It's going to be a blast going from city to city doing what we love. This will be a dream come true," remarked Melia.

I spend the entire day sending this press release out to anyone and everyone.

Tuesday, March 8

At 9:38 a.m., we got our first hit.

Good morning Steve(s),

My name's Tim Buckley and I'm a reporter/ meteorologist/avid Yankees fan over at WWAY.

Cacky forwarded me along your press release about your upcoming plans to hit the road for the entire baseball season, continuing your careers in comedy along the way.

I was wondering if I could catch you both before you hit the road for an interview and a quick/cool story.

Let me know if you're available next Monday morning for a brief shoot (probably around 9am or 10am). If that doesn't work hopefully we can schedule another date before the end of the month!

Go Yanks!

Tim Buckley
Morning Meteorologist
WWAY NewsChannel 3
Wilmington, NC

In Tim's own words:

In the world of local news, you truly never know what you're going to get. When I first read Steve's press release, I knew that it could be a story that would generate a reaction from viewers. Two guys hitting the road, seemingly against all odds trying to live out a childhood dream. As a lifelong Yankees fan myself, I was jealous. What could be better than following the team all year?

Of course, the story was met with quite a bit of skepticism when I pitched it to the rest of the staff in our newsroom. Their reactions captured what I expected people at home would feel:

"What're these two thinking?"

"Don't they know how much this is going to cost?"

"Wait, home AND away?"

> *"It's a great dream, but they'll never make it."*
>
> *"They don't have the money to pull it off."*
>
> *Steve Melia called me after receiving my email and we agree to meet next Tuesday, March 15th, and do a 90-second story.*

Thursday, March 10

The Rolodex Theory: It's not who you know; It's who *they* know.

I am getting the press release out to everyone in my network. I define a network as everyone in your circle of influence, plus their circles of influence. Best-selling author Harvey Mackey calls it the Rolodex Theory. Let's say you have 200 contacts in your rolodex. Each of them average 200 contacts as well. If you have a solid relationship and an idea worth sharing, you can now exponentially compound your contact base. 200 x 200 = 40,000. This is how many contacts you now potentially have.

I send one to Renee Olson as we have been conversing regularly over the last few weeks since my Dallas trip.

"Have you told Jeff yet?" she asked.

I'd been putting off telling Jeff as I don't want him to tell me not to do it.

"I'm going to talk to him today."

"Well, he is around. I just talked to him."

I hang up and dial Jeff's number.

"Hello?" Jeff answers.

"Hey man, I want to talk to you about my plans for the next six months."

I lay out the 162 idea. The idea has now morphed

into a movie. I acknowledge that I will have to miss the upcoming national convention April 8-10 in Oklahoma City. In our business, if you miss a national event, everyone thinks you quit.

"Who cares is you miss one event? There will be others. You should do it," Jeff astonishingly says.

"Thanks! It just seems like this is an important convention, with the merger and all."

"Nah, go for it. This is a sponsor's dream. Have you talked to the beer companies? You shouldn't have to pay for anything. Beer, tickets, hotels. You need to get some sponsors."

"Well that is another reason that I am calling."

Jeff's book *The Slight Edge* is currently selling like crazy. It is a great book and I have bought and resold thousands of copies to my sales force.

"I was thinking that *The Slight Edge* could be one of our sponsors. Maybe every day, we do an update from the road on our website, sponsored by *The Slight Edge*. Like "The Slight Edge Minute," or "The Slight Edge Thought of the Day."

Now the windup and the pitch ...

"I'm really looking for $25K." There is silence.

"Well, I don't know that there's a fit, but let me think about it."

I recognize a nice "no" when I hear one. At least I have his blessing.

I continue pounding the phones looking for media, sponsors, and comedy gigs. I also have an assistant named Karen who is working the phones as well from her home in San Diego.

Marcinowski calls.

"I talked to my parents today."

"How'd that go?"

"My dad is convinced that you're gay." He starts impersonating his dad. "So let me get this straight: This older gentleman is going to take you with him all over the country for six months and is paying for everything?"

We laugh.

"I told him that you like girls even more than I do."

Marcinowski is definitely out of his comfort zone. He, too, begins making all of the arrangements to be gone for six months.

Friday, March 11
Three weeks till Opening Day
19 days until we leave

Steve and I are on our first live radio interview with a local radio station. I am friends with the afternoon DJ, Brian Simms. After having lunch with him earlier in the week and running my plan by him, he invited us on the air.

I am learning that people are interested in this journey. It is generating some excitement. Brian has worked in radio all over the country and assures me that it is easy to get on the radio. He tells me that the trick is talking to the station manager, and some of the bigger shows have their own producer.

Steve and I meet outside the station.

"Are we doing this thing?" I ask.

"We are, Melia." We high five.

There is something awesome about doing something outside of the box. This will be our first time sharing the 162 idea over the airwaves.

We walk into the lobby and quickly get escorted back into the production room where Brian gives us a big smile and a Fonzie thumbs up. He finishes talking into the mic, takes off his headset, and meets Steve for the first time.

The interview starts and Brian asks, "Has anyone ever done this?" I'm not really sure.

"*We've* never done it." The reality is that I don't really care that much if anyone else has done it. We have to be the first comedy tour that did it.

Two comics … one mission.

He goes on to ask what inspired us, what our plans are, and how the heck we are funding this.

For me, the mission is simple and perfect: To attend every game while doing comedy along the way and make a movie about this incredible odyssey.

Steve is on board, but his mission is to make it as a stand-up comic and this is his chance to go on the road.

Saturday, March 12

As the days get closer I get more and more nervous. My biggest fear is that we won't be able to pull this off. My second biggest fear is that we do, but nobody cares.

I am using Facebook as my main promotional vehicle. Branding is paramount. Steve sets up a Facebook page and our Twitter account.

We are working with a friend, Sharla Patrick, to set up our website.

At around noon, I dial my brother Tommy who lives in Massapequa, New York. Tommy is a retired lieutenant with the New York City Fire Department and one of the biggest influences on me being a Yankees fan. He and his wife Lucy have five children, one of which is still living under their roof. I tell him that we will need a place to crash for a week or two while we look for an apartment in the city. He tells me we are welcome in his home.

The next call I make is to my best friend from

college, Steve Ferrara. Because we have the same first name and because of his very laid-back demeanor, I nicknamed him Slug in college.

Slug lives in Connecticut with his wife and three daughters. He's also a huge Yankees fan. We have stayed in touch over the years and were in each other's weddings. I tell him that we are looking for a place to stay, maybe every other home stand. He also tells us that we can stay whenever we want for as long as we want.

As I look at the schedule, I try to piece together the first month or so. The plan is to find a furnished place in New York City or even the Bronx. Subletting something for the summer would be perfect. Someone recommends couchsurfing.com. I go to the website for a few hours and try to line up places in New York City. Whatever it takes.

Monday, March 14

Today is the first day that I look at buying tickets. I have never been to an Opening Day at Yankee Stadium. I have been a customer of StubHub for years and have been trying to get in touch with a decision maker there for two weeks. Everyone I talk to from StubHub thinks that 162 is a great idea, but that is about as far as I get. A lot of people are asking me about my plans and are taken aback by my lack of planning. The reason that I have waited to book anything is that I am hoping an individual or a company will decide to sponsor us. As the days get closer, I decide to bite the bullet and start spending some money. So I spend the next hour buying tickets for the first few weeks.

Opening Day

3/31	$222.75 Section 205, Row 22
4/2	$47.95 Bleachers 201, Row 23
4/3	$75.35 Grandstand 410, Row 8 (4)
4/5	$31.95 Bleacher 203, Row 6
4/6	$19.95 Grandstands, Row 10
4/7	$19.93 Bleachers, Section 237

The tickets are only $4.99 x 2 = $9.98. The fees are $9.95. StubHub is making a killing.

$417.88 for six of the first seven games.

Now for Fenway tickets. April 7-9 is the Red Sox home opening series.

The rivalry continues.

4/8	$322.85 – Standing room only (who needs to sit?)
4/9	$191.95 – Standing room only
4/10	$202.93 – Outfield Grandstand 7, row 5 $717.93, of which $78.75 are StubHub fees!

$1,135.81 for the first nine out of 10 games.

Gulp … gulp! This is going to be expensive!

Tuesday, March 15

Marz and I meet outside of my apartment at 8 a.m. He has arranged to go into Home Depot a little late today. He shows up wearing his brown plaid top and jeans and sporting a brand new glove.

We make our way over to the other side of the

River, where we are meeting Tim Buckley from the ABC affiliate. Tim arrives and is as pumped as we are. We trade Yankees stories and I learn that he is from Syracuse. Tim is the weatherman, but such a huge Yankees fan that he personally wanted to do the story.

He interviews me first and then Marcinowski. He gets some footage of us playing catch. I haven't tossed a baseball in years and it looks as if Marcinowski never has. He crouches down in a catcher's pose as I sail one 10 feet over his head.

Tim fires off a series of questions: *Why you? Why now? What are your goals for this trip? How will you pull this off? Have you made any arrangements whatsoever? How can a Yankees fan pair up with some guy from Boston who doesn't even like baseball?*

"At this point, Tim, there are way more questions than answers," I said. "What we do know for sure is that we are getting in the car on either the 29th or 30th and we will be in New York for Opening Day on the 31st at 1 p.m."

Tim laughed at our lack of solid plans. I'm not sure he believes that we will do it. In his own words:

> *Their answers are full of infectious enthusiasm; especially Melia. It was obvious this was a dream of his. Heck, I wanted to go along for the season after talking with him. But the enthusiasm wasn't exactly matched with concrete details. No tickets, no flights, no lodging.*
>
> *In my head, my own skepticism was bubbling over. How could you be two weeks away from setting off on a six-month, grueling quest and still have so many question marks? The daunting financial burden seemed like something the two*

couldn't overcome.

I made them promise to stay in touch throughout the season so that we could do periodic follow-ups on their progress. I was impressed by their ambition, but in my head I was already dreading doing the story about how the plan fell off its track.

"Maybe by the end of the year the duo will be a fan favorite of the Yankees," he jokes.

I respond by promising, "You watch, by September we will be friends with Derek Jeter and some of the other Yankees. I guarantee it."

Tim films us driving away in the Mustang that is sporting a "FUNNY" vanity plate. They use this as the closing shot on tonight's newscast.

This is the article that accompanied the news story later that night.

WILMINGTON, NC (WWAY) -- If you're a baseball fanatic, you've probably dreamed about going to each and every one of your team's games. Well, two local comics are about to begin a six-month journey that will attempt to do just that.

Spring is in the air, and that means baseball. The New York Yankees are in the midst of Spring Training. While Jeter, A-Rod, and Posada are working out in Tampa, two other pieces of this year's campaign are getting ready right here in Wilmington.

Meet Steve Melia and Steve Marcinowski. No, they're not athletes, they're comedians. They typically spend their time at the Nutt Street Comedy Room making people laugh, but they're about to take a six-month hiatus as they hit the road on a quest to attend all 162 Yankees games.

"For about three years I've wanted to go to every (Yankees) game, and I kept talking about '162,' and that it'd be a great idea for a reality show," Melia said.

This makes perfect sense for this Melia, being a Yankees fan and all, but the other Steve is not a Yankees fan at all.

"I was born and raised in Boston, MA, so this is going to be interesting for me," Marcinowski said. "When it's safe, I think I'm going to try and wear some Boston gear. Because I'm not a really good fighter."

Allegiances aside, the two won't be spending all their time in the parks. They'll also be performing on stage across the country trying to book as many shows as they can.

"That's what I'm really excited about is just hitting as many stages as we can," Marcinowski said. "Especially in New York, we're going to be up there for a long time. It's such a big place for comedy -- and baseball."

Melia said, "Sometimes I think you're really creative when you're tired and exhausted, and I know we're absolutely going to be tired and exhausted. We're already looking forward to the All-Star Break."

The duo doesn't exactly have the logistics down pat just yet. With dozens of flights to book and tickets to buy, there's a lot of planning left to be

done, but they're just looking forward to the endless baseball and laughs to be had along the way.

While on the road, the two Steves will produce a documentary of their experiences to share with everyone on a live blog. We'll check in with them throughout the season to see their progress, so stay tuned for more updates.

I watch the 5:00 news that night with pure jubilation. Now we had a professional piece produced by a third party that we could use.

Chapter Four

YOU'RE AN IDIOT

Friday, March 18

Law of Momentum: An object in motion tends to stay in motion

In order to make this work, we need to line up comedy in as many cities as possible. New York has open mics every night of the week in various locations. I email and call 10 different clubs in New York. Most of them tell us to simply show up.

Getting gigs in road cities is tricky because most games are at night. I go through the schedule and start circling the available dates. Our first road trip is in Boston. I Google comedy clubs and find Nick's Comedy Stop. In Boston there is a rare Friday day game and a Saturday day game as well.

I called and they requested to see some videos. Progress!

The second trip is to Toronto. I put in a phone call to a veteran comic I know named Mark Trinidad who lives in Ontario. Mark is a rising star in Pre-Paid Legal and is more than willing to help. He tells me that he will book a show just for us on Monday, April 18. Mondays are always a night off for comedy clubs, so this works out great.

Our next trip is to Detroit for a four game series May 2-5. I find an open mic at a place called Laughtrax. They pencil us in for May 5th. My confidence is soaring as things are starting to come together. By the end of the day I get an email from John at Nick's Comedy Stop in Boston saying that we can both have 10-minute guest spots both nights in Boston. Wow. Things are moving.

I am literally working around the clock. My three main priorities are securing logistics, finding sponsors, and booking comedy.

Saturday, March 19

I think back to my guarantee of becoming friends with Derek Jeter. Maybe I overdid it.

I have had the opportunity to meet many of the Bombers in recent years. Probably the most exciting was in August 2005. The Yankees were visiting Anaheim and were staying at the Hilton. Kim and I were living in San Diego at the time. My brother Mike and his son, Willie, were at the series with us. We purposely stayed at that hotel because we knew that's where The Yankees stayed. They lost the Saturday night game and were on a three-game losing streak.

We strolled down to the lobby bar around 11:30 p.m. to find an almost-empty bar. Almost. I looked over to the left where there is a pool table. Racking the balls and asking if anyone wanted to play was the man himself, number 42, Mariano Rivera.

I immediately walked over and raised my hand like

I was a third-grader asking to go to the potty, and with a cracking voice mustered up, "We'll play!"

The four of us made our introductions and Kim and I got to play first. Mo was sensational. Of all the bars that I have played in, I have never seen anyone as good. The cue ball glided down the table like his cutter. The backspin was amazing. He was partnered up with a girl who worked at the hotel Starbucks and was not very good. We won the first game because she scratched on the eight ball.

"Yes!" I shouted with a fist pump. The Melias beats Mariano, the best closer in baseball history! We played again. Almost the exact scenario played out. But the 2-0 lead quickly vanished as Mo closed us down and won the next three.

The entire experience lasted about two hours. You always hope that when you meet someone you idolize, that they won't spoil the perception. Like he has so many times before, Mo delivered. Kind, gentle, warm, and funny, are just a few words to describe Mariano that night. We drank beer. He drank juice. Towards the end, we asked for a picture. He willingly obliged.

At one point Mike took out his cell phone and moved towards Mo. As he is dialing, he asked the future Hall of Famer if he could leave a message for Mike's youngest daughter, Dani. Dani was a student at NYU's film school at the time. Mo politely said no with a smile on his face several times, but no one can escape Mike's persistency! Mo left her a message and made her day when she finally believed it was him.

Over the next few seasons, we would run into Mariano several times and he always greeted us with a warm smile and a kind word. If he didn't remember us, he sure was a good actor.

Later that season I had a chance to meet Joe Torre in the men's locker room at the Hilton spa. It was the morning of Game 2 of the American League Division Series. The night before, the Yanks had won the first game of the series. Kim and I were in the workout room. This was definitely a place to see some Yankees in the morning. Michel Kaye, the voice of the Yankees, was sweating profusely on the exercise bike. Joe Girardi, the 2005 bench coach, was power lifting. I remember telling Kim that day that Girardi would be Torre's replacement eventually.

I was finished with my workout and decided to hit the showers and take a quick sauna. Just as I finished getting dressed, I looked up and opening a locker was the skipper himself.

I politely introduced myself and told Joe that I was a big fan. He shook my hand and greeted me nicely.

"Any chance that I can get a quick picture?"

"Sure."

"I'll be right back."

I took off back into the gym where Kim was supposed to be working out. I flew in there. The lone gym employee asked me if everything was OK. I told her that my wife had my camera. I looked furiously, but couldn't find her.

"You are not allowed to take pictures in here."

I acted like I didn't hear her. Kim finally came walking out of the women's locker room. I could barely speak. "Camera, camera!" I somehow managed to squeak out. She fumbled into her purse and handed me our disposable Kodak.

"Joe Torre!" I muttered, as I grabbed the camera and took off down the hallway. He had left the locker room and now was waiting for his manicure-pedicure wearing his white Hilton bathrobe. As we posed, I began to hold up the camera with my right hand for the classic self-shot special.

"If we are going to do this, let's do it right," the Skipper prescribed.

He started looking for his manicurist and was calling her by name to serve as our photographer. There was no sign of her, but now Kim was making her way down the hall.

I waved Kim over and she snapped a photo. Kim requested a picture as well. I think Kim and I may be the only Yankees fans with a picture of Torre wearing his bathrobe!

I always prefer a picture rather than having an autograph. Joe Torre was a class act and could not have been nicer. Based on these interactions, I believe that we will be spending a lot of time with the Yankees this year.

Tuesday, March 22

I am on a flight arriving in Melbourne, FL. My brother, Mike, is picking me up at the airport. He is the speaker tonight and is dressed in his suit. Normally, I would go with him, but I prefer to stay in the bar tonight. I have so much to do and it is hard to sit in a presentation for an hour.

When the meeting gets out, I see a lot of my friends and associates that I may not see for a while. My friend

Rich Kennedy is a huge sports fan. He is a good buddy and seeing me surprises him. He gives me a big bear hug.

"Stevo!" he exclaims. "I'm so happy that you are doing this. What a shining example that if you work hard enough, you can do anything you want."

Rich has a few prospective sales associates closely in tow. He introduces them and does an incredible job of encapsulating the 162 journey for them while edifying me and putting renewed wind in my sails.

"Steve, more than anyone I know, can pull this off," he says. "Can you imagine the kind of cash this is going to cost? Steve is the kind of person who does what he sets out to do. If Steve Melia says he'll do it, consider it done."

That was a huge compliment, and one that I'll do my best to live up to. I'm up for the challenge.

This may be the last trip that I am able to see my dad. I may be able to sneak over from a Tampa series in July. I last visited him in late January after the cruise. He is sound asleep when we get back and off to dialysis at 5 a.m. He has been on dialysis for over five years, going every Monday, Wednesday, and Friday for four hours. He was driving himself until a few months ago and now gets picked up and dropped off by a van. It is hard to watch someone that big, strong, and powerful in such a decrepit state.

Wednesday, March 23

My dad and I are sitting on the back porch. He is in good spirits, but awfully tired after dialysis. I have my laptop out and I am about to show him the WWAY newscast from March 15th. He has no idea that I'm leaving on the 162 Tour.

"I want to show you something, Dad."

"What do you got?"

"This was on the news last week."

I play him the 4 ½-minute feature. At first there was a long and thoughtful pause. Then he spoke.

"You are an idiot."

"What do you mean?"

"Do you know how much this is going to cost?"

I tell him that I am moving out of my apartment and plan on living on a budget. His facial expression is one of confusion. He looks like he wants to ask a question, but just shrugs instead.

I was definitely hoping for a more positive reaction. My dad does not like to see his children struggle or fail. I remember him giving me the startling statistics of how many little leaguers will never make it to the pros when I expressed my desire to play professional baseball. He did the same when I opened a lemonade stand.

"Dad, four more sales and I'll be even!"

He shook his head. "You'd already be even if you would have never started."

I love his brashness and his realist attitude. In my early days of business I used it as motivation. When we had success in business, no one was happier than him. I know the same will be true of the 162 Tour. My dad is very close to Kim and I think he is worried about her more than anything. Mike concurs when he tells me about a conversation he had with my dad after dropping me off at the airport.

"Your business partner is a wacko," my dad told Mike. Mike proceeded to tell him that it shouldn't affect our business much, and that maybe it would be good for me and Kim to spend some time apart. My dad doesn't just think I'm an idiot for the 162 Tour; he also thinks I'm an idiot for letting Kim get away.

Thursday, March 24

With Opening Day one week away, I start booking flights. I am booking the third road trip of the year, the first that will require plane tickets. I get a Spirit flight from New York to Detroit for $283.40 for two flights. We are there Monday through Friday. Then American Airlines will be taking us to DFW and then back to JFK on Monday morning for $640.80, a total of $923.40 for road trip number three. Marcinowski better not back out!

Mike and I sit and rack our brains about people he knows in different cities. He has gone to as many as 45 games in a season. He gives me a few names and numbers. There are 14 cities where we'll need places to stay, rides, and tickets.

Saturday, March 26

Word is spreading through Wilmington that we are hitting the road. We have a going-away party at the Front Street Brewery at 4 p.m. today.

We are excited to show the group of well-wishers our marketing materials. We have our 162 business cards and postcards. We have a huge thermometer banner that counts the games up to 162. Tim Boissey is the first to notice its resemblance to a penis. Hmm … I think he's right!

Around 10 friends show up to say good luck. My sister Mary and Burger have a going-away present. I open it and am blown away. A New York Yankees Jersey with the number 162 on the back. I had been trying for weeks to get one made but to no avail. I learn that Burger left no stone unturned to get this made. They also give me their E-ZPass for the entire season. I'm jacked as this will save me thousands on tunnel and bridge tolls going in and out of New York.

Later that night, Mark and AJ, two guys who run an internet radio show out of New York invite us on their show to tell our story. They love it. *Two comics … one mission.* They invite us to be on every Sunday night and give a report from the road.

Chapter Five

PLAY BALL!

Tuesday, March 29

Today is the day! My day is full of last minute arrangements and running around. I am moving out of my apartment today, as is Marcinowski. He is due here at 3 p.m. sharp. At 4:20 p.m., Marcinowski arrives.

I have our brand new Yankees-themed Flip cam. As the elevator opens, I catch great footage of Marcinowski getting out of his car. He grabs the wrought iron fence and jumps up and down. "Are we doing this Melia?" He's more excited than a college kid heading to spring break.

We keep the camera rolling. He looks at the Mustang that is almost full before he puts anything in there. I have constructed a pole across the backseat of the Mustang. I am bringing clothes for business as well. The back seat is so small that nothing really hangs, it is just stuffed in there.

The karaoke machine is jammed in there as well. This is key as it will allow us to practice or perform anywhere. I have two huge suitcases full of clothes. We also have all of our marketing materials such as the penis-shaped thermometer banner, two boxes of postcards, and lots of business cards. I have a bit of baseball gear, including my Yankees rally monkey and my glove.

We cram everything in and use every possible inch of space to begin our journey. The passenger seat has two boxes and a bag where Marcinowski will be sitting.

Our first stop is to my dream house that I bought with Kim in 2006. I am dropping a few things off and saying goodbye. This will be the longest time that we haven't spent together since we got engaged. I moved out exactly six months ago. It is nice to see and say goodbye to Kim. She will be one of our biggest cheerleaders. It is also very sad and difficult. Kim will be taking over all of the things that I have been doing like paying the bills as well as the accounting work for our business.

We pull away with a few horn blares and I definitely have tears in my eyes as I look in the rear view mirror yet again. Am I crazy? Well, I'm obviously crazy. I guess a better question is, am I crazy enough to pull this off?

We are dropping Marcinowski's car off at his friend's place. It is a huge house in a very nice neighborhood. My eyes get big as we pull up into their humongous driveway. I'm sure they are going to love having his car there for six months. He has the trunk open as he is sorting through all of his worldly possessions.

As we hit the road, we talk about a lot of stuff. This is the most time that we have spent together and we seem to be bonding pretty well. We are taping a lot of our conversations, which we think are enthralling.

Steve commandeers the radio and plays podcast after podcast of interviews with comedians. I have a lot of respect for his focus on his stand-up craft. We drive until 1 a.m. and pull into a hotel that we found on Steve's smartphone. We make it to a Best Western just outside of Baltimore for $66.

Tonight is the first night of many that we will spend in a motel, not a hotel. One letter can make all of the difference.

Wednesday, March 30

We awake at 8:30 a.m. to the sounds of Spanish-speaking maids outside our room. It is about 40 degrees.

What was I thinking? I can be crabby sometimes when I have a lot on my mind. This morning is definitely one of those times. There are more questions than answers. This is a running joke with Steve and I regarding our travel plans.

Tomorrow is Opening Day at Yankee Stadium. As a native New Yorker, the thought of doing all 162 is pretty cool. We have spent the last 30 days preparing for this trip. From a marketing perspective, things are on track. We have a website, a Facebook fan page, and well-designed postcards and business cards that all incorporate the same theme.

162.

To me 162 means "all in." No turning back. One hundred percent commitment. Commitment is doing the thing that you said you would do long after the feeling that you said it with has gone.

I am at the hotel's "continental breakfast." It is amazing how crowded it is. I am waiting for Marcinowski. I think he is most excited by the fact that he doesn't have to go to work at Home Depot today. Steve is a recent community college graduate. He quit his five-year job at Home Depot and gave up his apartment to do this journey.

He has been telling everyone at Nutt Street Comedy that he wants to go on the road. Welcome to the road. I admire him for having the courage to drop everything to do this. Of course, what are we really risking? If we change our minds or run out of money we can always move back in with relatives!

We are embarking on the comedy tour of a lifetime. I am a very goal-oriented person. I sit at the continental breakfast table and write some goals.

162 Goals

- We have produced an independent film: *162. The Movie.*

- We have written a best-selling book (the one you're holding!): *162. The Book.*

- Our comedy careers have received positive international attention.

- We are being parodied on *Saturday Night Live*.

- We have been guests on every major talk show and late night show including Conan, Leno, Letterman, Howard Stern, Regis and Kelly.

- By Sept. 28, we both have 45 minutes worth of solid material.

- We have successfully performed at major comedy clubs all across North America.

- The YES Network has given us plenty of exposure

and interviews once per series in a different city.

• We have been picked up by major corporations for sponsorship to the tune of 100K.

• We are friends with many within the Yankees organization and have had dinner with Mo by July 1st.

• I am in the best shape of my life by September 28th.

• We are world-record holders by attending and financing all 162 New York Yankees games in one season.

The authors of the wildly successful *Chicken Soup for The Soul* series, Mark Victor Hansen and Jack Canfield, once said that you should have a "wow of a business plan." When you share your idea or plan, everyone should respond with, "Wow!" Well, our idea of attending all 162 New York Yankees games, while hitting comedy clubs and producing a movie is definitely wow-worthy.

Marcinowski makes it down to breakfast, but doesn't have his laptop with him. Hmm.

"This is probably the best time to write, while the ideas are still fresh," I casually, but strategically mention to Marz. This is my way of hinting to him that we are writing a book.

"What are you writing about?" he inquires.

"I am recording my thoughts from yesterday. I'm also writing some of my goals for the trip. The idea is for us to both write from our perspective each day. I think it will be cooler if we don't see what the other writes. This way it won't affect what we write."

He nods and plows headlong into his Corn Flakes. I can tell that this is going to be work. I don't want to act like his boss, but he is going to have to be accountable if I am going to fund this entire tour. So far, Day One – I write, and Marcinowski does not.

We pull into my brother Tommy's place in Massapequa, New York, just after 3 p.m. Tommy gives us the tour of the house that I have been visiting for more than 20 years. There is a room on the main level with a queen-sized bed and a lot of privacy. Upstairs, there are two bedrooms across the hall like many Long Island layouts. Tommy and his wife, Lucy, are on the left and the other room has two twins and a crib for when the grand kids visit.

I give Marcinowski the big room on the main floor and move my luggage into the room upstairs. I want him to feel as comfortable as possible. I know that it is awkward moving in with someone you don't know. Tommy tells us to make ourselves at home.

We are less than 24 hours from first pitch of the 2011 baseball season.

Thursday, March 31
Opening Day 2011

The journey of a lifetime begins with one single step. My excitement for the season of a lifetime is matched equally by my anxiety of dealing with the details. The questions begin right away. Should we drive or take the train? I have a feeling that we are going to be partying hard for game one. We opt for the train. Tom drops us off at 9:45 a.m. It is windy and cold on the train station platform. I have my 162 jersey on over my sweatshirt. I have my baseball glove. We have our penis-shaped thermometer banner. I have a Sharpie to mark it. It is an hour ride from Massapequa Park to Penn Station. I spend $51 for two round-trip tickets.

At around 11:00 a.m., we greet my 26-year-old nephew, Shane, at Penn Station. He is one of five of Tommy's kids and the only Yankees fan. His siblings are Mets fans and thus will not be mentioned by name in this book. Shane is getting his master's degree in education and partying at Hofstra University. He reminds me a lot of myself when I was 35.

The three of us wait for the uptown train to the Bronx. I like the excitement of the Yankees crowd, but I am not a big fan of the subways in general. It is too crowded and subdued for my taste. The subway runs $2.50 per trip. That puts us at $61 for transportation costs … and we're not even there yet. I sit on the train and calculate expenses and time spent traveling. The subway ride, with the transfer, is another 45 minutes to the stadium. So, two hours each way is four hours per day just going back and forth.

We need to find a sublet in the city. The perfect scenario would be to find two girls who live in the city that we can also date.

At 12:15 p.m., we walk out of the subway and into the crowded corner of River Ave. and 161st St. There is an indefinable Opening Day buzz in the air. The neighborhood bars are packed with Yankees fans. Mike is meeting us in The Dugout, a sports bar across from Yankee Stadium. It is jammed wall-to-wall. We make our way to the back where we find Mike with four cold beers. They were only $3, and get a lot more expensive once you're in the ballpark.

The four of us walked in to the stadium together at around 12:45, and Mike snaps a great picture of me entering the first of what will hopefully be 162 games. Shane is sitting with Mike in field box seats off right field and Marcinowski and I are in the bleachers. We stop for a beer before finding our seats.

The beers are $12 each, and Mike breaks out a fifty. "This is not going to happen everyday," I warn Marcinowski. "This is definitely a rare treat."

I start doing the math again. Two daily rounds of beer for us would be $48 per game. 162x48 = $7,776. Are you kidding me?! That's just having *two* per game. I can't help but to multiply everything we do by 162. I am obsessed with keeping us on track financially.

We get to our seats in time for the festivities. This is my first Opening Day at Yankee Stadium. It is 42 degrees at game time. This is the first regular season game ever to take place in March. I hope it gets warmer soon.

The Yankees jump ahead early in the game, but the Detroit Tigers start chipping away at the lead in the fourth and fifth innings. In the middle of the sixth, we roll out the thermometer banner that we intend on marking off in the 6th inning at every game. Marcinowski holds one end as I begin to roll it open. A small crowd begins to gather as Shane and Mike watch with anticipation.

A security guard interrupts us. "What are you guys doing?"

A random fan adds, "Nice penis banner, fags."

This isn't as much fun as I envisioned.

The security guard is now warning me. "Don't do it!"

"We are going to all 162 games and marking the thermometer off," I explain.

He stares at our banner with a confused look. He thinks that I am going to draw something obscene on the banner. Against his wishes, I take the Sharpie and draw a thin line on game 1. We quickly roll the sign back up and acknowledge how awkward that was.

As the ninth inning begins, Yankee Stadium roars as Mariano Rivera enters to the blistering sounds of Metallica's "Enter Sandman." I think Marcinowski is enjoying this more than he thought he would.

Mo mows them down in order, notching his 560th career save to pull within 41 of Trevor Hoffman for the all-time Major League lead. The Yankees bullpen retired all nine batters they faced. Chamberlain, Soriano, and Rivera. Now that's a bullpen.

With game one of the 2011 season solidly in the win column, we take the train back toward the city. The guys all want to hang out in the city but I am a little stressed out. We spent so much money today. I am also pretty wiped out and think that if we are going to make it six months we should rest a little. OK, so I'm being a pussy.

I recall with such great fondness the first time Mike and I had attended an Opening Day back in 1999. We had only been with Pre-Paid Legal for six months and we were living in Atlanta, Georgia. Joining forces with this company was a total life-changer for the both of us. In our first six months with this company we had averaged over $20K a month. We had never made that kind of money. Believe me, that'll change a few things in your life. Because of the financial blessings of all of this, we were able to travel to Oakland and watch the Yankees Opening Day debut there. It was a magical night as I actually caught the first Yankees home run of the season, hit by Chili Davis.

Friday, April 1
Am I a Fool?

It's 4 a.m. and I am wide awake. Thoughts of doubt swirl through my head as rain pounds my brother's roof. I had imagined that there would be internal struggle as we move through the season. I just didn't expect it this early. If I am ever ready to abandon something, the right time would be now. I am seriously considering calling the entire thing off. I guess there are always downs after an up. The euphoria of attending Opening Day has worn off and I am seriously weighing our next move.

The cost of two round-trip tickets to Yankee Stadium was $61. Stadium beers are $12. In fact, 95 percent of every menu item is $12. We made sandwiches to save money but left them on Tommy's kitchen counter. He texted me during the game and told me the sandwich needed more mayo. This comedy tour is no laughing matter.

We are contemplating driving but I found out that the parking is $35. And $35 x 80 remaining games = $2,800. We need a place in the city, desperately. We need to be open to attracting the perfect situation. Every time we do something, I multiply it by 162. Anyway you break it down, this is going to be a challenge. I toss and turn for an hour-and-a-half. The thing with doubt is that once you ask the question, "Why is this a bad idea?" your mind starts to answer the question.

Can we maintain the nearly two-hour commute each way to the stadium? Will we have the energy to develop, practice, and perform stand-up? Can we navigate our lifestyle around this mega-expensive trip and be able to keep our costs down? We'll see. I feel badly about sharing my thoughts with Steve. I try and stay positive as I really believe that fans will be interested in reading the story of two comics with one mission.

Tonight is our first comedy gig on the tour. We are doing an open mic in New York City. This is what we love. Our goal is to perform at two or three clubs tonight. We walk into New York Comedy Club at 5 p.m. for a 5:30 p.m. show. We are the first ones to arrive. We pay $7 to perform and move inside to wait for the audience. At 5:30 sharp, the guy who was collecting the money walks into the room full of us seven comics. "Anyone interesting in hosting?" I wonder if they reimburse the host their $7.

We both go seven minutes in front of seven other comics and two couples that have wandered in. The New York comedy scene sure is glamorous. If the road to success is filled with shitty gigs, then we are on the right path. Neither one of us has a problem paying the price because we love the art of stand-up. I admire the fact that Marcinowski comes up with jokes in the car and delivers them right away. Tonight he does this bit about how Jesus Christ is a big prankster.

"People would be minding their own business, just walking along. Jesus would hide around a corner and jump out and scare people. They would yell 'Jesus Christ!'"

Changing voices he continues, "Don't use my name in vain!" Good stuff.

We have trouble fighting traffic across town and miss our second open mic. Instead, we meet up with Mike and his 25-year-old daughter, Dani. I knew that she and Marz would like each other because they are both fun to hang out with and a little goofy.

Like me, they are also both the youngest child. Dani works for Big Beach Productions. They make movies. I'm definitely biased, but think she is really great at her job and I hope she will be an important piece of the 162 puzzle. She is currently working on a film, *Our Idiot Brother*, with Paul Rudd. I am very proud of her and believe she'll have a very exciting career in the film industry. It has been her dream since she was a small child. At my constant request, she ran the 162 idea by her boss, the producer. He said, and I quote, "Your uncle is crazy." Well, at least that's better than being "an idiot." I think.

When Mike was getting started in the personal development industry, he would do his seminars in his New York City loft. Dani would often be there and picked up on many of the self improvement-type ideas. Simply put, she learned that you can create the life of your dreams. She learned that you are the author of your life. Mike would teach that the word *author* is rooted in the word *authority*. She has taken authority for her life and her own success.

Sunday, April 3

Today is the first day that we to drive into the Bronx. It is a nerve-racking experience.

I parallel park into a spot that maybe had a foot on each side. We get out and marvel at my parking job. We realize 10 minutes into the walk that we have parked way too far away. I'd put the Mustang at two miles from Yankee Stadium. At least we are getting our exercise.

Marcinowski has opted to wear plaid the first three

games. He is terrified today when a Red Sox fan is virtually booed out of the stadium. The bleacher creatures have a very loud and intimidating *Ass-hole! Ass-hole!* chant going. As the Bostonian went to the concession stand, a female fan poured beer over his head from above and he was eventually ejected. After asking a few security guards about the situation, we were told that he was "removed for his own safety." I don't think Marcinowski will ever wear a Red Sox hat again in or out of that ballpark.

We are joined today by two friends that are straight out of Jersey Shore. Jen and Kim Quigley live down in South Jersey. Kim was once married to Slug and Jen and I dated in the summer of 1994. I haven't seen them in at least a decade. They are fun, loud, and full of ideas on what we should be doing to get attention. They are dying for us to pull out the "penis thermometer."

We finally unroll it and are trying to conceal our embarrassment. Yankees fans gather around and have no idea who we are or what we are doing. Phil Hughes takes a pounding today as the Bombers lose 10-7.

Jen is sponsoring the game tomorrow and we follow them the two hours back to Jersey. We will be spending our fourth night in a different bed in our first week. Our phone rings at 10:00 and it is Mark and AJ for our second radio show. Those guys are good interviewers and we are happy to have the weekly spot. There first question to us was, "Inquiring minds want to know: Have you guys been arrested yet?" We both answer questions for a few minutes regarding the first week. By the next morning, Steve will have spliced together footage of our first webisode of the 162 journey. Steve has been great in capturing footage so far.

Tuesday, April 5

Today is the first day that I have exercised. I go for a two mile run and do some pull ups, abs, and push ups. I have been working out regularly since my late 20s and don't want to fall out of the habit.

Marz and I visit the local Pathmark and stock up on lunch meat and cereal. We have been making sandwiches every day. Our total cost inside the stadium for the last four games has been $48. We have nailed free parking the last three games as well. There is almost nothing more satisfying than parallel parking into a tight spot and then walking two or three blocks and watching other fans pay $25-35.

The Yanks go into the game with a 3-1 record. Tonight's game is 45 degrees and windy. We both are carrying tissues in our pockets and are fighting off colds. In the 6th inning, Marcinowski finds an open mic in Huntington that starts at 10:30. He texts and quickly hears back from the girl booking the show. They will squeeze us in for 10 minutes each. As the temperature drops our desire to beat the traffic rises.

The Yanks have this game. Tex slams another three-run shot. Sabathia looks brilliant, scattering two hits and a walk over seven innings. With one out in the eighth inning, we decide that this game is a lock. We turn the radio on in the car and learn that the Twins have tied the game at four. I hate being a fan who leaves early, but we have a comedy show to do. Soriano blows this game by walking three in the eighth. The Twins win 5-4 in 10 innings.

At 10:45, we walk up to Katie Mc's Irish Pub. One of the comics is smoking outside and greets us.

"You must be Steve and Steve. Heard about you guys. Are you really going to every game? You must be rich."

"We do OK," I said.

"How can you afford it? I go to one game and I'm broke for a month," quips Rob. Rob is there with the "booker," Jessica, and the headliner for the night, Tim. They are the most welcoming comedians I can recall.

"We are on a tight budget," I offer. "We have an uncanny ability to get free beer." We divulge a little of our cost-saving strategies.

"What are you guys drinking?" asks the 24-year-old Jessica, as we enter the Irish Pub. She is very cute … and very taken by Tim.

"Yuengling and a Blue Point," we eagerly confess as she forks over the $7.

"You guys got some scam going getting all this free beer," Rob jokes. Rob is hosting and precedes to bust our balls all night. It is hilarious. The crowd is made up of six comics, five customers, and a friendly bartender. We both have fun sets.

"We were told that you had to blow somebody to get stage time in Long Island. I'm not sure who we are supposed to see." This is my first joke.

A little after midnight, Jessica comes over carrying a coffee container that has written on it, "Donate to Haiti." The Haiti is crossed out, but it's still very readable. I think she is about to ask us for a donation. She begins counting out the money.

"We usually split the tips on comedy night, but since you guys are on the road and have come all this way, we want you to have it."

"Whhhhhaaaaaattttttttt?," I say to Steve as we get back into the Funnymobile. "Four beers, two shots, *and* $19.

"We have arrived, sir!"

71

Chapter Six

HAVE A GOOD GAY, GAYS

After a couple of days of rainouts and more comedy clubs, we are definitely starting to feel run down. But there are no sick days in 162. We must suck it up and figure out a way to keep going. After A.J. Burnett delivers a gem in a 4-3 matinee game, we hit our first open mic at 6 p.m. at Broadway Comedy where we perform for 30 other comics. At 11:00 p.m. we're performing the "real" show. We're getting the routine down. We have performed five times in the last 48 hours. We are both becoming a lot more comfortable on stage. At midnight, we begin our trip to Boston, via Connecticut, and we pull into the driveway of the lavish home of my former college roommate, Slug, at 1:30 a.m.

This weekend is the first company convention that I will miss in 12 years of being with Pre-Paid Legal. It's a good thing I have two of the most talented and inspiring business partners in modern times. They are hosting more than 600 of our sales reps from all over the U.S. and Canada. We host a reception for the entire company on the Thursday Night at every event. It'll be surreal to miss it.

Friday, April 8

We are on the road again. Slug and his wife, Tina, have a nanny who made us blueberry pancakes and Tina sent us off with goody baskets full of snacks.

We check into the Marcinowski Resort and Spa. His mom is very nice and full of questions. We sat less than 10 minutes and make our way to historic Fenway Park.

I feel my first bit of anxiety as I witness a sea of red. I immediately get some stares. When the train comes, I hear, "Yankees fans in the back," followed by some laughter. I am decked out in my 162 jersey and plastic helmet.

By 1 p.m., we are downtown just outside of Fenway Park. As a baseball fan, I am mesmerized by the tradition and history. Although the Red Sox are 0-6, there is still a palpable buzz around the stadium. Fenway is smaller and tighter than anywhere else I've been. This adds to the energy. We have Standing Room Only (SRO) tickets and are having a hard time figuring out where to actually stand.

Boston legend Carl Yastrzemski throws out the first pitch. I am filled with nostalgia for the entire pre-game, despite security continually telling us that we can't stand wherever we are standing. We visit the Green Monster, the famous 37-foot left field wall, the highest in Major League Baseball. The view is incredible. Just as we get there A-Rod rips a two-run homer and sends it right our way. Boston responds right away chasing Phil Hughes from the game in the second inning and takes a commanding 6-2 lead. Boston goes on to secure their first win of the year, 9-6.

We jump back on the train and are back downtown by 6 p.m. We are performing at Nick's Comedy Club at 8:30 tonight. But first, we grab a quick dinner with Slug and Tina Ferrara, who are in Boston for our show tonight and the game tomorrow. They have invited us to join them at Oishii, a swanky sushi place that's walking distance to Nick's.

Marcinowski and I excuse ourselves at 7:45 and make our way to our biggest performance of the tour. The Ferraras pick up the tab. John Tobin, the club manager, is outside. I'm still fully dressed in my Yankees gear head to toe.

"Let me guess, Steve and Steve?" John was gracious and introduced us around to the other comics.

I am introduced to a chorus of boos from the crowd. Nevertheless, I have a fun set. I love the Yankees/Red Sox rivalry and feed off of the energy.

"I hope my set gets off to a better start than the Red Sox season," I taunted.

I am feeling way more confident on stage. I do some 162 material. Our first gig in Boston is a success.

Saturday, April 9

The trip to Boston has been incredible. The biggest surprise is how nice the people are. I believe the media escalates the rivalry. Its still a great rivalry, but the people do not have to hate each other and be violent. I only received a few comments that were looking for trouble. Having Steve along is a good influence. Our mantra has been, "Do not engage."

We have gorgeous weather for the Saturday afternoon game and a much better outcome for the Bombers. The Yanks get off to a big start and never look back. Newcomers Eric Chavez and Russell Martin are the heroes today. Martin blasts two shots over the Green

Monster and Chavez chips in three hits in the DH role. Cano and Granderson also added home runs.

We are SRO again, but stand behind Section 2 in right field that has a great view of the field. A newer feature to many ballparks is the wandering photographer. They walk around and get paid $1 every time they snap a picture. They give you a ticket to an online feature that allows you to buy a copy.

Marcinowski and I are standing as the photographer makes his way to us. He signals for us to get closer together as the field is our backdrop. He hands us our ticket and says, "Have a good gay, gays." He doesn't even bother to correct himself. It takes a second after he walks away, but we turn to each other and both laugh. Did he really say that?

After the game, we visit the Red Sox bars and are treated respectfully. Most Red Sox fans will give you a hard time just to see how you will react. If you laugh and have fun, their defenses drop and you can have a great conversation. Like anywhere, you'll have an occasional jerk.

The game is over by 4 p.m. and we won't have time to go home and change before our comedy gig at Nick's tonight. We decide to stay around the stadium and have a few more beers. Bad idea.

"You guys look like shit," observes John Tobin as we walk up to Nick's.

"It is exhausting going to every game," I offer.

"The season just started! It's only the second week!"

He has a good point. It sure feels longer than eight games.

Steve's entire family is in the crowd tonight and they have secured the two front tables. There are about

15 in their party. Sometimes this makes a set easier for a performer, but not tonight.

I go up first and have a pretty good set.

Marcinowski is next and doesn't have his best stuff. He is thrown off by our generous beer consumption earlier and the fact that his family is in the front row. They are tough on him and almost have a prove-to-me-that-you-are-funny attitude.

Sunday, April 10

Today is the last day of the Pre-Paid Legal convention. I am Skyping into our team's breakout session at 10 a.m. I am live in OKC. [*By the way, since it's kind of a new word, I looked up "Skyping" just to make sure I'm spelling it right. The Urban Dictionary gives two definitions for it: 1) "To use the Skype program to video chat virtually online with friends," and 2) "The act of ejaculating, usually in the fashion of ejaculating on to another person." Just to be clear -- in this instance I'm talking about definition #1!*]

Anyway, Kim introduces me and I am live on a 12-foot screen. I am Skyping in from Marcinowski's childhood bedroom. I thank the team and about three minutes into it, I am informed that Rip Mason, the new CEO has just stopped in to address the crowd. He gets a standing ovation as I try to watch from my laptop. A few minutes later I complete my talk and throw it back to my partners. It seems like they have done an incredible job without me. This makes me breathe easier.

The game tonight is the ESPN Game of the Week and has a 8:05 p.m. start time. The Marcinowskis are throwing a huge barbecue for us this afternoon.

They could not have been nicer or made me feel

more comfortable. I am trying to act as masculine as possible in front of Steve's dad. The first question that he asked Steve about me a month ago was regarding whether I was gay or not.

His sister chirps in about Steve's set and has no problem advising him on what jokes should remain in his act. "You definitely shouldn't do the Jesus bit. It wasn't funny." I change the subject as we feast.

"Does anyone know who is pitching for the Sox tonight?" I ask.

The entire group of 12 fall silent as if I had asked about what causes gravity. I hesitate, before adding, "The Yanks are pitching Sabathia." No one says a word. I bet you can't find a house in a 50-mile radius that cares less about sports.

Steve's mom breaks the awkward silence as she addresses the group.

"They paid $300 for tickets and they didn't even get a seat."

"How could you be there for three hours and not sit? Can't you bring in a lawn chair or something," asks Steve's sister.

I start to answer but catch myself and cut it short. "No."

"I don't see why not."

Marcinowski is making a burger and chooses to stay out of the conversation. I can tell that he has been dealing with these people for a while. Steve's uncle looks exactly like his dad and I have a hard time telling them apart.

"You guys need tickets?" he asks. "You should have said something. I got connections. I know a guy."

We've spent more than $700 on tickets for three games and now he says this.

"Well, we'll be back two more times," I said, hoping this will lead to future tickets.

Steve's mom jumps in. "The Yankees are only here one more time this year."

I try to hold back, but can't.

"I'm pretty sure they play three times here. It's the same every year. They play everyone in their division three times."

We go back and forth, but nobody believes me and we leave it at that.

Wednesday, April 13

We have a great experience with the ticketing office. We wait in the customer service line and are greeted by Danny Hansbury. I hand him a card through the window and explain that we were the 162 Guys, comics attending every game.

"Sorry, I haven't heard of you."

"That's cool we are only on game 10. We have a few issues."

We have two seats in Section 305 thanks to Mike Melia. I accidentally printed out the same ticket twice. Unfortunately, Marcinowski doused one of the tickets that we do have with his beer that we drank in our parking spot.

Danny seems to like us and is feeling us out to see if we are real. A moment later he returns from the back and with two *free* tickets right behind home plate and two tickets to the Mohegan Sports Bar, so we will have a place to hang out if it rains. He knows that he is hooking us up, but downplays it and says that he wishes he could help more.

This is a breakthrough. We receive a ticket from the

Yankees. Game on!

I spend the first inning behind home plate, but the constant drizzle sends us to The Mohegan Sports bar. I didn't realize when Danny handed us the tickets, but these are valued at $100 each.

A-Rod rips a three-run shot in the first and the Bombers never looked back. A.J. Burnett notches his third win in as many starts. The win moves the Yanks back into a first place tie with the Orioles.

Only 152 to go!

Thursday-Friday, April 14-15

My dad took a spill two days ago. He is in the hospital now and my brother Mike is spending all of his non-sleeping time by his side.

Marcinowski and I are getting into the routine. I have been making sandwiches before every game. The stadium allows you to bring in any type of food you want. We leave at the same time every day, between 4:15 and 4:30. We bring a cooler and have two or three beers pre-game.

Tonight we are treated to exciting baseball. Steve and I are able to sit behind home plate again with some quick thinking. We use our ticket from the night before to get into the section. The lady in that section probably thinks that we are season ticket holders! It makes a big difference when you can see the entire game from that perspective.

I spend much of the day preparing for our upcoming road trip. On Sunday after the game we will leave directly for Toronto. We will be doing a comedy show Monday night and play the Blue Jays on Tuesday and Wednesday. Then we'll leave Wednesday after the game and start our trek back to Baltimore. We have places to stay in both cities. We should save a ton on this trip between airfare and hotels.

Mostly because of my Pre-Paid Legal business, I have a huge social network and people seem to like me staying with them. It is a win-win. I will be doing a recruiting lunch in Toronto on Wednesday afternoon.

In Baltimore, my host Ben Bradshaw hooked me up with his friend Matt from the Orioles ticketing office. I bought a total of eight tickets for $200 ($25 each). Ben offers for us to stay at his house for the weekend series.

Tonight we begin a three-game series with the Texas Rangers. They sent us home early last year in the first round of the playoffs.

Sunday, April 17
ESPN Sunday Night Game of the Week

We leave for the Bronx at 5 p.m. and are all packed for an exciting trip that will span two countries, three states, 1,200 miles, and 20 hours in the car. We are going to Toronto and then to Baltimore, before returning to the Big Apple. We will enjoy one comedy show, two PPL meetings, a birthday, and six games before we make it back to Massapequa.

Because the Yankees are the Yankees, the schedule can be more demanding than for other teams. For instance, the Yankees have more Sunday Night games than any other team, which makes traveling even more demanding. As most fans know, the last game of a series is usually a day game so that the teams can travel. It is called a getaway game.

The Yanks have the luxury of jumping on their jet

and heading for the next city. In this case it is Toronto. Us? Not so much.

As soon as I looked at the 2011 season, I realized that it would be way less cheaper to drive to Toronto as there is a day off Monday and Thursday. Because they play in a dome, we don't have to worry about a postponement due to rain or snow.

This is the fourth time we do the New York sports radio show. We find a quiet spot at Yankee Stadium to do the show. Mark and AJ are getting a kick out of our journey and are wondering where we are going to sleep tonight.

The radio show is turning out to be very beneficial as it keeps us talking about the tour. We notice that we are getting the same routine questions from fans as we do from Mark and AJ.

As the game winds up, we briskly walk to our car as we hear the stadium P.A. blaring *New York, New York*, by Frank Sinatra. We share a high five and are on our way to the Great White North. There is a light rain all night and that continues on the drive. We pull out of our free parking spot in the Bronx at 11:30 p.m.

The Yanks win the series tonight taking two out of three against the Angels and Mariano gets save number seven. We are exhausted and just want to make it to Binghamton. There are not a lot of hotels to choose from. We find a little dump for $55 named Roscoe Motel about 30 miles shy of our goal at around 2 a.m. Our fatigue and budget dictate that this is our place for the night. I highly recommend *not* staying here. The putrid smell in the lobby is barely sustainable. I am hoping the room is better as I am almost gagging handing the night clerk my credit card.

As we entered the room, the temperature seems the same inside as outside. Steve breaks out the Flip camera and starts taping. His teeth are literally chattering as he attempts to adjust the thermostat.

"What are you doing, Dude? There is a heat surcharge if we turn on the heat," I caution. The 25-year-old is sometimes naive when it comes to traveling, but not this time.

"Really? No way, Melia," he says as he continues to adjust the 1960-something thermostat. "I know you too well to think that you are going to sleep in here like this!"

I enter the bathroom to discover a dead cockroach in the shower. "We got a casualty in here," I announce. Marcinowski peeks in.

"Imagine how disgusting a place has to be for a cockroach not to be able to survive here."

I could tell Marcinowski is on to some great new material. He does an impromptu act where he pretends to be a bug dying. "It's too dirty here. I can't live like this! Gasp ... gasp." He falls over unto the bed and fakes a cockroach death with his arms and legs flailing.

In moments like this, at least we have our senses of humor.

Monday, April 18
Toronto bound

I have been traveling extensively for the last 15 years. I have been spoiled in that I get to stay in very nice hotels and resorts as I travel. This will be one of the biggest differences and luxuries that I will be avoiding this season.

I learn a valuable lesson today: Communicate clearly and understand exactly the living environment where you will be staying.

Over the last few weeks, I have been getting the

word out that I am looking for places to stay on the road. I know a ton of people in Toronto, but none that are very close to the Rodgers Center, home of the Blue Jays.

At the meeting in OKC last week, Kim stood up and asked if anyone would be willing to put us up. A woman named Alison stepped up and offered her apartment. I was quick to save a few hundred dollars wanting to endure the entire season. I accepted.

We spoke once on the phone for a few minutes and she certainly seemed nice. She is from the Islands, new to PPL, and lives downtown. She asked me on the phone if it would be OK if she could have people stop by and meet me during our stay.

"I'm not sure when," I said, regrettably. "We will be pretty busy."

"How about after the game?" she countered. She was anxious to have her prospects meet a successful PPL associate.

At midnight? I thought to myself. *And after a night of drinking beer?* I want to help, but there is no telling how long a game may last and what kind of shape we will be in. I told her that it would be difficult so late at night, but she should invite them to our comedy show or the PPL luncheon that I am hosting on Wednesday."

She was persistent and asked about possibilities during the day. Again, I delicately had to decline because I knew that we'd want to hit the city. She seemed disappointed.

I explain to Marcinowski that I don't know the people we are staying with, but I'm sure that it will work out fine. I don't tell him, but someone offered us a great condo downtown at $125 per night. I know that we have to cut back, so I politely declined.

At around 5 p.m., we turned into their apartment complex. We have a comedy show at 9:00 and I am really hoping to get a power nap in and to be refreshed for the set. We leave our luggage in the car and make our way to the 12th floor. We can hear noise inside as we approach. We knock, but no one comes to the door. After knocking several times with increasing volume, the door opens, and standing there is this Jamaican dude. He is holding a baby and has some killer Medusa-invoking dreadlocks. He is wearing a tank top that reveals his ripped physique. We both look surprised to see each other. Apparently, he's Alison's boyfriend, and we're told she would be home from work soon. As he describes where we should park, our eyes dart around our new pad. Instantly, we feel like this won't work for us. I like my privacy. This is sort of awkward.

Our host begins to hand his toddler to Marcinowski, so he can help me park the car. Steve's eyes are bigger than softballs as he holds his hands up in protest. He reads Steve's body language and keeps his baby. He gives us a key to the parking garage and additional instructions. Upon leaving the apartment, we couldn't look at each other fast enough.

I wait until we are in the tiny elevator before I start talking.

"Man, I'm sorry. This is certainly going to be a long few days."

"He tried to hand me his baby!"

We both laugh at the strangeness of this situation. We move our car and drag two big suitcases and our laptops back up to the 12th floor. Our host shows us to our bedroom.

I quickly notice that we will be sharing a queen size bed. I guess we will be getting closer on this trip.

Marcinowski's observation skills do me one better as he correctly observes, "This is their bedroom, Melia. We are sleeping in their bed!" We look at each other. It is time for action.

Our bags are still in the living room. As we make it out he asks us if we want to shower.

"Uh, no, we're OK. Hey listen, uh, is that your bedroom?" I delicately ask.

"Yes, we want you to be comfortable," came the oblivious reply.

The next few minutes is like watching a McEnroe vs. Connors tennis match. He deftly returns every one of my objections. Marcinowski isn't doing any of the talking. He reminds me of the character Silent Bob from the movie *Clerks*.

"Listen, we really, really appreciate it, but we can't take your bed."

"It's OK, mon," he says, using the stereotypical dialect you'd expect. "I work nights and Alison and de baby will sleep on de couch."

"This is very generous, but we have a lot of stuff. We are making a movie and we need to spread out our computers."

Marcinowski is standing still like a statue.

"Alison will be very disappointed if you don't stay."

Finally, I decide to make the break. This isn't an argument I am going to win.

"We have a big comedy show tonight. We still need to freshen up. We are just going to go now. I'll call Alison."

We say our good-byes and we are out of there as fast as we came. The entire episode from our first knock until we wheeled out our luggage could not have been more than 12 minutes. As we make it to the elevator, I feel as relieved as I do guilty for not staying. We try to figure out where we are and what hotel we are going to.

I am setting up the navigation system on the phone, when it rings. It's Alison.

"What's the matter?"

"Listen, we want to thank you, but we can't take over your bedroom. We really appreciate it, though."

"I'm sorry that it wasn't up to your standards."

"Oh no, no, it's not that. It's just that we are two grown men and we don't usually sleep in the same bed."

Thank God she laughs, because it breaks the tension.

"My entire family is coming from the Islands next week. We can fit a lot of people in this apartment."

We are crawling through traffic listening on speakerphone. I don't know the laws here, but I am sure I wasn't allowed to be on my cell phone. Alison and I repeat the same conversation I had with her boyfriend just minutes earlier. She finally gives up.

This is certainly going to be a long season as this is only the fourth away game of the year.

Wednesday, April 20

We check out of our hotel and make our way to a restaurant on the airport strip. We have a crowd of 30 that have come to hear about Pre-Paid Legal Services. I do a 30-minute talk on our company and my hosts buy Steve and I lunch. Later in the evening, we grab some dinner at the St. Louis Ribs across the street from the stadium. We begin to talk to a couple of Canadian businessmen on our left. They are extremely interested in hearing about our 162-game tour. We witness Canadian generosity firsthand when the checks come. Our new friend, Mike, takes our check and puts it with his on the credit card tray.

"This one is on us, fellas. You have a long season in front of you."

"You guys are definitely making the book!" I promised.

We express our genuine gratitude and we all take off for the game. With two free meals under our belts, we make our way to game 16. We are almost 10 percent of the way through the season.

Friday, April 22

I get the day started with a great workout. Marcinowski watches video from our trip and does his best to start editing Webisode 3. It takes a lot more work to put these together than I thought.

It is supposed to rain heavily in the late afternoon and ease up at night. We arrive at the home of Ben and Lauren Bradshaw just outside of Baltimore. We are greeted by Pablo, a large American Bulldog. They are supercool and we feel comfortable immediately. The Bradshaws are in their late 20s and were recently married.

Marcinowski was understandably worried about our accommodations after the Toronto trip. He's more at ease now and he is happy to meet some people his own age.

After getting all settled in, we head for Camden Yards, the home of The Baltimore Orioles. The bars outside the stadium are pretty packed. We decide on Sliders, which is featuring $2 beers.

The relentless rain will most certainly doom this game, but the vibe in the bar is pretty cool, so we hang out. I make eye contact with a young woman, who I find out shortly afterwards is a 31-year-old 7th grade teacher. And she's pretty hot. Her friend is a school teacher as well. The girls are down from Jersey for the games.

The hot one's game was to see how many drinks she could get bought for her. Steve and I have a very strict policy. We do not buy drinks for girls. We watch in amazement as several beers and shots get sent their way. The hotter one is definitely throwing off the vibe. Her friend tells us that her light is always on.

When the hot one comes back from the bathroom, she repositions herself next to Marcinowski. Within minutes they are making out like they have been denied each other for years. It is passionate, hysterical, and bordering on embarrassing. Marcinowski is horny and this girl is game.

We all walk out into the now-light drizzle to put my glove back in the car and move to our next location. We are parked in a garage that only allows parking for 30 minutes after the game. As we stand in the rain discussing what to do with the Mustang, we turn around and noticed the girls have disappeared. It is very strange. As much as Marz wants to get laid, he doesn't seem to care one bit. We laugh and start to walk back towards the bars. This is when we hit our first strip club of the tour.

Two fairly large strippers begin flirting with us. The bartender asks if we want to buy them a drink. When the cocktails arrive, she asks for $20. "No way," is my response. Before I realize it, Marcinowski has already forked over $20. She tells us that covers one drink.

We leave and agree not to hit any more strip clubs on the tour. We spent more in 10 minutes than we do for an entire night at Yankee Stadium.

Wednesday, April 27

The home games are becoming quite habitual. I make sandwiches, and now I'm adding a little macaroni salad and a snack as well. You can save a lot of money by packing your own dinner.

We continue to park for free in the Bronx. We need to leave by 4:15 to miss traffic and get a good spot. We pack a cooler and drink two beers each before the game in the car. Tonight we splurge and go to The Dugout for a

Pabst Blue Ribbon. With a tip, our cost is $8. We haven't bought anything inside the stadium this entire home stand. The tickets have been running us about $15 each for home games. With Mary and Burger picking up our tolls, gas is our biggest expense. I can make it to the stadium three times on a tank.

Earlier in the book, I referred to Tim Ferriss' *4-Hour Workweek*. In the book, he talks about having systems to maximize your effectiveness. The word *system* is an acronym for **Save Yourself Some Time, Energy,** and **Money**. I do a 12 p.m. conference call every day with our top 50 sales associates for 15 minutes. This gives me a chance to stay connected to them and give a little motivational chat every day. No one seems to be distracted by my 162 Tour. Efficiency is a beautiful thing.

Friday, April 29

I spend the morning doing last minute preparations for our trip to Detroit. I think that Marcinowski is on baseball overload. He has been watching less baseball and playing more "Words with Friends," a game that's sort of a modern-day Scrabble. Him attending a baseball game every day is like bringing your gay friend to a strip club every day. He is getting antsy as we have not performed comedy in two weeks.

Saturday, April 30

So far, we have had five home games this week. We spent a total of $5.50 inside the stadium. We've spent $18.00 on beers and $6 on tips at The Dugout. We brought all of our own food Tuesday-Friday. We drank two or three beers each in the car before the game. The only stadium purchase was a soda to mix our Jack Daniels that Marz snuck into the park for his birthday a few days ago. We spent about $120 on tickets this week. We did go to the grocery store a few times, though, and racked up about $90. Still, financially speaking, a pretty successful week.

The parking situation is very simple so far. Out of 15 home games, we have paid zero for parking! We leave Long Island everyday between 4:15 and 4:45. The trip takes 75 minutes. We sit in the car and tape as we drink our pre-game beers.

Marz and I agreed last night that it is time to step up the promotion. I will be in charge of media and he will head up the comedy scene. Today is the 24th game of the year and we have adjusted to our new lifestyle.

I am writing a new press release for our 25th game. We meet Mike and Dani in the city before the game. Mike and I have been inseparable for more than 17 years. I think he is as surprised as anyone that we are pulling this off.

Mike bought the tickets for today's game. Marcinowski and I snap a great picture with our sign that reads "24 down — 138 to go." I am wearing my Jorge Posada batting helmet. Spring is almost in the air as the game time temperature is 61 degrees and partly cloudy. The Yanks bounce back with a 5-4 win, as A.J. Burnett gets his team-leading fourth win of the year.

Meanwhile, in Florida, my dad was back in the rehab center in Palm Bay, Florida, about 20 minutes north of where Mike lives. Dad hadn't wanted to go back there because he was embarrassed to have fallen again. Right before Mike left for New York, my dad told him that he was real weak and had told the rehab folks he thought he needed a blood transfusion. Over the years, his kidney specialist recommended this type of treatment once in a while to "pep" him up. "Don't be surprised if you hear I've gone to the hospital," he told Mike. Sure enough, Mike got a call from our sister that Dad was admitted to The Palm Bay Hospital and received a blood transfusion. The doctors decided to keep him for a few days.

Sunday, May 1

Today is the first day that we do not have tickets in advance. We ask around in The Dugout to no avail. It seems like there is more demand today than supply. We are not able to get tickets until the top of the third when we score two tickets for $40.

We make our way into the stadium and security tells me that I can't come in with my New York Yankees helmet. I tell them that I came in yesterday and half the season with it. They won't budge. We attempt to enter two different gates and receive the same answer. I can walk all the way back to the car or ditch the somewhat busted-up helmet. They tell me to throw it in the garbage. I refuse and, instead, take it off and lay it on the ground. "If you want to throw it away you can, I'm *not* throwing away my helmet!" I declare. I am pissed at their sudden enforcement of a new rule that came out of, well, left field!.

The Yankees end the home stand on a good note. Tex hits a solo shot in the first and Granderson adds a three run bomb in the fifth. Nova pitched into the seventh inning scattering two runs

No, those aren't gang signs; we're flashing our accomplishment of hitting Game 25

and six hits. He struggles a bit today walking four. Mariano notches his 10th save in just 25 games.

We spend the night doing laundry, and at 10:45 Sports Talk New York calls for our weekly interview. After a few normal questions, the interview takes an unexpected turn.

"Here's a non-baseball topic. It has been confirmed that Osama bin-Laden is confirmed dead." Mark tells us that they just announced it in Philadelphia during the Mets-Phillies game and that the crowd cheered wildly. I do not even recall the next question, I just found it weird that they are asking *our* opinions. Marcinowski does the best he can do to throw in a one-liner before they go on to their next guest.

We might have one less terrorist in the world, which should allow us all to sleep better at night. But on this night, sleep doesn't come easy for me. Kim has been in Guatemala since last Sunday, and I'm thinking about our situation. This tour is supposed to serve as a time of healing for us. We were married for nine years and have been separated for eight months. As a comedian, you learn to find what is funny about a situation and exaggerate it with emotion. The reality is that I miss her very much and it is still very difficult. Ever since we met, she has been an important part of my life and hopefully she always will be. She has a servant's heart and continues to visit the orphanage that we have donated our time and financial resources to.

     I conceal my sadness with humor, but it is part of the deal.

Chapter Seven

MOTOR CITY MADNESS

Monday, May 2

We rush out without having breakfast. Tommy is driving us to JFK. He lost many friends in the 9/11 attacks, and the number of firefighters lost, 343, is still fresh in his mind almost 10 years later. The news of bin-Laden's demise brings all of that to the surface once again. Facebook is full of posts that are across the board. I stay away from posting stuff about this because it is such a sensitive subject. My comedian partner, however, fills our 162 Facebook page with his comedic take on the event. I sit in the front seat as we crawl in Long Island traffic listening to Marcinowski throw out one-liner after one-liner. My brother's reactions are stoic as I feel very uncomfortable. Know your audience.

11:50 a.m.

We land in Detroit and I learn that we are down to one camera because Marcinowski left our other one in New York with Dani. This is the first time we are flying and I want to capture as much footage as possible.

We wait for our luggage, which consists of one very large red suitcase. We are splitting a bag because Spirit Airlines charges $30 per bag. We are about to make a serious error in judgment. A taxi downtown will cost $60-$70. We call the hotel for a shuttle and discover that they do not have a shuttle service. I remember a trick I used in Vegas once. I took the free shuttle to another hotel and simply walked next door to my hotel. We venture over to the courtesy shuttles and figure that we can walk or get a cheaper taxi ride. We approach a shuttle driver.

"You can take the SmartBus," we're told. "It goes downtown and only costs $2."

We move our 58-pound suitcase over to the bus stop. There is a pretty shady group congregating. Ten minutes later the bus comes. The driver is a XXXL woman with an attitude. We ask her about going downtown, but she announces that she's on break and that she'll answer our questions when she gets back from the bathroom. She waddles away. When she gets back, there is a little chaos which ends by her yelling, "I can only talk to one person at a time!" I reach for my billfold and am chastised for not having my crisp dollars ready. "Have your money ready next time!" she barks.

"I didn't know I was going to be on a bus. Sorry for slowing down your day," I counter. She gives us a frown but provides no information or guidance.

At 12:45 p.m., our bus departs. We realize pretty quickly that this is a bad idea. The clientele on the bus is sketchy at best. Our illustrious driver stops every ¼ mile and has something rude to say to everyone coming or going. We use our GPS to determine that we are at least 20 miles away with a drive-time of 27 minutes.

It's now 1:15 p.m. and we are 30 minutes into the

trip; 17 miles and 24 minutes away. Our destination, the St. Regis Hotel, seems light years away.

At 1:45 p.m., the situation becomes laughable. Almost. The bus isn't even going *by* our hotel. We use our GPS to schedule our escape. At 2 p.m., we get off at Fort and 8th, which is another big mistake. We walk for 10 minutes with no sign of a taxi. Marcinowski is taping as some locals approach us to see if we need help. I warn him to be careful, that we don't want to get shot. It is downright scary.

We have not eaten all day. We walk into a Burger King at 2:15 p.m. that is perhaps the roughest fast food joint I have ever encountered. Half of the customers look homeless. The other half look much worse. I try not to touch anything. A guy at the next table has an entire conversation with himself.

I make a promise to Marcinowski: "We will never take a bus again!" He laughs. He enjoys it when I am constantly modifying the rules. "Seriously, read my lips, this is our last bus ride." He takes out the Flip camera and makes me repeat my promise.

2:27 p.m. We begin our quest for a cab. It is cold and beginning to drizzle. It seems like we are in an area not known for its wide variety of limousine services. We walk six blocks with our computer bags, big red suitcase, and Flip camera in tow before we spot the first available cab. We run while waving our arms frantically, much like Gilligan and the Skipper might do after spotting an airplane flying by their tropical island.

"St. Regis Hotel, please," we beseech the driver. At this point I don't care how much it costs or even where it is, I just want to get off of the street.

Four miles later, at 2:45 p.m., nearly three ours after

we landed, we pull up to what was probably a really nice hotel at one point in history. I pay the driver $15 and we check in. As we begin to walk away from the front desk, Marcinowski semi-frantically begins checking all of his pockets repeatedly before he realizes that he has left camera number two in the cab!

I am really pissed. This is about the maddest I have been since leaving North Carolina. He makes what he considers a great attempt to get the camera back by calling the cab company a total of one time. Not exactly a valiant effort.

We are exhausted and settle in for nap time. This is turning out to be the greatest movie never caught on tape.

After our much-needed naps, we make it to Hockeytown across from Comerica Park. We meet a really cool bartender, Rebecca East. She is a bubbly blond and loves all things Detroit. She also loves the 162 idea and rewards us with a shot of our choice. In the stadium, we move around quite a bit in an effort to stay warm. We enjoy walking around Comerica and search to find the best deal on beer. We meet an ambitious beer vendor who informs us that she would refill our beers for $5 (under the table, of course). The regular price is $8.50 per beer and comes with a cup. She has obviously performed this scam before. Every time we go back she makes us promise that she is not being set up. This becomes very stressful as she constantly looks around to make sure that her boss is not in sight. Marcinowski wishes we had someone like her at every stadium! The Yanks edge Detroit tonight 5-3, improving their record to 17-9.

Tuesday, May 3
Octopuses and Lebanese Thugs

Late in the day, we make it back to Hockeytown. Our new favorite Detroit bartender, Rebecca, has the night off and is going to the game. She greets us both with a hug. She introduces us to Scott, a Scottish dude, who is in Detroit for a week. This is his first Major League Baseball game. We can't tell if their relationship is anything more than friends. He has a constant huge smile and is easy to be around.

A local radio station is sponsoring a promotional event and the DJ announces a pre-game contest that involves throwing octopus for distance. We quickly order and eat our dinner as we do not want to miss this. Luckily, Dani is overnighting camera #1 from New York. These are the kind of things you film when making a movie. There are about 30 puss tossers. The smell is so gross that we have to wash our hands after every toss. The contest is being held in the backyard of Hockeytown with the temperature hovering around 40 degrees and an even colder windchill.

The Octopuses are stored in a big, smelly container. Each participant must reach in and pick their own puss. I have a hard time even putting my hand in the makeshift aquarium. Very little direction is given. Marcinowski and I discuss our strategy and whether they are alive or dead.

The first contest is for distance and we do not fare very well. The accuracy portion of the contest is next. There is a plastic target on the ground some 25 yards away. I am getting a rhythm down as I toss the squid like a bowling ball. All of our afternoon bocce ball matches are paying off; two full steps and proper follow up. After three grueling rounds, I somehow make it to the finals alongside two Tigers fans. Turns out, the winner will be rewarded two

Red Wings playoff tickets for Friday night. I technically lie when I fill out an application and say that I live in Detroit. I even make up an address. I don't find it fair that you have to be a local to win. This was not announced earlier.

The finals include three tosses each. I get booed when I step up to throw. I use the energy of the crowd to get in a zone. All three tosses wind up on the tarp and adrenaline surges through my body as I take first place. We win Red Wings playoff tickets! Only one problem: we obviously can't go since we will be in Dallas on Friday.

The game is freezing, windy, and rainy. We leave our seats and spend several innings at an indoor bar, The Upper Deck. Our runny noses and sniffles have not gone away since the trip began. It is nice to be inside for a change. We are seated at the bar in the 5th inning and Steve is playing his usual Words With Friends. I am watching the game on TV. A guy is waiting in line to place his order and can see over Steve's shoulder.

"Seriously, Dude?" he says incredulously. "You are at a baseball game and you are playing a game on your phone?"

Without even looking up, Marz replies, "I go to a lot of games." No further explanation. His answer and demeanor are classic.

The Yanks lose this one 4-2 and we make our way back to Hockeytown. Rebecca and Scott are happy to see us. Also with the group is another off-duty bartender, Danielle, and a Lebanese guy named Rudy. Rudy is very threatened by us right away for some reason. We proceed to do a round of shots and we present Rebecca with the Red Wings playoff tickets. She is super-appreciative. Rudy doesn't take the news as well.

We get invited to hang out for the night. It becomes

obvious that we have too many people for Rudy's Mercedes. Steve and I begin to back out, but Scott won't hear of it. This is when things start to get exciting. Scott volunteers to get in the trunk. At first, Rudy argues and isn't going to allow it, but he finally gives in as Scott piles in the trunk. Scott is a big boy. I'd put him at 6'-2" and around 240 lbs.

Rudy slams the trunk closed and mumbles, "He'll be sorry." He proceeds to squeal out of the parking lot, pounding on the accelerator. He fishtails around a few turns while maneuvering the car from right to left as many times as possible without overtly alerting the police. I am seated in the back on the driver's side holding the handle for dear life. Marcinowski and I exchange a glance that has "WTF" and "this-dude-is-nuts" all rolled into one. Ten intense minutes later, we arrive at an Irish Pub.

Scott slowly gets out and declares that he is feeling a little dizzy. As we make our way to the bar, we hear Scott yelling something profane at Rudy. We look back and see Scott's hands gripping Rudy's collar. This is the Scottish way of letting him know how he felt about his driving. Rebecca is sandwiched between them. Rudy quickly karate chops away Scott's arm and unleashes some threats of his own. We reluctantly decide to get between them as Danielle yells for our help.

Steve and I are the kind of guys who usually run and wait inside the bar when a fight breaks out. This is when Rudy gives the speech of a lifetime.

"I don't give a f--- about you, about you, or you," he says pointing at us individually. His rant goes on as bystanders begin to gather. I believe he actually loves the attention. He continues, "You don't know who I am. I am from Lebanon. I am Rudy. I will f------ kill you." Marvelous.

Marcinowski is smiling apprehensively as I look over. He's not sure whether he should run or break out his notebook and start writing this down. The group cautiously moves to the pub as I keep one eye on Rudy. One minute they are yelling and the next they are hugging. It becomes apparent that Rudy has a thing for Rebecca and perhaps a small anger management issue. She is supercool and highly intoxicated. Finally, Scott storms off into the night. We both like Scott a lot but we are sort of glad that the two are not around each other anymore. I've hung out with a few Scottish guys in my day. I wasn't surprised by his gift of gab, his short temper, or his ability to drink heavily. He promises to buy a copy of *162*.

We must not have learned a lesson as we actually get back in the car with Rudy and the girls. Rudy drops us off at the MGM casino where I proceed to win about $25 playing Blackjack. Marcinowski uses a slot machine to turn a $20 into $75. He is so jacked that you might have thought he won the Michigan State lottery. I see cigarettes in his future.

Wednesday, May 4
Stress Cracks

I awake at 4 a.m. to violent vomiting in our hotel room. It sounds like a small animal is being slaughtered. Marcinowski is puking up a lung. When I get up again at 8:00, he is not moving. I go to the YMCA a few blocks away and work out. I sit at the desk and begin to write for the day. This is becoming part of my daily ritual. I know that it is vital for us to write everyday if we are going to create a book and document this adventure. It is also very therapeutic to review the journey daily. It does require a certain amount of concentration.

Marcinowski finally wakes up, grabs the remote, and turns on the TV. Seriously? I am really pissed. It's bad enough that he isn't writing, but now he is going to disrupt me? I realize he doesn't even know that he is bothering me. I ask him to turn it off. A minute later, he begins watching rap videos on his phone at the exact same audio level. I have to get out of here and have some alone time. It was easier being married. I finally decide that we should vacate the room and let the maid clean it, since we skipped our cleaning yesterday.

"Where do we go?" Marcinowski asks.

"I don't give a f--- where you go. Anywhere but this room."

I move to the lobby with my laptop for the next 2 ½ hours. At 1:30 p.m., I am interviewed on Mike Lindsey's' ESPN radio show in Syracuse. We connected on Facebook and he was intrigued enough to have me on the air.

As I worked out today, it was the first day that I thought about sending Marcinowski packing. It's not so much because of him, but because of the environment that he is helping to create. I hate having the TV on in the background. I hate being with someone who is always thinking about their next cigarette. I have way more respect for people who exercise and take care of themselves. I like Marz, don't get me wrong. I just don't want his habits to negatively affect me.

When I get back to the room, Marz asks me where I have been. I can tell that he is pissed that he didn't get to do the interview. If you want to be on TV or radio, start picking up the phone and book something. The stress between Steve and I is at an all-time high.

On Monday night, we drank a lot at the stadium via our $5 hookup. We couldn't find them on Tuesday. We run into them again tonight and make plans to hang out after the game. Ashley, the more attractive one, seems to be the leader. Her friend, Angela, must weigh more than 350 lbs. Her tits alone must weigh 50 lbs. — each! These gals are from the ghetto. We go back to our hotel after hitting a very sketchy liquor store where they are both on a first-name basis with the manager. We park and receive some very curious looks from the local clientele sitting inside and outside. Luckily, we had a good buzz on or I would have been terrified in this part of town.

I don't know this until reading my texts later, but Marz is convinced that they want money from us. I spent $25 on drinks at Hockeytown and $34 at the liquor store and I'm not paying for anything else. I'm not sure if it is my naiveté or his paranoia, but I miss all of their hints at us about paying for anything of an extracurricular nature. They say a few things like, "I'm here for the paper. I'm a paper chaser. I'm here for the money." Right over my head.

They are pounding shots of tequila and roll up a blunt. I am freaking out because they were getting loud and we were in a non-smoking room. Ashley thinks that I am being a pussy. "You paid for this room. We can do whatever we want!"

The more tequila they drink, the crazier it gets. Big Angela takes off her shirt and unveils the largest breasts either of us has ever seen. They are the size of two volleyballs. Ashley begins to lick them. Oh, jeesh. Because I am insistent to uphold our non-smoking room policy, the three of them go downstairs to have a smoke. This is when I check my phone and realize that Steve has been texting me.

These chicks want $$$!

Right. I send a text back:

F--- em…ditch em.

I start to look around the room and make sure that nothing is missing. I quickly spot my wallet, computer, and phone. A few minutes later, they come back in and it is quite awkward. I put an end to the night. During the course of the evening, though, we got plenty of interesting video. They did not mind talking to the camera. The most interesting footage is Marcinowski getting a fully-clothed lap dance from big Angela. I am not sure that he was getting any physical fulfillment or just thought that it was hilarious. For the record, *nothing happened*, and once again we added some fun memories. Luckily they had to be back at Comerica park at 9 a.m. So if you consider 1 a.m. an early night, it was an early night.

Thursday, May 5
Cinco De Mayo

I am hung over. Marcinowski has a tequila hangover, which is way worse. It appears that his community college education has prepared him for the real world of partying. I have always been proud of my ability to bounce back and party one more time. He is a gamer.

The day starts with us hustling out of the hotel and off to Hertz Rent-a-Car. We are going to be doing an open mic tonight that is about 45 minutes away. We need a car and don't want to have to pay $70 for a taxi ride to the airport tomorrow. So we will rent a car for one day at the rate of $34 plus tax. Not bad.

The Yanks lose the day game for their third straight loss. They also lose Eric Chavez to a broken foot. We decide to hit the casinos one last time. Today we choose The Motor City Casino. The other nights we hit MGM and Greektown. They are all pretty much the same. They are very smoky and have a lot of local folks who are wasting away in theses money pits. I like the thrill of gambling, but to watch people spend their lives this way is depressing. Unlike Vegas, most of the patrons are locals. I am up about $200.

We thought we'd have time to go back to the hotel and shower and get ready. We are wrong. We leave the casino in haste for Lafftracks in Novi, a city about 30 minutes west of Detroit. We pull up and realize that Lafftracks is also a billiards and dart hall.

"This sucks, let's get out of here," I said. I hate performing in front of three people. This is my type-A personality kicking in.

"Let's just go in." Marcinowski wins the argument.

We find the "comedy show" in the back room. There are about 20 comics who are in a roundtable format around two long tables. Ken, the host, welcomes us. "You must be the infamous Steve and Steve," he deduces.

The audience is all comics and they put us on last. This is either a sign of respect or they want us to stay until the end. The most interesting thing about the experience is how similar the comics are compared to our comic friends back at Nutt Street Comedy. My opening includes that observation.

There are two black dudes. One well-dressed and one with dreadlocks. *Check.* There is one token female who looks like a librarian and that all the other comics want to secretly (or not so secretly) have sex with. *Check.* There is a super-sized biker dude who looks like Kevin James and would kick your ass if we was inclined. *Check.* There are also had a couple of stoner dudes who forget their set because they were too high. *Check* and *check*.

After the show, we say our good-byes and head for the hotel. As we drive back, I reach for my phone in my pocket and everything in my wallet falls to the floor. I pull into a dark parking lot and find everything except my driver's license. I get out and check all of my pockets and start growing frantic. After searching everywhere we go back to the club. I have all the waitresses looking and the owner gives me his flashlight. I take it out to the car and look feverishly. No license means no flight to Dallas for games 30-32. Ugh.

We head back to the St. Regis. We are not sure what to do. As we pull up, I tell the valet that I have lost my license, but I think that it might be somewhere in the car. I offer him $20 if he finds it. He doesn't bite.

"If you can't find it, how am I supposed to?" he asks. I guess he never heard the expression, *Look at something with a fresh pair of eyes.*

I toss and turn all night knowing that the license is still somewhere in that rental car.

Friday, May 6

I wake up today with the biggest dilemma of the trip. How in the world am I going to get on this flight? We have an American Airlines 11:25 a.m. flight to Dallas and a game tonight at 7 p.m..

Because of this dilemma, we decide it probably makes sense to get to the airport earlier than usual. I am racking my brain thinking about what other forms of I.D. I might have with my picture on it.

As the car rolls around, we conduct one more

search. We both run our hands along every opening in our very compact car. Marz finds an old Bugle corn chip.

"This must be old," he says. "I don't even think they make these anymore."

"The car is a 2009. It can't be *that* old."

I give up looking and defeat begins to set in.

"I got something!" Marz squeals. "Oh Melia, you're going to love me." With that, he holds up my North Carolina driver's license. "Let's hug it out," he suggests. We do. I am so relieved. The tour will continue. It feels like the weight of the world has been lifted.

"You just bought yourself another month," I joke. Little did I know.

We make our way back to the airport in much more comfortable fashion. We rehash our four nights in Motown. Can our bodies continue to take this kind of abuse? I thank him repeatedly for being so persistent and not giving up. "That valet could have been $20 richer if he had your determination," I remind him.

Marcinowski starts laughing. "The funny thing is that I was downloading a podcast to my phone and was trying to buy a few more minutes."

Either way.

Chapter Eight

THE END OF THE WORLD AS WE KNOW IT

Our journey takes a turn for the better. We are picked up by Renee Olson in her Lincoln Navigator. The last time I saw Renee was in February when she gave me the thumbs up and inspiring words of encouragement on the 162 Tour. Jeff and Renee remain great friends and have a beautiful daughter, Amber, who just turned 26 and is recently engaged.

Marcinowski is blown away by the Olson home. It is huge, and its pool in the backyard hovers over Lake Lewisville. His eyes are wide open as he takes it all in. Marcinowski is most impressed that they bought the home from former NBA player Roy Tarpley. He is running around taking pictures and posting them on Twitter, labeling them as Tarpley's former digs. Ironically, more people would be impressed that he is staying at multi-millionaire businessman Jeff Olson's former home than a former NBA player with serious substance abuse issues.

"Don't get too comfortable," I remind him. "We are only staying here one night." Tomorrow, we move to a friend's apartment in Arlington. We will be right next to the ballpark. We are going to the game with 14 people, which is our biggest group yet. Amber's fiancé, Damon, and her best friend, Lola, meet us at the house for a pre-game celebration. The game itself moved along nicely as we were bombarded with the normal questions about our trip. It is nice to go to a game with someone different, and we wind up talking through most of the game.

That night, we all sleep in at the Olson house. It is great to sleep in and not be awakened up by a surly maid. As I am doing my morning journaling, I get a text from my friend Chip from Arlington:

> *Bad news...can't make it today...not my fault. My boss, (s.o.b. backwards) won't let me go.*

Blame and lack of responsibility are two things mentioned in Jeff Olson's *The Slight Edge* that unsuccessful people do.

I text back.

> *Does that mean we can't crash at your place tonight?*

No response. No call. No text back. He told me that we could stay all weekend and, even though he was working an hour away, he would leave the key for us. I also bought him a ticket to the game. So now, rather than saving me money, he is costing me money. I am thinking of adding a column on our website: One for contributors and one for people who cost us money.

Then again, this may be the best thing that could have happened. We now get to stay at the Olson Resort and Spa for the entire Mother's Day weekend. But now

I'm scrambling to make plans. We are an hour away from the ballpark with no place to stay and no rides to the two remaining games or the airport.

Renee takes us out to an incredible lunch at a local Italian eatery.

"Can I give you some advice?" Renee asks.

"Of course."

"You need to loosen up and have more fun. Don't let all of the logistics bog you down. Every guy I know would love to trade places with you. You are living out a dream. You should be enjoying every single minute of it."

Renee is right. I have been way too stressed all of the time. I decide right there and then that there will be no more problems, only turns in the road. Enjoy the journey. Renee asks a lot of great questions about marketing and gives us advice on getting more help from our social network.

Marcinowski and I are certainly enjoying living like millionaires for a few days. Renee picks up the tab. Rauly Williams, my musician friend who wrote and produced our theme song, *All 162*, is coming in from Austin to go to the game tonight. Rauly is one of the first people I shared 162 with in early March and is a big supporter.

Rauly picks us up and is impressed with our temporary quarters. He is a huge Rangers fan and we talk baseball the entire way to the game. He then plays us a song that he wrote about our 162 journey. It is brilliant. He tells us how they individually laid down the tracks and then went into the studio.

"All 162"

When I woke up this mornin'
It was time to hit the road,
Leaving the house that the Babe built
Back in '27 or so.
I'm on my way to Fenway, then Baltimore for a few,
and baby, you can catch me at all 162.

Andrew Jones, A-Rod, and Teixeira,
They're no strangers
Hey, didn't all those guys
Used to be Texas Rangers?
Rivera, he will set you down
With his cutter and his heater,
And I wanna be very best friends
With Derek Jeter.

Yeah, I plan to stand-up for things
That I think are funny.
Tomorrow night at the comedy club
Telling jokes for your money
I'm following the Yankees
In pinstripes deep and blue,
And when they make the playoffs
I'll go to those games, too.
Until then you can catch me at all 162.

Melia and Marcinowski just like Butch and the Kid.
Everybody wants to do it, we'll be the ones that did
The bases are loaded, baby how 'bout you?
You don't have to be from New York
To love that Yankees blue
And baby you can catch us at all 162.

Rauly is good buddies with the Rangers' team photographer and is able to snag three tickets with the employee discount at $25 each. Rauly is officially sponsoring game 31.

The Rangers get off to a 5-0 lead as Colon does not have his best stuff. The bombers fight back and tie it 5-5 in the sixth with Nick Swisher's solo blast. It isn't enough though as Texas scores two more in the bottom part of the inning. The Yankees end the day tied for first with Tampa. Boston is four back.

Rauly is happy that he gets to see the Rangers beat the Yanks today.

We get dropped off to an empty house as both Renee and Amber have a pretty active social life. It is nice to just go to sleep without partying.

Monday, May 9

We are in the midst of playing 31 games in 32 days. Today is the only day off. In Dallas morning traffic, it takes almost an hour to get to DFW airport. We learn that you can indeed get on an airplane in 2011 without a government-issued I.D.

As we get to ticketing, Marcinowski informs me that he has left his passport at Renee's house. He recalls exactly where it is. Renee has just pulled away from the curb and the thought of asking her to go back an hour only to come back again isn't very appealing.

The dude checking us in is more consumed with the 162 idea than he is at getting an I.D. "It's not a big problem," he informs us. "Answer a couple questions, maybe a little pat-down and you'll be fine. Happens all of the time." He then fires away some more questions about our tour. A few minutes later, I am in the security line and

Marcinowski is on the other side waving. The dude is right. Just answer a few questions.

When I bought the airline tickets, I made the mistake to seat us next to each other, rather than getting a window and an aisle. I am so used to flying for years with Kim that I do it automatically. I took the window to Detroit and let him have the window to Dallas, mostly because I was grateful that he found my I.D. I hate sitting in the middle seat.

I decide that it would be a nice touch to get postcards from each city and send them out to all the people helping make our journey possible. Marcinowski boards while I'm still in the gift shop. As I move towards my seat, I am shocked when I find him next to the window for our three-hour trek home. I grow more pissed as he sleeps and snores the entire time. I grow even more pissed later as he recounts how great it was to sleep on the flight.

Wednesday, May 11

I redo our press release today and send one to all of the major papers, ESPN, and Michael Kaye. I write one letter and cut and splice it and send it out to every reporter with T*he Daily News, Newsday* and *The New York Post.*

Neil Best from *Newsday* is one of the sports writers that I have been emailing regular updates. Today I get my first bite from New York media.

Here is my letter and his response:

Neil,
Thought that you might be interested in a great story.
Myself and another comic are attending all

162 New York Yankees games, hitting comedy clubs along the way, and documenting our escapades for a film.

I included our press release and a local TV spot from our home town of Wilmington, NC.

We would welcome an interview. We are currently being featured every Sunday night on Sports Talk New York with Mark Rosenman and A.J. Carter.

Thanks in advance for any interest.
Steve Melia

His response:

Hmm.
-Neil Best
Newsday

It might not seem like a lot, but the story is picking up steam. I know that this is a cool story, because I meet people every day who tell me so. At least I know that his email address works. I am jacked! "Hmm" could mean so many things!

Another major breakthrough today. On our daily 1:15-minute drive to The Stadium, I call in and talk to Michael Kaye on 1050 ESPN radio. Michael is the voice of the New York Yankees on the YES network. He also has the 3-6 p.m. slot every day on ESPN New York 1050. I have met him several times over the years at the team hotels. Getting his ear has been one of my major goals.

"Steve from Massapequa, you're on The Michael Kaye show."

"Hi Michael, I am living out a lifelong dream of attending every New York Yankees game. All 162."

"Home and away?"

"Yes, we just got back from Detroit and Dallas. Home and away."

"Wait a second, how are you doing this?" Kaye asked.

"I have a business that does well and I can run it from the road."

"Pretty cool. So you didn't have to quit your job or anything."

"My buddy did. He worked at Home Depot. We are both stand-up comics, so we are on a six-month tour hitting every game and as many comedy clubs as we can along the way."

"OK. So you might be at Yuk Yuks in Cleveland and then see the game there as well. I get it."

"That's the idea."

"Cool. Anything you want to say about the Yanks?"

"I predict that Jeter will hit .300. Even if he doesn't, he offers so much as far as leadership, working the counts, he is still one of the best defensive shortstops in the game."

"Well, I'm glad someone agrees with me, I'm getting killed. Don and I have a bet on whether Jeter does it. If Jeter hits .300 he [Don] has to wear full Yankees gear to the stadium."

"I look forward to seeing that. I wear a 162 jersey to every game. Look for me on YES."

That was it. Short and sweet and worth every second. We are on our way to national exposure. This was a key day!

Friday, May 13

Tim Buckley, from *WWAY NewsChannel 3,* recalls:

> *The great thing about technology is that a satellite interview is only a webcam away. After about six weeks on the road, I set up a Skype meeting and had a quick face-to-face with the crew. Laughing and joking along the way, they assured me everything was going according to plan.*
>
> *From the looks of things, they were right! A couple of bumps in the road to be sure (like rainouts and snow) but all in all the trip was succeeding. Not only were they still going, but the two had maintained a good amount of enthusiasm through their first 35 games. Thankfully for me, plenty of videos and photos chronicling their action from the road made for an easy TV story to show their progress.*
>
> *While it looked like things were going great, I still wasn't completely convinced that they were on the fast track to the finish line. I mean, they are comics — they can put on a smiling face, right?*
>
> *Steve told me that flights, tickets, and lodging were kind of a day-by-day process. I think that was the hard part for me to grasp. As one of those guys who has to have everything hammered out to the small details well in advance, it was hard for me to grasp how a monster trip like this could keep going "on the fly." All it takes is one missed flight and it's game over.*
>
> *I thought I'd find out quickly whether or not they'd hold up for the long haul. A daunting road trip to Seattle, Oakland, and L.A. was coming up*

for the duo in just two short weeks.

At 10 a.m., we Skype in to WWAY's newsroom from Tommy's kitchen. Tim interviews us and seems to be as excited as we are that we haven't missed a game. We have our Yankees flag taped to the wall behind us. Tim says they will have it ready for the 6 p.m. news.

The next morning, we wake up and I immediately go to my email and play yesterday's news clip. Tim Buckley proceeded to put together a news masterpiece lasting 2:08. He used video from our site and pictures from the trip. He did a nice job of capturing the drama and undying enthusiasm of the trip.

WILMINGTON, NC (WWAY) – Back in March, we brought you the story of two local comedians just crazy enough to attempt a road trip to all 162 New York Yankees games this season. Well, it's now mid-May and the two are still going strong.

Steve Melia and Steve Marcinowski have been on the road since March 29th, and haven't missed a beat since Opening Day.

"We're at 35 games as of (Thursday) night," said Melia. "The first couple weeks were honestly very difficult."

Even though they're only through 20 percent of the season, their trip has already spanned two countries, five states, and two time zones. Along the way, they've been faced with mental and physical exhaustion, a few financial woes, but even some problems with Mother Nature.

"It started snowing in Buffalo," recalled Melia. "And that was really one of the parts of the

trip where we were like, 'What on Earth are we doing?' Have we told too many people that we can't back out now?"

And yet, the two haven't backed out just yet. They've met fans in Boston, Toronto, Baltimore, Detroit, Texas, and of course New York. So far, there have been two main reactions.

"One is, 'You're the craziest people I've ever met,'" said Marcinowski. "The other one is, 'That's something I've always wanted to do. You guys are awesome.'"

But outside of their quest to hit each and every game, the two had set some loftier goals. Back in March they assured us they would eventually become best buddies with Yankees start Derek Jeter. As we found out – they haven't exactly excelled in that department.

"Absolutely nothing. We've had no player interaction," said Melia. "We thought it would be easier to find their team hotel, but as of yet we have met zero New York players."

"We thought he made eye contact with us once," added Marcinowski. "But it was the girl behind us."

With 35 games down, and a whopping 127 to go, their budget is understandably strained. But they're not bogged down with mountains of financial stress. Instead, they're surprisingly upbeat.

"What's great about credit card companies these days is they give you five years to pay off the balance. So we should be right on target to have this all paid off by 2020 or so," joked Melia.

We'll be sure to have more updates about the two Steves' trip, along with their finances in the coming months.

I am getting a lot of texts and well wishes from my family down in Melbourne, Florida. My niece's wedding and reception are this afternoon and it's killing me not to be there.

My brother recalls a conversation that he has with my nephew, Tim.

"So what do you think about Uncle Steve not making it to the wedding?"

"I think that he'd love to be here, but he made a commitment."

"A commitment? Shouldn't family take priority over a baseball game?"

"Normally, sure. But he is doing something that is important to him." Mike does a good job of getting to the point. "Didn't you miss Patrick's wedding a few years ago?"

Tim is the biggest guy in the family. The former Marine stands about 6' 2" and weighs in at a solid 235.

"Well, yeah. I was in Iraq, though."

"Whose decision was that?"

"It was mine. But that is totally different. I *had* to be there."

"It seems like you made a choice to go and reinforced it with your decision. Same as Uncle Steve. I am proud of him. You do not usually run into people who do what they say they are going to do."

I'm sure he isn't the only one who questions me. Am I a little sad that I am not at a very important event in my niece's life? Yes. Am I feeling a little lonely as most of the people I love are all in one place? Yes. Does this change my mission or commitment? No. Commitment is doing the thing that you said you were going to do long after the feeling in which you said it with has left you.

This is the second of five weekends that I see as a major sacrifice. If this were easy, I am sure that more people would have accomplished it.

Monday, May 16

At 6 a.m., Steve and I pull out of the driveway and head to the Sunshine State. We are flying into Orlando and are being picked up by Mike and Kim.

I wonder what the sleeping arrangements are going to be. I know that Mike has rented two rooms, one of them being a suite. Will it be Kim and I? Or Mike and I? Hmm, that would leave Marcinowski and Kim. Mike and Kim take the suite as I get to keep my new roommate.

Tonight our group will consist of 15 people. Some of the family has stayed in town to take in a game. My sister and Burger are driving over and are being joined by Tom, Lucy, and their youngest, Kevin. My cousins, Trish and Kevin, join us as well. My friends and PPL associates Rich Kennedy, Chip Humphrey, and Mike

Kim and I at "The Trop."

Odessa will be going as well. It is fun having everyone there, but it is quite exhausting moving from section to section and trying to spend time with everyone.

The game starts nicely. We are up 5-1 with AJ on the mound. Things unravel quickly and we lose our sixth straight tonight, 6-5.

"This is going to turn," Yankees manager Joe Girardi said. "We are going through a really tough stretch right now. This is where you are tested as a team. You have to get to the other side."

We are 40 games in and we have not even come close to meeting any of the Yankees. We are hoping that our luck will change tonight as we pile into a cab and head for The Renaissance Vinoy. Over the past few years, we met David Cone, Reggie Jackson, Don Mattingly, Jason Giambi, Andy Pettitte, and even Alex Rodriguez at this five-star hotel. My stalker crew includes Kim, Mike, Tommy, Marcinowski, and Kevin, who is a huge Mets fan. We have all changed clothes and are wearing no Yankees paraphernalia. We do not want them to see us coming.

As we walk into the bar, we can feel that the energy is different than before. It doesn't take long to figure out that the Bombers have changed hotels. We order a round of very overpriced drinks and take off soon after.

I get the feeling they are trying to avoid me.

Tuesday, May 17
3:15 a.m.
Snore ... snort ... snore ... snort. This is the sound emanating from Marcinowski. This is awkward. I *Shhhh!* I *ahem*! I get up and give his mattress a nice shove. Just 30 feet away, Kim sleeps soundly. Ironic, I think, as Kim was amazing at getting me to not snore. The trick was easy. She wouldn't allow me to sleep on my back or stomach.

Sleep on your side. She would elbow me to turn over and it always worked.

I lay there and become increasingly annoyed at his snoring. Then all of a sudden, it was like he didn't make a sound for 10 minutes and then it would start up again. This went on for most of the night.

Wednesday, May 18

Tonight we are going to the game with Lauren Bradshaw's sister, Nicole. We hung out with Nicole last time we were in town and she can certainly hang with the best. Nicole's friend, Joey, is our designated driver tonight.

Nicole is a thrill seeker like us, and a blast. Joey is a baseball fanatic. He knows a lot of statistics about baseball. But he hates the Yankees. He actually was drafted in the 24th round by Philadelphia. Due to an injury on the practice field, that was the extent of his pro career.

It's after midnight, and Game 41 is the best game so far. Bartolo Colon pitches a masterpiece for eight innings. He threw 87 pitches that yielded only three hits and no runs.

Girardi opts to go for a fresh arm and brings in Mo to start the bottom of the ninth with a 1-0 lead. The concourses at Camden Yards are filled with "Let's go, Mo!" chants. Two one-out singles and a sac fly by Vladimir Guerrero later and we are in for some free baseball. It is Rivera's third blown save this season.

"Of course, there's a thought to leave him in there, but I have Mariano Rivera," Girardi said. "That's why I made the move. I wanted someone who was fresh, and it didn't work out. Bartolo was outstanding."

Every stadium has a fun thing that they do. In

Baltimore, during the seventh inning, a guy with a banjo acts out Cotton-Eyed Joe while the song plays along. Tonight, we get to see him twice … in the 7th *and* in the 14th!

This is the first 15-inning game that I have ever been to and can't remember the last time the Yanks had a game this long.

To open the 15th, Tex and A-Rod single and Cano follows with a double off the right field wall. Three pitches later, newly-acquired Chris Dickerson is beaned in the head. Camden Yards quickly goes silent as the slugger lays there with a golf ball-sized knot growing from his temple. The pitcher, Michael Gonzalez, is booed and immediately ejected.

We are sitting so close you get to *feel* Joe Girardi's passion for the game. His intensity is awesome. When Chris went down, Joe sprinted out there to his aid. His natural instinct was to run out to help his player. When he got there, he slammed Dickerson's shattered helmet in disgust.

It is refreshing to see how badly Girardi and the Bombers want to win. It is easy to question their desire lately, but not tonight.

Friday, May 20

I wake up with a deflated air mattress underneath me. I gave Marcinowski the bed. I'm trying to keep the sleeping and living conditions fair. We've spent the last couple of days at Ben and Lauren's home in Baltimore. I am excited for this weekend as this will be my first subway series.

We are in Ben's car on the way to be dropped off at the MVP bus terminal in downtown Baltimore. The math was too simple. $249 for Amtrak or $40 for the bus including Wi-Fi. Ben warns us this he is taking us to a very shady part of town.

"Sorry Marcinowski," I announce. "I hate to break a promise. But I do have a fiscal responsibility to make sure our money lasts the entire season."

"See you in August, dudes," Ben laughs as he sees us make our way inside the terminal. The smell is immediately revolting and I can't even eat my breakfast sandwich. Marcinowski takes out his camera and begins taping. He wants to have a record of my broken promise.

The game is over in 2:47 tonight and the story is all Mets pitching. Knuckleballer R.A. Dickey goes six innings allowing four hits and the Mets bullpen is perfect for three innings.

Our luggage is back at The Dugout. It is not fun to drag a big suitcase through the subway with 47,000 fans. We take the subway to the Long Island Rail Road and then grab a taxi and arrive back in Massapequa a little after midnight. We are not the only ones who are exhausted.

Joe Girardi is complaining to the media about their rigorous road schedule.

"We have been in three cities in five days, all night games, including Sunday night. Getting in at 3:00 or 4:00 in the morning takes a toll on our guys," he says.

Saturday, May 21

Today is the end of civilization as we know it according to a fundamentalist radio host named Harold Camping. Camping predicted that Judgment Day would take place today, and it was (and I quote) "beyond the shadow of a doubt." Many of his followers believed it and made the necessary preparations for The End.

Unfortunately it has been 22 years since my last confession.

Camping said that The Rapture would start at around 6 p.m. local time and would start sweeping the globe time zone by time zone.

At 5:55, Marz and I are sitting in the Mustang on River Ave. making jokes about the end of the world. I really do not believe that the world is about to end … but you never know. At 5:59, we stare at the clock on the dashboard and as the clock moves to 6:00, we begin to celebrate by popping open another beer.

"Wait a second, why does it have to be EST time?" Marcinowski quires. True. Maybe we still have an hour or two, depending on the time zone where the rolling judgments begin. So, with the world safe for at least another hour, we continue our daily rituals of locking up the car and make our way to The Dugout to celebrate our new (although maybe short-lived) lease on life.

The Yanks use the long ball to get back to their winning ways tonight. Tex homers for the third night in a row and Grandy, Martin, and A-Rod join the party. According to MLB.com, the Yankees have scored 52.2 percent of their 226 runs this season via home run, having hit 70 homers that account for 118 runs. Chicks dig the long ball and so do the 162 Guys. The Yanks even the series with a 7-3 victory.

Sunday, May 22

Today's 1:00 p.m. game is the TBS Game of the Week. We often move around and rarely sit in one spot for too long. Marz and I are standing in the bar area in the outfield, when Marz gets a text from Zac Burke, a fellow comedian back in Wilmington: "Just saw you guys on TV!"

Within minutes we both receive about 10 similar texts. My brother Jim was the first to text me.

They just had a close-up of you coming back from commercial break.

For a minute I thought that maybe they had picked up on the story and knew who we were. Nope. It was just a random camera shot coming back from commercial. TBS had inadvertently spotted the 162 Guys. Within minutes, our Facebook accounts were blowing up as several friends took a picture of us on TV and posted it.

> *Mike Melia*: Nice!!!
> *Zack Burk*: I was flippin out - had 2 to do a double take, thank you dvr
> *Mike Melia*: They look like they just mugged somebody and they are ducking into the crowd
> *Terre Mack Krotzer*: Very cool!
> *Sean Webb*: Well I'll be a monkey's uncle....
> *Matthew C Turner*: Well done. Pulling for ya.
> *Jon Ripley*: You guys look pissed!

It is funny how we looked miserable. Maybe it was because the Yanks were losing 3-1 for most of the game. It may also have been that we are tired, cold, and worn out.

As the 7th inning stretch concludes, the Mets fans are extra loud in the stadium and making a lot of noise. This doesn't last for long. By the time the 29-minute bottom of the seventh is complete, the Yankees have sent 13 men to the plate against four Mets pitchers in their biggest barrage of the year. An eight-run inning sends the Mets fans running like cockroaches at 3 a.m. when the lights get turned on.

Monday, May 23

I am beginning to look at the next phase of the trip. We leave for Seattle in two days and have a list of 17 things to do as we will embark on our longest road trip of the year. They mostly center around travel plans and accommodations. After Seattle, we'll hit Oakland and then L.A. for 10 games, two comedy shows, and four PPL meetings

We fly out of Newark Wednesday night after the game at 6:30. We'll need to take the train in at 10 a.m. Then we will drag our luggage from Penn Station to the subway and leave it at The Dugout. After the game, we will take the subway back to Penn and out to Newark.

The airfare for the trip was $1,250 for both of us. In Seattle, we should have a place to stay. In Oakland, we are staying at a Days Hotel for about $60 per night.

Accommodations for L.A. is up in the air. We only need to rent a car in L.A. as we will have rides in Seattle. In Oakland, our hotel is walking distance to The Coliseum. I should have my degree in travel and hospitality by October. I will also be doing a media blitz for the next 30 hours contacting print, TV, and radio in Seattle, Oakland, and Anaheim.

We have a planning meeting this morning and dole out what we should be doing the next 48 hours. Marz is putting together our fifth webisode and calling comedy clubs. We are both growing frustrated at the amount of comedy that we have not been doing. I told him that I am committed to doing it two or three times per week, but that he has to help find the gigs. We do have a gig this Thursday night in Seattle at a bar called Stonegate Pizzeria, which is owned by a friend's uncle.

In Yankees news, Jeter is only 25 away from 3,000

hits. This will be a fun ride for the next few weeks as he enters yet another prestigious club. Much of the talk all year long has been about him supposedly losing it. Well, the Yanks are in first place and he has the third highest batting average, with .268 amongst yesterday's starters.

Tuesday, May 24

I call this morning and talk to my dad. I try to call him every few days and check in.

"You still going to all of the games?" he asks.

"Yes sir. Tonight is number 47 and we head to the West Coast tomorrow."

"Well, I never thought you'd do it."

Technically, I haven't done it yet, I suppose. But just hearing my dad start to believe (in his own way) that I might just be able to pull this off puts renewed wind in my sails.

Chapter Nine

GO WEST, YOUNG MAN

When we get to the airport, I tell Marz that I have good news and bad news. The bad news is that he is sitting in the middle. The good is that I would start getting us a window and an aisle from this point forward.

Marcinowski settles into his seat for our longest flight of the year. He has never been to the West Coast and is excited. Things have been a little tense lately and we bond by sharing a headset as we watch "Gran Torino," a tear-jerking Clint Eastwood film that is riveting and makes the flight go by quickly.

Mike is flying in from Hawaii and meeting us in baggage claim. He has just spent a week there doing a few presentations and soaking in the rays. Our ride and housing accommodations are with KC Call. KC and his wife Elena have three beautiful children, and their gorgeous home overlooks Puget Sound.

Thursday, May 26

The weather is supposed to range from 44-57. We

have a night off from baseball tonight. Yeah! We are doing a PPL training at 7 and then we have a 10 p.m. show.

KC will be handling hosting duties at the club tonight. My brother is doing five minutes in his comedy debut. This should be fascinating. The old saying, "It looks easier than it is," comes to mind. Having four frantic comics in the same house is difficult. Mike keeps to himself most of the day. I told him to come up with three subjects and then to have three jokes per subject.

When writing a joke, you want to have a premise. Rodney Dangerfield, for example, had this down pat. He'd open with something like:

"I live in a tough neighborhood!"

Next is the set up.

"Last week I saw a guy rotating my tires …"

Then the punch:

"… From my car to his!"

The punch should be a surprise, a curveball, if you will.

The audience wants to laugh, but they do not want to see it coming. Throughout the day, the four of us continually practice material on each other. Even though Marcinowski and I haven't performed in two weeks, we feel like the veterans and are freely doling out advice. The entire house is on edge.

KC has done stand-up twice. When he was in Wilmington a year prior, he made his debut at the Nutt Street Comedy open mic. He is very personable and has been speaking in front of people for well over a decade. Marcinowski and I will go 15 minutes each in our longest gigs of the tour.

KC opens and does very well. My favorite joke is when he talks about his wife Elena being from Russia.

"We are perfect for each other," he gushes. "She is everything I wanted; a blond, beautiful, and voluptuous woman. I was everything that she was looking for, too. I was an American citizen over 18. So it's worked out."

After his set, he introduces Mike. Right away the audience loves him. He has incredible stage presence. They know it is his first time. My favorite joke of his also revolved around a Russian woman.

"Meeting a female can be tough. I sent away for a mail-order bride. The mailman wanted me to sign for her. 'Sign for her? Take her back. I don't want a deaf one!'"

He pauses for effect.

"I said I wanted one that didn't speak English!"

His pause is perfect as he owns the moment. For a first timer, he nails it.

Next is Marcinowski. He has a way of being as big as the moment, much like Derek Jeter's performance is elevated during clutch situations. I can tell that his confidence is at an all time high.

Steve's funniest joke was about meeting the nicest guy in New York.

"I met the nicest guy in New York," he starts before going into a heavy New York accent. "Hey asshole … dumb ass … you dropped your wallet."

He gets an incredible applause. He is 11 minutes in and still could have kept going. He knows that he has a few more minutes, but decides to say good night on his biggest laugh of the tour.

I am next. I feel like the night is already a success and the audience is ripe for having a good time. I go about 15 minutes and feel like I clear the bases. You can usually tell how good a show is by how long the crowd stays afterward. It must have been great because we wind up hanging out until almost 1 a.m.

Mike has invited a young lady named Nicole Wong to the show and she is coming to the game with us tomorrow. She is beautiful and has a sweet demeanor. We had actually been getting to know her through her Facebook profile during the day. Marcinowski and I are both vying for her attention. We are both working the crowd, and, as usual, Marcinowski spends most of his time talking to the attractive females.

When I go to bed, Marcinowski and KC are still up reminiscing about their killer sets.

Friday, May 27

I am set to be interviewed at 1:15 by Bob and Groz, local radio personalities on ESPN 710. We are sitting around KC's house listening to the show while I am on hold. Legendary pitcher Rollie Fingers is on right before me. The hosts move on to me and interview me for a good 12 minutes. It is a great interview. I am keeping the story alive.

On the comedy front, I am having no luck getting a gig in L.A., but I talk to the La Jolla Comedy Store. They are very open to having us. I email them our YouTube videos and within an hour of the initial phone call, we both have eight-minute spots next Thursday.

As happy as I am that we are firing on all cylinders, I am quite frustrated as well. I am booking 100 percent of our gigs. Besides a few open mics, Marcinowski has booked nothing. He is not happy that I am now doing these radio interviews by myself. I tell him if he wants to be on the radio he needs to start picking up the phone.

The biggest thing that pisses me off is that I am

writing everyday and he is not. I want to be able to look back and say that the 162 Tour didn't cost me anything, because the book paid for it. Every morning I write. Every morning I watch him *not* write. I believe that having two people's perspectives will make a much more interesting and dramatic book. Today, he has spent most of the time playing with the three kids and watching cartoons.

His main responsibility is to produce our five-minute webisodes. We decide to do this one from KC's deck overlooking the Puget Sound. We must have done 12 takes trying to get it right. This is the only productive thing that he does now outside of writing his comedy. The tension is growing thicker.

Tonight we are going to the game with Kirk Thomas. Kirk is a season ticket holder and volunteer extraordinaire to the Melia Family. He likes to help and to be part of the action. He has secured us tickets for all six of the games in Seattle. Tonight is game 49 and for game 50 tomorrow, he has organized a huge celebration.

Kirk picks us up a good hour away from the stadium. As we are driving, I ask Mike about Nicole Wong.

"So, do you have any claims on this girl?"

"She and I have been friends for a while. She's my daughter's age, though. I appreciate you asking."

KC has arranged for us to stay with a woman named Heather for the next few nights. I met her on the phone today and she is more than hospitable. She even agrees to pick us up after the game at a bar close to the stadium.

The four of us are driving in as I spot Nicole Wong on the corner in our meeting spot. I announce to the group that I will go wait with her as they find a parking spot. I learn that she is a personal trainer in addition to being a part-time PPL associate.

Keeping Marz (far left) and Wong (far right) apart.

Our seats are killer. We are in the first row of the right field stands. This is directly behind where Ichiro Suzuki, the star right field from Japan, plays. These are Kirk's seats and have been for many years. As we sit, I make sure that I am next to Wong and that Marcinowski is not. Joining us is another PPL big hitter, Kevin Dunn. Kevin is the biggest Yankees fan I know in Seattle. He is a ton of fun and has a huge heart. We have been buddies for 13 years.

I thought that Safeco Field had a roof, but apparently it doesn't close all of the way and the 54-degree temperature calls for a chilly night. We are using the Yankees flag as a blanket. I feel like Wong and I are hitting it off big time.

After the game, it somehow gets decided that Heather will drive Marcinowski and I will be getting a ride from Wong. Marcinowski gets our suitcases and we agree to meet up later. Wong and I spend two hours sitting in her car talking and getting to know each other. She is not going to let me stay at her place and is more than happy to drive me back to Heather's.

Saturday, May 28
Game 50

The PPL Super Saturday event goes from 10 a.m.-2 p.m. We begin having a few drinks in the lobby bar. The game is at 7 p.m., but we are renting an entire section for 75 people so we get to go in early.

From 5 p.m. to 6 p.m. all beers are only $5. I have never seen a happy hour in any of the previous 49 games and we are certainly taking advantage of it! By the time 6 p.m. hits, we are feeling good. We have banners hung up commemorating our 50th game and are having a blast.

Wong is out with friends for the night and could not join us. I have found a new friend named Krysten. She is really cute. She is here with her mom and stepdad. As the game progresses, we hang out together more and more. Her stepdad comes over after every half inning and invites her to come back and sit with them. She tells him over and over that she prefers to stand with us and stays put. At some point he tells her that I am married and that this doesn't look good. I explain that I'm separated. Awkward.

During the fourth inning we go for a walk around the entire stadium. I honestly have no idea how long we were gone, but apparently long enough to ruffle a lot of feathers. As we entered back into the party area, Kevin pulls me aside and Krysten's mom grabs her and drags her away. They are keeping us apart like Romeo and Juliet.

The game turns out to be exciting as the innings roll by. Krysten's folks are ready to leave in the 10th inning. Most of the non-partiers from our group have already left for home. Her parents are sitting in an area where they are not even watching the game. If she is going to get to stay, I am going to have to get involved. I decide that when the Yankees' half of the tenth is over I will make my way back and see if they will let her stay.

I have about a quarter cup of a beer left. I don't want to take it with me because it will make me look less responsible and more drunk. It is not the look that I am going for. These folks were at my Super Saturday event and have a great deal of respect for me, so I'm hoping this will be easy. I approach Marcinowski and say, "I've got to go talk to Krysten's parents. Since they stopped serving beer three innings ago, I need you to watch this for me. I'll be back in less than five minutes." My tone could not have been more serious. "Please, protect this beer for me and do not drink it. Thanks."

With that, I walk back and do my best convincing act. The stepdad and mom are both sitting.

"Great game, huh?" They politely nodded. "Hey, I know you guys are ready to leave," I continued, "but it would be great if Krysten could stay. I promise to get her back to the hotel safely as soon as the game is over."

"We have a problem with this," came the reply from her dad. "You are a married man."

I explain to him that I have been separated for almost a year. He is most concerned with what other people are thinking.

"Well, people do not know that," he says.

"What do you want me to do?" I ask. "Explain my personal life from the front of the room?"

We go back and forth, but they are not budging. Well, I did my best, back to baseball. I get back to the group just as the bottom of the 11th is getting underway.

I see my cup, now empty, sitting on a table surrounded by Heather, Marcinowski, KC, and a handful of others.

"What happened?"

Several in the group start to giggle.

"This is a joke, right? You poured my beer into another cup?" Marcinowski stands silent, much like he did back in Toronto as we escaped from our first apartment fiasco.

I try again. "Where's my beer?"

"It's gone," is all that he musters up. The group is holding back laughter.

"Is that all that you have to say."

He nods. With that I take the bottle of water that I am holding and spray it on his shirt and up to his face.

"Good. This makes us even," I explain.

He appears shocked and stomps away.

The game continues on with no sign of Marcinowski. He reminds me of the kid who runs away, but never goes too far because he is not allowed to cross the street. He doesn't have any money, so I don't think he will go very far. I see Mike and tell him what happened. He laughs and shrugs. I ask him to talk to Marz if he sees him and make sure that he is OK.

The game is now in the 12th inning and is approaching four hours. We have been "celebrating" for almost eight hours now. It is probably good that beer sales were cut off 90 minutes ago.

With Mariano in the game, it looks like there will be a 13th inning. With that, a deep fly is hit toward us in left field and crashes against the wall sending home the Mariners' winning run.

The obnoxious fans explode, many of which have been drinking all day, like us. They start right in on me and the other Yankees fans.

"Yankees suck!"

"Why don't you go back to New York?!"

"Go Home!"

I have been in these situations many times and the best course of action is to leave immediately.

Heather heads right for me.

"You should know something," she confesses. "I drank your beer. You should apologize to Steve."

"I don't care who drank my beer," I said. "I asked *him* to watch it."

She keeps going. "You should really be nicer to him."

"You should mind your own business," I tell Marcinowski's new squeeze.

This goes back and forth for a few more minutes and the language and emotions get much worse. At some point she listens to my advice and falls back into the group bursting into tears. As we reach the street, KC approaches me.

"You made that girl cry. You need to go apologize."

"Mind your own f------ business! You have no idea what is going on!"

Apparently, Heather and Marcinowski stayed up all night and she gave him advice that he needed to start sticking up for himself and stop being bossed around by me. Her drinking my beer must have served as some kind of lesson in defiance. Whatever it was, I am done with this girl.

KC and I, who have been friends for over a decade, are now yelling in the middle of the street outside the bar. My brother comes over and pulls me away.

"I threw water in his face," I yelled. "*Water*! Big deal!"

We all make it into a bar named The Elysian Fields. Mike and I separate from the rest of the group and saddle up to the bar. Marcinowski and I haven't talked since I doused him with water. KC comes over and offers to buy me a shot. I shrug. He insists and hands me a Jägermeister. I nod and slam it.

"OK, the girl is over there crying. Now will you go and apologize?"

"F--- you. You think that you can buy me for one shot?"

We go back and forth even louder now as Mike and I walk out and jump in a cab. This would make a great movie. We are laughing as much as anything. I wonder if they know that Marcinowski is not a cheap date.

I stay in Mike's room at the Hilton. Fifty down and a measly 112 to go.

The next morning, Marcinowski comes rolling in with his luggage. He is pouting and looking for an apology. I tell him I am sorry that things got out of control. We argue about how much beer was left in the cup. He tells me that he was embarrassed in front of the group. I tell him that I was as well.

During the course of the weekend, I notice that Marcinowski has a new Facebook friend in Nicole Wong. He sits there and texts much of the Sunday game.

Monday, May 30

We are celebrating Memorial Day in Oakland by going to a baseball game. Marcinowski is moping around like he lost his best friend. Since our responsibility meeting back in New York, he hasn't called a single comedy club. We are in Oakland for three more nights with two nights off of baseball. I remind him again about finding us an open mic in the Bay Area.

He checks some stuff online and sends a few emails. I walk though every comedy gig that we've had and point out that none of them have come from email communication. Not one. You must pick up the phone to get gigs.

I need to get out and exercise. The temperatures are in the low 50s and it is overcast. I put on my shorts and sneakers and head out for a run. We are just under a mile from the Coliseum, so I decide to jog in that direction. My endorphins start to release and I feel better almost immediately. It is approaching 11 a.m.. and the parking lot is already alive with barbecues and tailgaters.

I run to an area that is roped off a bit and notice a big luxury BMW pulling up to two security guards. And out walks Mr. October himself, Hall of Famer Reggie Jackson.

"Good morning Reggie!," I yell, a little out of breath.

"Good morning!" he shouts back with slight wave of his left hand. Reggie Jackson! Three consecutive home runs in the 1977 World Series. I may have only been 7 years old, but I remember that night clearly. I do not have my phone with me, and thus no camera, so I decide to just keep running. I am now in a great mood. I just talked to a Hall of Famer!

My niece, Jessica, is sponsoring the game and is driving in from Sacramento, which is about 90 minutes away. Jess is Mike's oldest daughter and is currently employed as an attorney. She did her undergraduate at Wesleyan and graduated at the top of her class at the University of Miami's law school.

I get back to the room and shower quickly. Marcinowski is not moving very fast and I tell him that I'm going to pick up some beers. When I get to the very ghetto gas station across the street, I notice that they sell the highly scrutinized Four Loko. This is an "energy drink" that has the equivalent of four beers in it. The name "Four" is derived from the original energy drink's four main ingredients: alcohol, caffeine, taurine, and guarana. Four Loko contains 12 percent alcohol by volume and is packaged in 23.5 oz. cans. It's also been banned in much of the U.S. and I am surprised to see it on the shelf. We will see why over the next few hours. They are on sale for $2.50 each. I pick up a couple.

Marcinowski and I start to walk toward the Coliseum. Jessica is notoriously late and I will be happily surprised if she is close to being on time. Three sips into the Four Loko and I am buzzing. We are some sight. Two exhausted comics drinking 23.5 ounce Four Lokos out of paper bags walking along the side of the highway with cars zipping by.

As we approach the Oakland Coliseum, we are about halfway done with our drinks and feeling the effects. Marcinowski wants to chat. He is unequivocally looking for an apology from the "water incident." We have one of those conversations where we both want to be heard and get a few things off of our chests. I reiterate that I'm sorry that things got out of hand, but I would do the same thing again and did not see throwing water at him as a big deal. He continues to defend his lack of watching my beer and continually goes back to what percentage of beer was left. We dance around the issue for 20 minutes or so and get no closer to a resolution.

Jess arrives and we make our way to our seats. The Four Loko has definitely kicked in as I proceed to tell her the same story three times. In the third inning, I look up at the scoreboard and announce to the group that the Yankees are winning 3-0. It is the first time all year that I can recall having no idea what was going on. I literally did not look at the scoreboard until the third inning. I'm glad this product is being banned. One can had me buzzed most of the day.

Wednesday, June 1

We made it to another month! I get asked a lot if I am tired of baseball after 53 games. I am not. I am tired, though. We have another day game today.

We are getting a bit of a late start and I ask the hotel manager if I can use her computer to print out the tickets for today. After three nights there, the entire staff is aware of our venture. As I sit in the manager's office I go to my StubHub account and realize that we do not have tickets for today. I spend another 20 minutes searching my email. I am usually pretty organized, but soon realize that I do not have tickets for the game.

Just before 11 a.m. we walk into Denny's. This is our fourth time eating in this establishment. It is the only real restaurant within walking distance. I did run this morning, but still feel like I am getting less and less healthy by the day. Sometimes I feel like Morgan Spurlock, the guy on "Super Size Me" who eats at McDonald's every day and starts to see the havoc it creates on his body. We should have doctors checking our vitals.

Marcinowski loves Denny's. Nevertheless, he's distracted and staring at his phone for most of breakfast. I am not sure if he is really doing something or just avoiding talking to me. We meet a nice couple from New York who are sitting at the booth next to us. He just retired and she is taking her vacation days. They are doing the entire West Coast swing. They started in Seattle and are headed to L.A.

next, just like us. They are blown away by the tour and we chat across the aisle the entire time. They inform us that the game starts at 12:35 today, which is 30 minutes earlier than I had been planning on.

As we get outside, it starts to drizzle. We hustle back to our palace and I leave for the stadium to see about scalping two tickets. As I cross the street, I see two policemen directing traffic.

"Hey guys. I don't have tickets to the game today. Is it illegal to scalp tickets?"

"It is not illegal for you to buy them, but it is illegal to scalp them."

I walk away and try to decipher his interpretation of the law. I do not want to get arrested.

As I make my way into the parking lot, a gentlemen on the corner wearing an A's jacket and a headset is holding up a lot of tickets. I walk by and look uninterested. I casually look up and ask how much the cheapest ticket he has is going for. A minute later I have my first two scalped tickets at just $10 a piece. I'm sure there are different factors in play, but this new information on getting less expensive tickets is a revelation. So far on the road trip our total cost for tickets to six games is $20. One third of the way through the season and we are definitely staying on budget!

Thursday, June 2
The Hand That Feeds You

We are performing at The Comedy Store in La Jolla, just outside of San Diego, tonight. This is one of the bigger venues that either of us have played. We have eight minutes each. We have a 6 a.m. flight out of the San Francisco airport. Our morning starts off with a 3:30 a.m. wake up call.

After a ridiculous comedy of errors, we end up missing our flight and having to pay $150 in additional fees to get us on the next flight. I'm beyond pissed. At the airport, we sit down to have breakfast. Marcinowski is texting with his right hand and holding the menu in his left. The waitress asks if we want something to drink. I order a coffee. I don't have to wonder who he is texting. I just can't believe it. I know that Wong gets up early as she is a personal trainer.

Without his eyes leaving his phone, like he couldn't be bothered, he says, "Yeah, I'll get an orange juice and a coffee." I glance down at the menu and do the math.

"Hey slick, you just ordered $10 worth of liquid."

"Huh? Oh, sorry."

I am fuming. I like orange juice, too, but we are on a budget. $6.25 for the juice and $3.95 for the java … you have got to be kidding me! The only way for us to last all year is to cut out all luxuries. To me, orange juice is a luxury. I don't know it at the time, but today will be a critical turning point of the tour.

As we get on the I-5 to San Diego, Marcinowski again winces at the two-hour ride. "Well, get used to show business, big guy," I tell him. "It's a lot of early flights and, yes, San Diego and L.A. are two hours apart. Deal with it."

He is seriously engaged in the texting process. I don't know for sure, but I suspect he is texting Nicole Wong. This guy is something else. I have been paying for everything for 10 weeks. I flew him to Seattle, Oakland, and now L.A., and he is flirting with a girl that he knows I like. I start thinking about breakfast. $40. Orange juice. Unbelievable. I am driving and can't text, so his texting is driving me even more bonkers. *I'm glad you are having a good time,* I'm thinking. On a positive note the weather is spectacular in southern California.

We have The Comedy Store tonight and we are both anxious and a little on edge. We are both going over our set lists in our head. Steve practices his out loud and times it twice.

"You want to do your set?" he asks.

"I'm good," I said. I feel very self conscious doing my set for him. I feel like he doesn't think I'm funny, so I'd rather do it in my head than have him just sit through it and not laugh. The other reason I don't want to do my set is that he seems bothered by one of my jokes. In Seattle, I told this joke:

"When we first got to New York, we were at an open mic and another comic said, 'You gotta blow someone to get any stage time in Long Island.' So I don't do Long Island. But Marcinowski is headlining there three times a week."

I ask him if he minds, and he says it's cool. Still the tension is thick. I am pissed because I feel like I do everything and he takes it for granted. I booked us at The Comedy Store. I'm the one setting up the entire trip and financing it. Everyday I get a little more agitated with his laziness. I have also been working the phones and have 25 guests coming to the show. The Comedy Store will be pleased.

The 25 guests who are coming tonight are a mix of PPL associates and friends. Over the last few weeks, I became Facebook friends with a cute Yankee fan named Sara. She seems enamored by our tour and can't wait to see us in action. She is coming with a friend tonight and joining us for tomorrow's game.

My friend, Dan Eaton, and his daughter, Julie, are

already there when we arrive. Dan is always early. He is in his mid-sixties and was diagnosed with stage four cancer several years ago. I know that it takes a lot of effort for him to be there.

Thirty minutes prior to the show, the place is already packed. Like I normally do, I got a feel for the room. I like to go on stage and visualize the audience. I also like to meet as many folks as I can. I heard once that Jay Leno used to stand at the door and greet every single person as they came in. I always encourage Marcinowski to do the same. He is very personable. In Seattle, he did it well. Tonight he seems more distracted as his head is planted in his notebook. He is really nervous. The performance list has him performing fourth tonight and I'm sixth.

The very attractive Sara and her friend, Misty, show up and hang out at the bar for a few minutes. Just before the show, Misty's boyfriend joins us. So much for a double date. They move into the main room as the show is minutes away.

"I call June," says Marcinowski with a devious smile. At the beginning of the trip we came up with this game that if you liked someone, you could call the other guy off once a month.

"Nice try. That's for a girl that we haven't met before," I remind him. "I've been talking with Sara for weeks. She's here tonight because I invited her."

The show begins and Marcinowski kills it. The audience likes the 162 idea and he has a great set going just over seven minutes. I can tell by Sara's expression that she liked it too.

He did his bit on how the photographer from Fenway thought that we were a gay couple and ends with his new tag line, "Have a good gay, gays."

Ten minutes later, it is my turn. There are 200 there, so my 25 fit nicely in the crowd. They are spread out, so no one can tell that I have a crowd. Other comics tend to think that you may not be as funny if you bring a lot of people. They call you a *bringer* and it is a negative term. To me, I am building a fan base and I'm sure the owner likes me "bringing" as many as possible.

I open with the intro, "Hello, my name is Steve and I'm a recovering Yankees fan. It's been 27 hours since my last game." There is a lady in the first row who says something about my shoes. I engage the heckler and get more laughs. I am off to a great start. I ask her if it would be OK if we moved on since I had actually some spent time and prepared some material. More laughs.

My next challenge is to do my separation material. Kim is both well known and well liked by many of my friends in the crowd. Our separation is a new topic to some and news for others.

"I am just getting out of a long term relationship … AKA marriage." [laughs.] Marriage is derived from the French word *mirage*, which means an illusion that seems better from a distance." I actually got booed from the people who knew us.

"Don't boo me, " I jokingly warn the crowd. "It's all about being happy. Happiness is a choice. There are those who decide to be happy and those who decide to stay married." I get a nice laugh.

"When people find out we aren't together anymore, they freak out. It's like you have a disease. They lower their voice. 'I'm soooo sorry, I heard you were separated.' We prefer to call it newly free." A few more laughs as I am building momentum.

"Heard you were split up (I use my hands acting

like I am pulling something apart). "Just operating independently." More laughs.

"Heard you were broken up."

"No, happy as shit, thank you for asking."

My set is rocking.

"I like being single, but I hate going out to restaurants by myself. There is always a super-smoking hot blonde with blue eyes hostess that asks that same annoying question as she looks you up and down: 'Just one?'"

"*Just*? No not *just*. Melia, party of one. There is nothing *just* about me. Are you *just* the hostess?"

I fixate on one woman right in the front row and deliver all of my lines right to her.

"Seriously, at this point in your life … with all the career possibilities … with DeVry Institute right down the street, this is what you do? You're *just* the hostess? How does that feel? I guess I'm still a little bitter.

"The other thing is that when you are single they won't even give you the dignity of an announcement. It's like they reserve it for parties of two or more. They don't announce you when you are alone. They look at you and put down the mic. 'You. Come on. Follow me.' They put you in the back by the cigarette machine. It's like they don't want the other patrons to know they can come by themselves.

"If it was my restaurant," I continued, "not only would I announce the single people, I'd let them write their own bio. I'd have a stack of index cards by the hostess stand. Write whatever you want: 'Now seating Table 5. He considers himself to be one of La Jolla's most eligible bachelors. He is financially independent and in his free time he likes to volunteer at an orphanage in Guatemala. He stands an erect 6 feet, with piercing blue eyes. Table 5 welcomes party of one, Steve Melia!"

I get a nice ovation as the emcee takes the stage.

To me there is nothing more exhilarating than having a killer set. We'll spend the next four months cheering on grown adult millionaires. It sure is nice to be cheered *for* once in a while. Sara comes over and congratulates us both. She is on her way outside and guess who joins her? Hmmm.

By midnight, the party moves to a pub in Del Mar. It is crystal clear that Marz and Sara are hitting it off. I am definitely the third wheel. Their cigarette breaks are getting longer. I am hanging out with a few comics from the show and haven't seen Sara and Marcinowski for a while.

Once 30 minutes go by, I realize what is going on. Just like Jorge Posada, I am being benched for a younger up-and-coming prospect. My mind is jumping. I can't believe what is happening. I start adding up how much money I have spent on this kid. I am not only insulted, I am raging.

Should I call him? That will only make it worse. We have been getting on each other's nerves for a month now. I gave him the stage tonight. I booked it. I filled the crowd. I bought his beer.

As the minutes turns into an hour, I make the decision.

Marcinowski must go.

Do I have the balls to send him home? I still can't believe it. The tour is absolutely rocking. We are officially a third of the way in. To me, we have already proven that we can do this. Tonight we proved that we are good comics and that we can hang with anybody. I start adding up how much money I'd be saving if I did this by myself. This trip to the West Coast alone has to be costing me $3,000.

I text him.

WTF? Bar closes in 10 minutes.

He texts back.

Sorry bro. Gonna crash at Sara's place. Call you in a.m.

I pay the tab for all of us and jump in a cab and head back to the hotel. The site of his suitcase pisses me off more. Thoughts are swirling through my brain. I look at the hotel clock at 4 a.m. and I still haven't slept. Am I overreacting? I start to rationalize his behavior. I know that it is probably Sara who initiated this little tryst. It's still not right. Ungrateful. What else has he been doing behind my back?

I start role-playing the conversation of me telling Marcinowski that his trip is over. Then, for the first time in a while, I begin doubting that I can make it the entire season. Maybe this just was not meant to be. I am missing way too much of life by doing this. Maybe I can still get to Cancun and join my colleagues. I wonder if my brother will let me crash in his room. I bet I can get a decent flight out of San Diego. All of my friends and associates are in Cancun. This is where I should be. If I quit the tour now, I can be there for the Orlando event next month.

I finally drift asleep only to have my dreams full of more Marcinowski.

At 9:30 a.m., Casanova knocks on the hotel room door.

I open the door. He offers a weak, "Hey."

"So what do you think about what happened last

night?" I waste no time.

"I think that we had good sets."

You are not getting off that easy. "That's not what I'm talking about. You stole Sara from me and then left me at the bar."

"It wasn't my idea. She came on to me."

"I don't give a shit whose idea it was."

"You would have done the same thing, Melia."

"Maybe. Maybe not. That's not the point. The point is that you won't have the chance to do it again." My heart is racing.

He tries to drive the point home that he is an innocent participant here.

"She starts kissing me. What was I supposed to do? You would have done the same thing!"

"You left me sitting in the bar like an idiot."

He says nothing and continues to stand in the doorway.

"Well, I have some thinking to do. This might be it for you."

"Seriously?"

"I didn't bring you on this tour to steal girls from me."

He gives me a look of disbelief. "You can't have them all."

"Listen, what you don't seem to get is that I'm paying for everything. It would be like if I was the headliner on a comedy tour and I bring you as an opening act with me. I pay for everything and you steal girls from me in every city. You'd be off the tour."

"You would have done the same thing."

"That's what you are not getting. It's not about last night. Last night is over. Now it's about ensuring that it won't happen again. We have four months to go and I'm not giving you the chance to do this again. I've got to do some thinking. I'll be back later."

I take off and head for the beach. I lived in Encinitas from 2000-2006. My favorite place to get breakfast was a place on the 101 called Mozy's. They have the most incredible burritos. As I pay with a five dollar bill, I think how great it is to not have to pay for two. I glance up at the menu to see if they sell orange juice. I laugh to myself as I can hear him ordering a f------ orange juice!

I take a drive over to Moonlight Beach. This is the beach right off Neptune Ave. where we used to live on a cliff overlooking the pacific. I sit in the car and dial Mike's number. I quickly and emotionally tell him the story. Mike likes Marcinowski and is able to look at all sides of a problem fairly. He agrees that it is time for him to go. I then dial Jeff Olson and recount the story to him as well.

"Sounds like it will be a good lesson for the book, *Don't Bite the Hand That Feeds You,*" he says. He agrees and votes strongly for sending him home. Two people whom I trust for their opinions concur.

I guess people were right. Two guys traveling together for six months — no way. A Yankees fan and a guy from Boston who doesn't even like baseball — no way. A 40-year-old guy and a 25-year-old — no way. Just when the movie is start to get exciting. Cut. I feel like Joe Girardi slowly walking to the mound and signaling for another pitcher. I'd like to let him stay in the game, but it is time for a change.

Friday, June 3

Since I have already paid in advance for the hotel,

we are stuck there one more night. I told Marcinowski from day one that if either one of us decided that enough was enough, I would give him an airline ticket home.

The drive to Anaheim is awkward. I am pretty hungry and make my way to a place that sells sandwiches. I order, and guess who decides to stand right next to me in line? It is another moment of awkwardness as he waits for me to give him permission to order. As usual, I pay for his meal. Unbelievable. That was the last thing I bought for him that night. No beer for this guy.

I was supposed to bring Sara to tonight's game. I sell her ticket outside the stadium for $20.

The game goes by quickly as the Yankees fall to Jared Weaver and the Angels 3-2. We make our way back to San Diego. At around midnight, Marcinowski informs me that Sara is picking him up in a few minutes. That seals it for me. I stay in my $109 hotel by myself for the second straight night.

I get up early and go for a run and clear my head. Within minutes the endorphins are going and I feel better. Should he stay or should he go? I know the answer. If he still had a chance to be saved, he blew it last night. Now my decision is 100 percent certain.

The drive to Anaheim is one hour and fifteen minutes. From the time we leave until the time we pull into the parking lot, not a word is uttered in the car. Marcinowski has been planning the entire trip to visit a friend of his in L.A. Even though it is a rental car, I tell him that he could borrow it as long as he was back by 1:00. It would be an hour ride each way. So his schedule will be tight. I break the tension as we pull into the parking lot.

"Well, I guess we have a few things to talk about. I have pretty much made the decision that the tour is over for you. Unless you have something to say to try to talk me out of it."

"I thought that we made a commitment."

"We did, and you are more than welcome to tag along as long as you pay your own way."

We both knew that that wasn't going to happen.

I get out of the car and hand him the keys as I grab my suit jacket off the hanger from the back. I straighten my tie and do my best to leave my problems in the car. Speaking in front of 2,000 people needs a certain amount of positive energy. We exchange civil good-byes and I make my way into The Grove, a beautiful facility that is a perfect venue for many musicians and bands. As I walk in I am greeted by lots of old friends who congratulate me for the 162 Tour. I quickly make my way backstage to where the other speakers are located.

As I sit on the couch, I share with my friend Sean Mikeal about the developments of the tour. Sean is running this event and is one of the leaders of Southern California.

"Why are you keeping this guy around?" he asks.

"I sort of feel badly. We made a commitment to do the whole season."

We talk a little more and then I break out my laptop. I go directly to the JetBlue website and check on flights from JFK to Raleigh, Durham. Bingo. $59. That is less than I spend on him for food and beer everyday!

As I pull out my wallet I decide this is the right decision. Ticket purchased. Tour cancelled for Steve Number Two. A wave of relief comes over me as I have just released an incredible amount of pressure. The constant financial burden of taking care of someone else is finally over. His flight out is Tuesday night. A few more hundred dollars is all I'll have to spend on him.

Sean Mikael takes the stage to introduce me.

"Many of us join Pre-Paid Legal because we have big dreams and want to achieve financial independence. This next gentlemen is living out the dream of a lifetime. He is one of the most sought-after speakers in our industry and his family continues to lead by example. They were recently recognized by the company for earning more than $500,000 in one year. Many know that I'm not really a huge sports fan, but this next speaker is and I'm sure that others fans will be jealous when you hear what he is doing. He was recently featured on the news and we will let that clip introduce Mr. Steve Melia."

The May WWAY news piece is projected onto the two mega screens on each side of the stage. As the clip finishes, I make my way out to a standing ovation. I deliver a 15-minute speech in which I reference the *4-Hour Workweek* and talk about designing the life you want. It is amazing how many people come up to me afterwards and share what their big dreams are and how they are inspired to achieve them. It's ironic that I'm supposed to be living the dream and sometimes it feels like a nightmare.

After the event, I walk across the street and grab a bite to eat for lunch. I am ready to duck out and change clothes, but Marcinowski isn't due back for another hour with the car and my clothes. I order some food and as I am waiting, I see him pulling into the parking lot in our economy rental. Hmm, he's early. I call his cell and learn that he never left and has been close by the entire time. It turns out that he spent the entire time talking to Tim Boissey, his parents, and anyone else who would listen.

Besides the awkwardness of the situation, we have a fun-filled day in front of us. I have lined up a few friends to go to the 7 p.m. game with us. It will be nice for us to have some other people around. But first, we are off to Dave & Busters where a few hundred people from the Super Saturday are joining us. Marcinowski and I officially break up on the way over. We've often talked about how we are both really bad at confrontation and specifically breaking up.

I tell him that with everything that has happened I am not willing to finance the trip any longer. He isn't happy, but takes it well. We film one last time. As we are leaning against the trunk talking into the Flip camera, a couple approaches on their way to their car and inquire as to what we are doing. We tell them that we are making a movie about attending all 162 Yankees games and they are blown away. They are firing the usual questions at us and Marcinowski is just going through the motions. He plays along and we don't tell this couple that they are the first people to meet us after the breakup. Technically though, the tour is still moving on, as Marcinowski still has two games to go.

I give him the option of sitting out the last two and hanging out with his friend, but he says, "No, I made a commitment and I am going to live up to it." I guess this is his way of saying that I did not honor mine.

Several times during the trip, mostly in jest, I referenced a Ghandi quote, "My commitment is not to consistency, but to the truth the way I see it moment to moment."

This sums up how I feel. It is a new moment.

Sunday, June 5

Today is the day of good-byes and is met with mixed emotions. My friend, Dan Eaton, and his daughter,

Julie, meet us at Edison Field. Just like always, Dan beats us to our seats. His spirit is strong but his body is weak.

I first met Dan through PPL. He was a very successful attorney in San Diego and even argued before the state Supreme Court. He joined as a marketing associate and rose to the top very quickly. We loved to showcase his experience and leaned on his credibility in the legal community. He also first helped us start the Melia Foundation and did all the legal work pro bono.

When he found out that Kim and I wanted to learn tennis, he willingly offered to help coach us. For several years we would meet once a week and hit yellow balls. We spent hours together talking about tennis, life, and our mutual adoration of the New York Yankees.

He is a patient teacher, a generous soul, and a proud family man. Like myself, Dan is very stubborn and I was thankful that we usually saw eye to eye on stuff even though I am seven inches taller. I have a feeling that this may be the last time I get to spend with Dan and I embrace the hours.

We settle into our seats. It doesn't take Dan long to point to the mound and recall his playing days of amateur ball. "I pitched on that very mound. Jeez, I bet it's been 40 years." I have heard his pitching stories before and love how he lights up when he tells them.

As we watch from the upper deck, Dan is on my right and Marcinowski is on my left. Today will probably be the last time I go to a game with either one of them. Sitting next to Marcinowski is awkward. We have shared some incredible moments in 57 games over 68 days. We have been to New York, Boston, Baltimore, Toronto, Tampa, Dallas, Detroit, Seattle, Oakland, and now Anaheim. It was us against the world trying to do something special.

He has been such a big part of the tour. I know that he feels he was helping me live my dream. I am very thankful for that. He is heading back on Tuesday night. It is scary moving forward alone, but yet a big relief as well. There has been a lot of tension lately. We barely talk on the way to or from the stadium. Silence has become our preferred method of communication.

With most of our PPL leaders in Cancun, I am left to run our Sunday Night PPL call. I hope to finish in record time. Mark and AJ are supposed to go out to us at 10:25 EST. At 10:20, with my PPL call still going, they introduce me. I hand the phone to Marcinowski as I am on with 200 people. He unwillingly takes the phone as they go over to him for a weekly report.

"Hey guys it's Steve Marcinowski. Well, the tour is over for me. Melia decided that he couldn't afford both of us anymore."

I give him a dirty look. I can only hear his side and am listening as much as I can.

"We had great sets in San Diego at the La Jolla Comedy Store. I'm not a baseball fan anyway. This was Melia's dream. I was happy to help him live it out, but I guess it is over. I've got a flight home from New York on Tuesday."

He signs off to Sports Talk New York for the last time. The announcement to the world has been made.

Monday, June 6

We are up at 4 a.m. to catch another early flight departing out of LAX at 6:00. My brother is picking us up and I called him quickly on Saturday to let him know that one of his tenants would be checking out early. When we get to the airport, they inform us that we are not sitting next to each other. We are both relieved. This should make things easier.

We get back to Tommy's and Marcinowski has 24 hours to pack his stuff. He packs as much as he can and I promise to send him the rest. He periodically ducks outside and makes a phone call. With the sun still out, we play our last few games of bocci ball. This has been our favorite way to spend downtime and a regular daily activity. We joke around a little and try to ease the tension.

There is no game tonight and we stay in for a quiet evening. Steve seems to have been comfortable at the house over the last two-plus months. It is never easy staying with someone you have just met and he was well liked by the family. He always did his best to get along with and has a great knack for it. I believe it is one of the things that make him a great comic. He relates well to people and people like him and his stage persona, which is one in the same. Sara certainly liked him.

He thanks Tommy and Lucy for everything the last few months. They were always very kind to him, and continue to be on his last night. The tension is in the air but at least it has a clock on it and it will stop ticking at 5 p.m. tomorrow when I drop off Marcinowski for the last time. This is why employers get rid of employees who are no longer part of the future. Escort them out of the building ASAP.

Chapter Ten

MELIA, PARTY OF ONE

Tuesday, June 7

I call my buddy "The Breeze" to come to game 58.

"Really? Man, I've never been to a Yankees/Red Sox game. That would be awesome! I'll have to come straight from work."

So I officially have a date for the first of 105 remaining games without Marcinowski.

Meanwhile, Marz and I drive to New York City for the last time and we recall some great times over the last 10 weeks. Fifty-seven games is quite the milestone for someone who doesn't like baseball and hasn't been to a game since he was 9. His flight back to Raleigh leaves at 9:55 p.m. It is just before 5 p.m. as we get closer to JFK. I'm not going to miss getting a good parking spot.

The ride to JFK is less tense. He asks me what I liked most about the trip (which, by the way, is a great network marketing technique for getting someone to focus on the positive.) "Well," I say, "I enjoyed our ride in to the city together every day. I will miss our daily routine." As much as I'm unhappy with the way this is ending, I sincerely appreciate Steve's commitment to the tour and I'll always cherish our time together. I also acknowledge that I am not the easiest person to get along with.

It seems like he is suddenly having a burst of energy and is probably relieved it is over as well. He is more talkative today than he has been in a long time.

"How are you going to go to 105 games by yourself?" he inquires.

"I won't," I reply. "I'll piece it together. At this point it's like I'm in the jungle and I just have to plan the next few days. I'm in survival mode. I made it one-third of the way, now it is time to piece together the next third."

"I guess that is where we were thinking differently. I never thought I was so … dispensable."

I don't know what to say, so I just say nothing. I just let that hang. I pull into the JetBlue terminal and up to the curb.

We wish each other the best, do a half hug and that is it. The first chapter of 162 is quickly over.

When I get back in the car, the adrenaline pumps through my body. I feel like I just broke up with a girl. It's the feeling you get when you extricate yourself from a toxic relationship. Not that Marz was toxic, but the vibe lately certainly has been. I believe it was the Seattle trip when he spent the night chatting it up with Heather that might have put some thoughts in his head. I'm not sure what they were, but I think they centered around him not being respected. As a comic, he'll do fine. He eats and breathes comedy. It's his passion and he is very good. I hope that this experience won't tarnish our relationship.

In the meantime, there's a lot of baseball still left to play. And tonight is all about one of the greatest rivalries in Major League Baseball: Red Sox versus Yankees.

I meet The Breeze at The Dugout. He told me that he would be coming straight from work. I guess I didn't realize what that meant. He looks like he had just been pulled out of a mine after being trapped for a week. He is dirty, sweaty, and has his own unique aroma. Don't get me wrong; I love The Breeze, but he is filthy tonight. I laugh when I see him.

The Breeze and I at Yankee Stadium

I first met The Breeze in Wilmington last September. It was when Kim and I split up and I first moved out, and he and I instantly became buddies. He was in town for a month to help a friend who had cancer. He is back in Brooklyn now working construction.

We sit in Section 236 — the left field bleachers. There are plenty of Boston fans in the house. I am more of an observer at this point than a participant in rowdy fan behavior. I have been treated well on the road by opposing fans and I always do my best to return the favor.

There is a Yankees fan behind us who refuses to move and is blocking a female Red Sox fan from getting to her seat. Maybe funny for a second, but that's about it. He finally moves and lets her get to her assigned spot. There are no actual seats in the bleachers, just numbers, and everyone sort of squeezes in. The Red Sox fan is very nice and certainly not looking for trouble. Her boyfriend is a Yankees fan and finally has to tell the guy to knock it off.

The loudmouth is seated behind me and to the left. He is very obnoxious and is yelling in the girl's ear, who is on my right. I see her make eye contact with her boyfriend, as if saying, "This guy is driving me crazy." The Breeze is on my left. He stands a good 6' 2" and is built like an armored truck. He has a full mustache and beard. He looks like the love child of ZZ Top and Dukes of Hazard's Uncle Jesse. To me, he is one of the most gentle people I have ever known. Others are scared shitless by him.

The loudmouth behind us is constantly running his mouth like bad diarrhea. He is also "chattering." This is the constant yelling and piecing together of various thoughts and sentences without any structure. When I played little league, it would go, "Hey batter …" and then you added in whatever you wanted. Very early in the game, he starts talking about Girardi and how he is such a piece of shit. His constant stream of discombobulated chatter is beyond annoying. I would have rather heard fingernails on a chalkboard.

Then the unthinkable. He calls Derek Jeter a "f-----ing douche bag." He says it loud enough for everyone to hear and I can't take it anymore.

I turn around and tell him to shut up. I'm sure that there was an extra word or two in there. He doesn't like this at all and starts including me in his chattering episodes.

"Hey, 15-year-old. Hey, brings a glove to the game like a little kid. Hey 15. Hey 15! Hey little punk …" he keeps going and going.

The Breeze and I make eye contact. I look over to security and they are way too far away to grab their attention. After a few minutes, he keeps growing louder and louder. The Breeze stands up and turns around. With a very calm demeanor he addresses him.

"Excuse me. I see what you're doing to my friend here. I want you to stop right now."

The guy is petrified. "Hey man, I'm a Yankees fan."

Breeze's eyes must have been burning a hole through him. I never saw anyone backpedal as fast as this guy.

"I don't care what kind of a fan you are. I'm only going to ask once."

"OK, OK," was the last peep that we heard from this clown.

I wanted to laugh as much as I wanted to put my arm around my new hero. Security gets there by the time The Breeze turns and sits down.

"Is there a problem here sir?"

"No, we were just talking," The Breeze says calmly as he stares straight ahead and re-engages in the game.

"Are you sure?"

"No problems here."

I definitely learned some lessons in game 58. I can hear Marcinowski's voice, "Don't engage, Melia." Dirty or not, I'm sure glad that The Breeze was here tonight. The Yankees fall again to Boston 6-4. The rivals are tied for first place.

Thursday, June 16

Today I go to the game with Mike and my niece, Katie. Although the sun is shining brightly today, my cold and runny nose have not gone away. It seems to be getting worse. I am run down and need a rest. We watch from the left field box seats as Brett Gardner provided the game-

Mike, Katie, and me.

winning hit in the 12th inning. It is the third walk-off of the year as the Yanks sweep Texas and win six out of seven.

I am flying to Chicago on the 8:45 Southwest to Midway Airport. I get to ticketing and they ask me if Steve Marcinowski will be checking in as well.

"No, he did not make the trip."

When I get to my seat, I can feel his presence as the seat next to me is empty. He has been gone 10 days and this will be the first road trip without him. In that span, the Bombers have played 10. They are 6-4 without him. Of the 10 games, I have been to five with friends and five on my own.

The city train delivers me to the beautiful Palmer House Hilton. I was describing the 162 Tour to a gentleman on the airplane. He was excited as a sport fan. He was impressed when I told him about the Palmer House and, by his reaction, must have thought that I was loaded.

The reality is that I booked the hotel online for $ 532.74 for four nights. This is a smoking deal for downtown Chicago.

For this trip, I will get to split the expenses with my buddy, Danny Vulin, who is flying in from Wilmington. Danny took over as the Regional Manager there since I left. We play three games here in Chicago, ending with the Sunday Night Game of the Week. This is a rare appearance by the Yankees at historic Wrigley Field to play the National League Cubs and we have our tickets lined up for all three games of the interleague series. I do not want to take a chance on scalping for this much-anticipated series. We paid $143.76 for Friday, $278.00 for Saturday and $130.60 Sunday, for a total of $552.36 for the three-game weekend. Gulp.

Friday, June 17

Today will be a packed day as our day game will be topped off by having dinner with the incoming CEO Rip Mason at 7 p.m. He is in town for a Super Saturday in Chicago. He is a huge Yankees fan and I invited him to go to the game with us, but his schedule wouldn't allow it. His invitation to dinner, though, is happily accepted. He has been traveling around North America conducting town hall-type events.

At 10 a.m., I am having my daily writing session at the hotel room desk when Danny Vulin knocks on my door. This is the first time I have seen him since leaving Wilmington in March. He is my best friend back home and was nice enough to let me store all of my stuff at his house.

The Yankees day record is incredible so far with a 16-5 record. Garcia is good, but not good enough. We watch the Cubs silence the Yankee bats 3-1 on a beautiful Chicago summer day. The bars around the area never stop. We don't have time to stop, but notice a bar there called "162." This will make a good place for the book signing.

That evening, we get to the restaurant and Rip Mason greets us with a big smile and handshake. Rip is a good listener and a great conversationalist. Meeting Rip and spending some time with him does a lot for me. He is very gracious about the tour. One of the things that I respect about him is that he never has a bad word to say about anyone. In fact, just the opposite; he had something nice to say about everyone in the company whose name was brought up.

Towards the end of dinner, I ask about Jeff Olson's role in the company. He knows that Jeff is our guy and does a good job of sidestepping the issue. "I flew down to Florida and met with Jeff," Rip says. "We certainly know how talented he is and the ball is literally in his court." I have a feeling that he took time to meet with me because he is aware of our allegiance to Jeff Olson.

Danny Vulin, Rip Mason, and me.

On the way to driving Rip back to his hotel, we see two of our provider attorneys in the parking lot walking towards their car. I've known Frank Moscardini and David Shimanovski for at least a dozen years and have a ton of respect for their work ethic and professionalism. They are just leaving a leadership meeting with our sales associates.

Frank sticks his head in to say hello and I introduce them to our new leader. They share a hardy greeting. The attorneys are as anxious as the field to get to know Rip. Like my family, they have spent the better part of the last two decades helping to build PPL. The provider lawyers are compensated by earning a percentage on their state's membership base. For many of the law firms, their PPL members have become their biggest clients. While they still have traditional clients, many of the bigger firms are receiving monthly checks from $500,000 - $1,000,000. Because they are paid this way, there is a built-in accountability system. Many of our firms have grown from a few lawyers to dozens that service only the PPL base.

Over the years, I have developed some great relationships with some very cool lawyers. Frank is at the top of the list. He and I have done many presentations together. Usually I'll open the meeting and share the concept and then Frank comes in and adds the credibility and sprinkles in some real-life stories.

"Are you guys coming tomorrow?" I ask.

"No we can't. The rules have changed. We can't speak at any recruiting rallies anymore. The state ABA sees it as solicitation if there are prospects there. That's why we are here tonight."

"Ahh, too bad. We always made a great team. Did you hear what I'm doing? I'm going to every Yankee game the entire season."

"Get out of here! Wow. You know my firm has a connection for White Sox tickets."

"I'll be back August 1st through the 4th!"

Frank tells me to call him and he can get me tickets. Yes!

As we pull around, Rip tells me that the lawyers really wanted to take him out to dinner tonight.

"As much as I want to get to know these guys, I

am a field guy. I have been doing this a while, Steve, and I want you to know that the most important people in the world to me are the leaders in the field. I feel like our strongest asset is this company's leadership. This is the best I have ever seen."

With a vote of confidence like that from a man of Rip's pedigree, it just confirmed for me once again that I am with the right company at the right time.

Saturday, June 18

We show back up at the Comfort Suites hotel in Orland Park. There is a buzz in the air as Rip Mason is standing in the front of the room gripping and grinning. Also in town, from Charleston, SC, are Frank and Theresa Aucoin. I could write an entire book on this couple. I have known the Aucoins for 17 years and they are close friends.

Frank is almost impossible to describe and easy to describe at the same time. He is somewhere in his late 60s. He is rarely spotted without a Waffle House styrofoam cup full of Diet Coke. He has never had a drop of alcohol in his life and is a self-made millionaire. At any one time, he owns a few dozen homes and is constantly turning them over. The Aucoins opened up a chain of sign stores and bookstores. Over the last few years they bring me in to do a comedy show at their annual team sales meeting. The Aucoins are also competitive and for years we have been competing in the business. The competition is friendly as they are some of our closest allies in PPL. Theresa is opposite of Frank in that she is always very health conscious and on stage is Frank's "straight man."

The Aucoins open up and do a compelling business overview. Rip Mason is next and delivers a very presidential-type talk. He is a welcomed breath of fresh air. The game is at 2:20 today and I am constantly peeking at my watch. We have to be out of there by noon and drive an hour back and then return the car.

At 11:45, they begin to play the WWAY piece from May. Most of the crowd has no idea what I'm doing. Some love it and some are just confused. I deliver a talk on designing a life and how I was able to use the PPL business model to do it. It may seem hard to believe, but I am stopped in the hallway to sign a dozen autographs and snap a few pictures. Usually I am very accommodating. Today, I am doing it with one foot out the door. We rush back and, after changing, quickly decide to jump in a cab to Wrigley. We miss the first pitch and arrive at 2:30.

As the game gets into the later innings, a few fans start to head for the streets. Danny and I move up. We make it all the way to the first row, down the right field line. As we settle in, we notice that there are three Yankees fans to our right that are way too drunk. They are getting yelled at by Cubs fans in every direction. Not to assign blame, but they are breaking the *DO NOT ENGAGE* rule. The Cubs fans are yelling with the usual hometown bravado, and rather than letting it go, the drunk Yankees fans respond to every insult with a more obnoxious one. It gets so bad that it is hard to watch the game.

As the ninth inning comes, one of the Yankee fans threatens a Cubs fan a few rows in front of them. I'm guessing at Wrigley that the security guards must have tenure, because they all seem to be over 70. The argument has been taking place for more than 20 minutes and not one police officer has shown up. A 75-year-old guard tells the Yankee fans to knock it off. It does nothing as he walks away.

The game ends with a Yankees victory and the fans stay put and get louder. Cubs fans began to close in and also get louder. A Cubs fan open-hand slaps the loudest of the New Yorkers. Then all hell breaks loose. Danny and I stay put and are staying silent. As the first blow is thrown, though, Danny starts to move towards the fracas.

"Don't, dude," I yell as I hold him back. "Let's get out of here."

There are a few more pushes and maybe a punch or two are thrown before three uniformed officers appear on the scene. Better late than never, I suppose. Without asking any questions, they handcuff the three Yankees fans and escort them out to cheering of rabid Cubs fans. I am mad at the really slow response time. The Cubs should take some responsibility for this one as the situation could have been avoided altogether. Just like anything in life, if you deal with things early enough, you can stop them from escalating.

The outside bars aren't much better as we get yelled at for simply wearing our New York gear.

I think that they should show the Bryan Stow documentary regularly at ballparks. Bryan is a Giants fan who was beaten to within an inch of his life by some Dodgers fans on Opening Day. His care is estimated to cost more than $50 million. He'll never be the same again.

The Yanks take one back from the Cubbies today, 4-3. The trip has been great so far and we still have the Sunday Night Game of the Week to play. Danny is wearing me out!

Sunday, June 19
Father's Day
Danny and I spend most of the day walking around

downtown, as this is the first chance we have to see the city. No sick days on this tour. I call my dad and wish him a happy Father's Day. He asks me how it's going now that I'm solo and asks if I can really make it alone. I tell him that it is going great and that I have not missed a beat. He sounds good and I thank him for being a great dad.

I read in the *USA Today* the next day that Joe Girardi got up early and drove three hours to visit with his father in Southern Illinois. A six-hour hour round-trip to visit his ailing father in the hospital on Father's Day. I can relate to the players and staff who have to juggle their personal lives for nearly eight months every season. As I read the article, I got tears in my eyes as it reminds me of my dad. One of my biggest realizations is how hard it is every year to be away from your loved ones and miss a lot of family events. I know the players must appreciate their loved ones who pick up the slack while they are gone.

Monday, June 20

I wake up with the realization that I am still unsure of how I am getting to Cincinnati. Airfare was ridiculous from Chicago to Cincinnati and the Amtrak train would not get me there in time.

The Megabus is an option. It is $44 and a six-hour trip. The first one left at 7 a.m. and arrived at 1 p.m. — too early. The second one leaves at 11 a.m. and gets into downtown at 6 p.m. Too close a call and too many things can go wrong. I didn't want to miss a game and be stuck on a bus.

Many of the rental car companies don't allow one-way out-of-state drop-offs. Others have a $200 fee. Hertz, however, would be my choice. I worked them down to

$109, plus tax.

    At 10:45 a.m., I drop Danny off at the train station in my rental any head for Ohio. I am exhausted and my nose will not stop running. For two weeks now, my cold has turned into a bad cough. Before the drive, I started consuming the non-drowsy Robitussin. I went through an entire box of tissues in Chicago. I am trying to get some rest in between games, but feel very run down.

    In addition, my cell phone is really low on batteries and I do not have a car charger. Then I learn of the time change in Indiana and how I have already lost an hour. Great.

    I look over at the empty passenger seat and chuckle to myself. I guess I am the only one crazy enough to do

With Beth and Steve

this. It has only been two weeks since Marz left. Fifteen more games have passed since his departure. Was it a good decision to go solo? I believe it was.

    I am staying with Steve Maguire and his wife, Beth Mountjoy. Steve was an original programmer with Microsoft in Seattle and has been financially independent for years. He has been involved in PPL since 1998. He and Beth are incredibly philanthropic and have been friends for 15 years. When the 162 Tour was announced in March, they scooped up tickets for this series.

    They were the very first to call and tell me they have tickets for me. Although they had not been to a game in their four years living in Cincinnati, they bought a season ticket package to be able to get the Yankees tickets.

Tuesday, June 21

I am doing a luncheon seminar from noon until 2 p.m. I look forward to taking a long nap during the break. As I put my suit on, I tell myself that I just have to muster enough energy to get through it. There is a crowd of nearly 25 today and they are thrilled to have a top PPL associate in Ohio. It is a nice break from baseball.

My hosts, Steve and Beth, are off to their PPL meeting. At 6 p.m., just as we are walking out the door, we get news that the game has been postponed. A wave of relief comes over my body as I knew it was going to be a long, wet night. This is the first time all year that a game

Me and April.

is called prior to my leaving the house. They also announce that tomorrow will be our first day/night doubleheader of the year. 12:35 and 7 p.m. Just what the doctor ordered.

Any normal person would see this as their chance to get some much-needed rest. But I know that April Gillespie, who was supposed to be going to the game with me, was looking forward to spending some time with me and skipped the meeting to do so. So, we go out and have a great time. I make it back to the Maguires' place around 11:30 and head straight for bed. My body is pleading with me for some rest. I am so congested it feels like my head is going to explode.

Thursday, June 23

I am in the Cincinnati airport, which is in Kentucky. I feel horrible. Cough, congestion, and an equally unhealthy hangover. Four hours of sleep was not what the doctor prescribed. Thankfully, today is one my 18 days off from baseball. This will also be my last day of being 40. In one of my sets, I call this my Midlife Crisis Tour.

"Guys have it pretty good. Girls go through midlife crisis and they sit around and eat Häagen-Dazs. They go through menopause and have plastic surgery. Guys start to work out, drive sports cars, and attend 162 baseball games. This may be one reason that women live longer."

Just when I think that I will have a nice relaxing day, I learn in Philadelphia that our connecting flight is cancelled. Two hours later, we board the next available flight and I doze off. Just before I pass out on the plane, I notice a gentleman sitting across the aisle with a huge championship ring that looks like it has a CR for the Colorado Rockies.

The Rockies are our foe for the next three days. He is by himself so I deduce that he is probably a scout. He is a little old to have played for the Rockies, as the organization has only been around since 1993 and they didn't win for a long time.

"Are you going to the series this weekend?" I inquire across the aisle.

"Yes, my son is pitching on Saturday," he boasts proudly.

My adrenaline starts pumping. "That's awesome! Who's your son?"

"Aaron Cook."

"Wow! Is it his first time pitching at Yankee Stadium?"

"It is his first time in the new stadium. He pitched three innings in the 2008 All-Star Game, which was held at the old Yankee Stadium."

I come to learn that Cook is 32 and in his ninth Major League season. I learn later that he signed a $30 million contract three years ago.

I ask about his ring. He tells me that his son gave him his NL championship ring and bought another one for himself. I like this kid already. I give him a card, a rundown on my 162 journey, and tell him to call me over the weekend and that I'd love to interview him for the book. The pilot then announces that the flight is cancelled and we need to check with the gate agent to re-book. It's a good thing that there is no game today.

We continue to talk as we grab our overhead luggage and walk down the aisle.

"The Rockies flew all of the fathers to Cleveland last weekend for Father's Day and picked up the tab," he tells me. "I wanted to go to see him pitch in Yankee Stadium instead, though."

"Is this your first time to New York?"

"Yes, it is."

That prompts me to give him a brief layout of the different airports and advise him to be flexible as there are a lot of options with the New York area airports. I was hoping to speak more, but we were getting off of the plane and everyone scatters to make reservations.

Tuesday, June 28

I am in my favorite seat tonight in Section 110. These are the seats off the right field line. The game is out of hand with the Yanks up 11-2. I am gloveless tonight as I forgot my leather in the house. I should have paid attention to the omen.

With one out in the 8th, 3rd baseman Casey McGehee rips it foul down the right field line. I immediately stand in anticipation. I position myself so I can reach and get the ball rolling against the wall. It is moving so fast that it clears the wall and grazes off of the security guard's hand. I step forward and put my body in front of it.

CRACK!

The ball hits me on the left side of my nose. It's hit so hard that the ball immediately changes direction and bounces onto the field. I hear an instant groan from the crowd. I'm not sure if it is because of my injury or the fact that I did not make the play. Even Nick Swisher winces.

The ball boy retrieves the ball and tosses it back, but by this time several other people are vying for it. Of course, he throws it to some dude with a glove. He plays the nice guy and hands it to the kid next to him. The kid gets the ball. The dude gets the glory. I get a headache and a possible broken nose. A few people ask me if I'm OK. I constantly touch my nose for the rest of the game. I vow to bring my glove to every game from now on.

As I'm driving home, I realized that I should have hit the ground and milked it. The cameras would have stayed on me, and this was my biggest opportunity to get discovered. Oh, well.

Wednesday, June 29

It is shortly after 1 p.m. and I am walking through the Sunrise Mall in Massapequa, shopping for some sign materials. My cell phone rings and it is Jeff Olson. I immediately think that Jeff is either confirming or canceling his appearance at our summer event which is a training by our top associates and includes a golf tournament, luau, live auction, and tons of fun. We are expecting about 400 this year.

"Listen," Jeff says with a serious tone. "This is just between us. I am leaving to start my own company."

After 13 years, the call is finally coming. There have been rumors about Jeff leaving for years and now they are being confirmed. I am half freaking out and half excited. Over the years, I have said to Jeff many times that if he was going to do something else, he had better call us.

"I am not calling to recruit you," he said, which is legal jargon for *I'm calling to recruit you.*

"This is something that I have been working on for two years and I will be launching sometime over the next 90 days. The only reason that I am calling you is to give you the option of not having me speak at your event."

"Wow. What's your company about."

"Man, I am so excited," he says. "I can't tell you any specifics. I can tell that this is going to be the most exciting thing to hit the network marketing industry in years."

"Can you tell me anything?"

"We are going international right away. I bought the worldwide rights to market this particular product. But like I said, I swear I am not trying to recruit you."

"What will your role be?"

"CEO and Founder. I have told Rip Mason as well. He understands and they want to keep me on board as a consultant in some capacity. I will not be going after any PPL people at all."

All that I can muster up is, "Wow. Well, I am not even going to be in Orlando, so let me talk to Mike and

Kim. Kim gets back from Guatemala on Friday."

"I just wanted you guys to know so you can be able to make a decision about me coming or not."

"I imagine that we still want you there. There will be more questions if you do not show up."

We say our good-byes.

I call Mike. We spend a few minutes contemplating what this means to us. We have always said that if Jeff left to go do something that we would heavily consider it. It is hard, though, when he won't tell us anything. We have always believed that it would be easier to leave because there are three of us. One could potentially start to build something else while the others continued to run the business. We rack our brains trying to figure out what kind of company he would launch.

Meanwhile, my nose is still very sore, but I don't think it is broken, although I'm having a hard time breathing out of it.

Friday, July 1

This weekend is my first trip to Citi Field, the home of the New York Mets. The stadium opened in 2009. It replaced Shea Stadium as the Mets home. There is a big argument between Mets and Yankees fans about who has the better stadium.

Things have certainly changed over the last 24 years. I couldn't help but flash back to my old journal, dated June 25th, 1987: Shea Stadium.

I turned 17 yesterday. I am on summer break up from Florida. We are seated just off the left field foul line. Our original seats were back about 10 rows. *It is a hot, sleepy afternoon. It is the top of the eighth and the Mets have taken the field and are warming up.*

I am at the game with my brothers, Mike and Jim. Mike's sons Luke and Willie are with us as well. Jim and I have moved up to the third row from the field.

"I've always wanted to jump on the field," I offer to Jim.

"You don't have the guts."

Within a few seconds, he has added a few incentives to the deal. He offered me an honorary membership to his "gang." Gang is probably a little strong. It's more like a "group" of cool guys. I hand him my wallet, lean my hands on the wall, and use my body weight to make the jump.

Kevin McReynolds is the left fielder. I land on the dirt and quickly make it to the well-manicured grass. This is my first time on a Major League field. The same field that the Mets won the World Series a few months ago in dramatic fashion. My adrenaline is flowing.

McReynolds is roughly 20 yards from me as I continue my jog. There is no turning back now. My goal is to meet McReynolds and shake his hand. I reach him and he still doesn't notice me as he plays catch with the center fielder, Lenny Dykstra. I tap him on the right soldier.

"Excuse me. Could I get a handshake Mr. McReynolds."

He gives me a smile and obliges.

"I'm a big fan, Sir."

"Nice to meet you." He is a little startled,

but friendly nonetheless. I weigh 140 lbs. soaking wet and probably don't pose a threat.

Goal accomplished.

I begin to jog back as a Shea Stadium security guard is now jogging towards me. He is halfway between myself and my seat. I turn left. As I do, a few of New York's finest descend from the left field bullpen. There are at least five of them chasing me now. I do a few figure-eights in hopes of prolonging my birthday excursion.

Within seconds, I am in the arms of the NYPD. I am being escorted out with my left hand behind my back. I use my right to wave to the crowd. I give the thumbs down with my right thumb and the fans at Shea boo the authorities.

They often make the announcement that anyone running on the field will be ejected from the park. I've arranged with my brothers to meet me back at the car.

I am escorted through the visiting Cubs' bullpen. A giant of a man, veteran Lee Smith is warming up. He pats me on the back and asks, "What are you doing, kid?"

"Hi, Mr. Smith."

I am expecting to be dumped outside, but surprisingly, I am led to the stadium drunk tank. I am thrown in a caged cell with the other trouble makers from the day. I quickly recognize a guy who had tried to run the bases an inning earlier. When I can't produce an ID, an officer tells me that it is going to be a long night. I tell him that I am at the game with my brothers.

"Too bad. Since you are a minor, we can

only release you to your parents."

An hour later, when I am sufficiently scared, they write me a ticket for trespassing and let me go. My brothers and nephews are waiting in a reception line and are quick to give me high fives.

I had a court date later that summer that would require a court appearance. My dad wrote a letter and was able to use his clout as a FDNY chief. I received a $25 fine and had to write an apology essay. To this day, it is the best $25 I have ever spent. I was on the same field as Darryl Strawberry, Dwight Gooden, and Keith Hernandez.

If you tried that today in any stadium, it would be an entirely different story. It would begin with an open-field tackle, continue with a weekend imprisonment, and would be followed by a hefty fine for as much as $5,000. In nearly half a season, I can only recall four fans running on the field, two of which were completely naked.

I am in line at one of the beer stands when I hear a woman behind me ask her boyfriend, "What do you think that 162 means?" an obvious reference to my jersey.

"It is how many games are in a baseball season."

I turn around and agree. "I'm attending all 162 Yankees games this year." For the next few minutes we chat about the tour. I answer the "how" part by discussing how I am an a budget most of the time.

It turns out that the guy, John, is from Encinitas, Ca. This is exactly where I lived in San Diego. As we get to the front of the line, I place my order and he insists on buying me a beer. I more than appreciate his $10 contribution toward my trip. Meeting folks like John and his friend Sherry keeps me going every day. I give him a card and we promise to stay in touch.

Meanwhile, news from Mike isn't quite as good:

This night was horrible for me. I was out and about taking care of some business and hanging with a lady friend. I got home way, way late to find all the lights on in the house. It wasn't a good sign. Inside, I found my father sprawled out on the kitchen floor where he had been lying since early evening and most of the night.

I've never felt so bad in my entire life (and I've done a few really bad things!). I totally felt like it was my fault and I still do. I called the ambulance and he was whisked away. I met him in the ER. He had re-injured his ribs. Thankfully, it wasn't as bad as before. This was his third spill since New Year's Eve.

Chapter Eleven

HALFTIME

Saturday, July 2

Kim is back from Guatemala and is really freaked about Jeff Olson leaving. Jeff has been one of the constants in our lives, and business without him won't be the same. Mike, Kim, and I get on the phone and discuss our options. Those who know us personally know that the three of us are tight no matter what happens. We all have each other's back no matter what.

I sit quietly and look over the sea of Mets and Yankee fans. There are a few more Yankees fans today. I fondly remember the last game that my dad and I attended together. It was at Shea Stadium in 1985 and Dwight Gooden pitched a gem. As much fun as we had, my dad vowed never to go to a game again. He would get so mad when fans would get drunk, loud, and curse. He kept his promise.

After a 4-0 victory by the Yanks, I walk to the parking lot and silently congratulate myself. Eighty-one games. I am halfway home. I am exhausted. I am run down. Yet I am beyond excited that I have decided to live out a dream. It's halftime.

Monday, July 4
Independence Day

As I do most Mondays, I email every sports reporter I can. Halfway and no major bites. But, hey, Derek Jeter is back tonight! The Yanks went 14-4 in his absence. There is a lot of chatter on sports radio that they are better without him. Give me a break. Jeter returns just six hits away from 3,000!

I am headed to Cleveland with no tickets. I've come a long way in a month. Just a few weeks ago, I was neurotic about not having tickets in advance. Logistics are much easier with one person. There are three night games on

this short trip, so once again there will be no comedy shows.

I am in a great mood. I am celebrating my independence at the Philadelphia airport, waiting on my connection. I have my neon green sign and my computer bag in tow. My flight arrives into Cleveland at 3:18 p.m. This is about the closest I have pushed it. I have a nervous energy about this trip. I am not sure what it is, but I am very jittery. This could be due to the fact that I'm now halfway finished. Eighty-two down and 80 to go. Maybe it's also the fact that this is my first real road trip that I don't know anybody. No visitors, no friends. Lonely, yet liberating.

"Now boarding, Silver Preferred," comes the

announcement from the gate agent. This is my cue.

A girl seated to my left is smiling at me. I'd put her in her mid 20s.

"What's on your sign?" she asks.

"It's for Derek Jeter. He is six hits away from 3000."

"I know. I'm going to all of the games in Cleveland," she says as she smiles widely.

I unroll the sign and let her get a glimpse. We say our good-byes and I board the plane. She certainly has me guessing. She is cute, young, and apparently traveling by herself. She sits four rows behind me as we occasionally make eye contact and smile.

Could she be traveling out to the games because she is a huge fan like me? Not likely.

Later at the baggage claim, I am standing next to two businessmen. They are seated on a bench as we wait for the belt to start moving. There is no sign of the cute Yankees fan. They ask me if I'm in town for the games. I tell them that I am on my way to game 83 tonight of 162. One of them says something that I hear frequently: "I wish I could do something like that."

I immediately think, *You can if you want to!* Life is all about choices. Choices and consequences. I personally do not like to say "I wish," because it is disempowering. It is like saying, "I have no control over my situation. I might as well close my eyes and hope for the best." I choose my words very carefully.

Anyway, I'm sure my fellow traveler was just making friendly conversation.

I sometimes avoid the 162 conversation. I know all the questions and I know the answers. I know that it will lead to a 10 minute commitment. Right now I'm more curious as to where my new friend is. The bags are still not coming out. I walk outside and loop around through another set of doors, before noticing her at the Help Desk. I wait behind her and can hear the conversation. She looks frustrated.

She is explaining to the lady that she is supposed to go to The Ritz. Then she says something that catches my attention. She claims that she is meeting one of the New York Yankees. As she walks away from the desk, I ask her what she needs help with. She tells me that she is in Cleveland visiting one of the players.

"He told me that everything would be taken care of. I don't even know the name of the hotel. I thought it was the Ritz. I can't even call him now. He is already at the stadium and doesn't have access to his cellphone."

I am taking the train to my hotel which is close to The Ritz Carlton. I tell her that I know where it is and that I'll bring her to her hotel. We get on the train together. She really looks like she needs help and I can use some companionship. I'm not sure why, but I buy her ticket as well. It is just the two of us on the train. She has no idea what she is doing. She has no ticket for tonight's game and she doesn't appear to have any spending money. She does know her name, though. It's Stephanie.

My curiosity is killing me. Which Yankee is she here to see? I want to ask her almost as much as she wants to tell me. I think it is very uncool to ever give up anyone's name. I will not be naming the player that is getting a Spanish visitor from the Bronx. I can tell you this. It isn't Jeter, A-Rod or anyone else making over $10 million a year. As far as I know, the player is not married, either.

Players live in a different world than a few decades ago. Alex Rodriguez was busted in Toronto a few years ago by a reporter for entering his hotel with a blond bombshell. With the moral implications aside, I think that it was a sad state of our media. In the new world of social media, these guys have to be extra careful. The liberty given to celebrities and sports stars of an era ago no longer exists. I wouldn't want someone following me around telling my business to sell newspapers. So let's just say that she was on her first date with a New York Yankee. I learn that Stephanie had worked for both the Mets and the Yankees in the old stadium. When she found out that I was writing a book, she developed a gift for gab. She shares with me a few ballpark scams of how employees rip off their bosses. Nice.

She then launches into this crazy story of how Derek Jeter supposedly got her fired. After listening, I conclude that he did not have anything to do with it and probably wouldn't even remember her. The short version is that she brought Derek a gift and gave it to him one day at the stadium. (Keep in mind that they didn't know each other. Hmm.) The next day she was fired. She is convinced that DJ complained about her bothering the players. "I really did not think it was him," she says, "but after talking with some of my friends, they convinced me that it was."

Now to her current flame. She quickly tells me that they had met outside of the stadium a few weeks prior and have been trying to get together in New York. He went online last night and purchased her ticket. She is excited. I am excited. It is exciting. I am selfishly hoping that this is my "in" to the players. At least I know where they are staying. I drop her off at the Ritz Carlton and call the DoubleTree shuttle for a lift. We exchange cell phone numbers and I agree to pick her up at her hotel at 6 p.m. The Ritz is right next to Progressive Field.

After quickly checking in, I walk by the hotel bar and see that they are selling Molsons for $2. I pick up two with my luggage in tow and head up to my room. I pound one while changing clothes. Glove? Check. 162 jersey? Check. Money? Check. Wallet? Check. Tickets? Nope. I text Stephanie, but do not get a response.

I make my way over to the stadium. It is the Fourth of July and I'm sure tickets will probably be a little higher than normal. Within a few minutes, I have traded a twenty dollar bill for an upper deck ticket. I text her again as I make my way over to the Yankees hotel. I wait in the lobby, but still no sign of her. I start to make my way back when my cell rings.

"It's Stephanie. I just got in the room. They had a hard time finding my reservation. The ladies at the desk were so rude to me."

They must get a lot of groupies who pretend they are girlfriends of the players. According to Stephanie, they had a hard time believing her. She seems very upset, even frantic.

"I haven't eaten yet. He didn't leave me a ticket and I can't get in touch with him. I'm just going to stay in the room."

I thought that she was a huge Yankees fan.

"Seriously? Come on. You came all this way. It's the Fourth of July and Jeter's first game back." I get a quick idea. "How about if I get you a ticket tonight and you get your friend to get two for us tomorrow?"

"What if I can only get one tomorrow?" she hesitates. "No, it's OK. I'll just stay here." I'm sure that she doesn't want to tell him about me.

I do not take no for an answer. "I'll tell you what. You order room service. Tell them you want it ASAP. I will get you a ticket and be there as soon as I can. If you can't get me one tomorrow, no sweat."

She agrees and I make my way back to the stadium and trade another $20 for a ticket. I laugh to myself how easy it is to secure a ticket.

After arriving at her hotel, she appears and hands me two mini bottles of Jack Daniels. Well, it's not the way I would have scripted it, but it looks like the New York Yankees have finally bought me a drink.

It is a few minutes after 7 p.m. and I do not want to miss DJ's first at bat. I'm doing my best to move her along. We pass a scalper on the way into the park who "upgrades" me for $40 with two tickets right off of the first base line in the second row.

By the fourth inning we are on our third beer.

"Are you trying to get me drunk for [*player who shall remain nameless*]?", she asks giggling.

I guess I am. I am being a gentleman and think it's cool that I am entertaining one of the Yankee girls. At $8 per beer, a ticket, and her transportation, I have now

At the game with my new friend, Stephanie

spent about $50 on her. It is nice to have someone to sit and watch the game with who loves the Yankees. As much as I enjoy the freedom of going by myself, I am thoroughly enjoying her company.

The Yanks lose this one as DJ goes 0 for 4. There is a fireworks show immediately following the game. It is pretty spectacular as I watch with Stephanie. The minute it is over, she is all about getting back. The night ends as fast as it begins for her as I drop her back at The Ritz Carlton. We hug good night.

I change clothes and make my way to the part of downtown where there is bar after bar. I bounce around by myself and just before 3 a.m. I find myself in a taxi headed for the DoubleTree.

Tuesday, July 5
Tips and Tricks

I wake up and call my dad in the hospital. We talk about my mom who would have turned 82 today. They would be celebrating their 62nd anniversary this summer. He tries to sound upbeat, but I can tell that he is getting tired of the fight.

With half of the season gone, I have learned some things. One of my frequently asked questions is "How do you get tickets?" I have learned a lot and I believe that I can save my readers a ton of money.

Here are some pointers:

- *Sold out never means sold out.* There are 162 games in a season and roughly 50,000 seats. It is a buyer's market.
- *The person with the most information wins* (or is prepared to negotiate better.)
- *Check the attendance from the previous series.* This will give you an idea of how many seats are available. I recommend checking StubHub up to 2

hours before the game. This will give you an idea of price range and seat availability. If there are 1,000-plus seats on StubHub, when they stop selling, what happens to these seats? I believe these are the tickets that scalpers are selling. This is a good way to identify where an open killer seat is.

I sit in my hotel room and map out what seats are still available. Singles remain open a lot; it is rare for one person to buy one expensive seat with only a few hours before first pitch. I write down 10 seats around the Yankees dugout. It's simple, really. They have a search button that allows you to look in each section for the amount of tickets that are still available. I write these seats down on an index card (ie. Section 120, Row AA, Seat 1.)

Ten minutes prior to first pitch, I walk right down to the a premiere single seat that I located on StubHub. I opt for an aisle seat. I notice that the three next to me were taken by a man with two kids.

• *Act like you belong there!*

I hold up my $8 ticket and follow the row numbers with my eyes and utter just loud enough to hear, "Here I am, great seat." Indeed it is! Directly behind home plate, in the third row. This seat was listed on StubHub for $235.

Some things to consider any time you opt to sit in someone else's seat: Be prepared to have that person show up. Most people embarrass way too easily and care what others think way too much.

• *Have an exit plan.*

Pick a seat nearby that is open and when approached make your move quickly. I always like to have a laugh with it and break the tension. Some folks who pay big bucks for seats bring their pretentious attitude with them.

When they throw the snooty "You are in my seat" at me, I usually quip something like, "Man, I thought that you were never going to get here! Was traffic that bad tonight?" or "There you are! If you were any later, I was going to charge you for keeping your seat warm!"

• *Don't let security notice that you are seat jumping.*

Make contact with the usher when you first get to your section. I like to compliment them on the stadium and ask them some questions (ie. *How long have you been working here?*). This is not only smart, but you will meet some of the biggest fans and coolest people this way.

As I sit down following my new favorite song, I get a tap on the shoulder. My fight or flight reflex kicks in as I begin to gather my things. Not so fast. It's Stephanie. She spotted me from the section behind me. Looks like I got a better seat than the Yankees can score! She settles in the seat directly behind me.

This night stands out for a couple of reasons. The guy I am sitting next to is traveling around with his son and a friend visiting several stadiums on their summer vacation. He is also a Yankees fan. Early in the game, with Jorge Posada in the on-deck circle and the Yankees racing to an early lead, a foul ball rolls over slowly in his direction. This guy, his kids, and most fans in the area stand up and yell for the ball. Posada flips it into the dugout. The guy next to me in seat 2 does not take it well.

"You get paid millions of dollars and you can't give the ball to a kid? You are a bum!" He keeps going and going. The rest of the game, he rides Posada. He goes on and on about how much he makes and how ungrateful he is. This gives permission for the Indians fans to join in. Up to that point we had been making small talk. I cut off any further contact.

As a supposed Yankee fan, who are you to talk to a 17-year veteran with five championship rings like that? I am appalled. This guy has no idea what is going on with Jorge. Maybe his son is back in the hospital. Maybe he is under a lot of stress. Maybe whatever. You can fill in the blank. My point is, have some class, dude! Give a guy the benefit of the doubt. You sprang for the big seats. Enjoy the game. Also, what kind of example are you setting to your kid and his friend? It was one of the uglier and more disturbing moments of the year.

• *Be a spectator not be a spectacle.*

As a Yankees fan I feel like I represent the Yankees and work to have as much class as Derek Jeter. As the "162 Guy" I decided to be an ambassador for goodwill. Remembering back to Opening Day in San Francisco, I shake my head. This is supposed to be fun.

Jeter raps two hits in his first two at bats. Stephanie leans in asks if it's possible that Jeter could do it tonight. The fans around me are doing the math. Four away and it is still the second inning.

Superfan is Born

I have my Captain's Countdown sign with me that I unroll every Jeter at-bat. This is quite a task, while keeping score and wearing my glove on my left hand. A zealous Indians fan five rows back notices me early in the night. He directs many comments in my direction. He is good natured and I don't mind the ribbing. As the game gets into the later innings, he is sure to point out my fanny pack, 162 jersey, glove, and my score-keeping. I even laugh with him a few times.

In the ninth inning, it looks like DJ., who is now 2 for 5, would get one more at bat. The Yankees are winning this one easily, 9-2. The front row is lined with padded leather chairs and several fans have already left. Jeter enters the on-deck circle following the first out. I stand up and begin to make my way to the VIP seats so I can be closer to Jeter and get a picture.

My heckler does his best to draw even more attention to me. He starts chanting louder, "Superfan, with your fanny pack. Hey Superfan!"

I try to ignore his catcalls, as I awkwardly carry all my stuff. Fans are laughing along with him as the security guard follows me with her eyes. Another tip for seat jumping is to not have a lot of stuff, which can make you stand out. The only thing I don't have is my big red suitcase.

"Superfan, you can't sit there. Get back to your seat!"

Security agrees. The female usher calls over, "Sir, do you have a ticket for that seat?"

Now the entire section is watching me and laughing along. Here I am, 41 years old, wearing a glove, carrying a neon green sign and wearing a fanny pack. I don't embarrass easily, but I am turning red.

I try to plead my case. "Come on. My seat is two rows back. It is the ninth inning." At this point I'm

within 5 feet of Jeter. The stocky female security guard
is not budging and I make my way back. The "Superfan"
chants continue. A young boy of about 12, who is seated
directly in front of me, leans back and tries to console me.
"Don't let that guy bother you," he says sagely. I chuckle
as I appreciate his kind words of encouragement as Jeter
records an out.

The nickname Superfan is born and I make a
difficult decision that night. I opt to never wear my fanny
pack again. What was I thinking?

As the game ends, I notice a cameraman trying to
get my attention. He is signaling for me to unravel my sign.
I immediately oblige. He does a still shot for 10 seconds
and begins to put his equipment away. A gentleman with an
MLB shirt on seems to be the one in charge. He approaches
the dugout as I get his attention. He is producing an HBO
special called *3K*. It is a story about Derek Jeter's chase for
3,000.

I get his card. His name is Jeffrey Spaulding and
he is an MLB producer. I tell him quickly about the 162
idea and he is very cordial and seems interested. This could
be the huge break that I am looking for. I look up to see
Stephanie waving impatiently. This girl is something else. I
have been waiting all year to make a contact this good and
she is hurrying me along. She hasn't paid for a thing since I
met her. I would have fired her, too.

As we move forward, I recognize a familiar face
and it takes me a split second to register. Wow! It is
Dr. Jeter, Derek Jeter's dad. I walk right up to him with
Stephanie closely behind.

"Mr. Jeter, can I trouble you for a picture?" I am so
nervous that I forget to call him "Doctor."

"How about a handshake?" he offers as a concession.

"That would be great." We shake hands.

"Can I tell you what I'm doing real quickly?" I hand him the 162 card. "My name is Steve Melia and I'm going to all 162 Yankees games this year. Tonight is game 84." I

Dr. Jeter and I

tell him that I am writing a book about my journey.

He looks at me with his full attention and contemplates. He is a very serious man. I read Jeter's book, *The Life You Imagine* and feel like I understand his dad pretty well. He was an educator and respect is important to him.

He is impressed enough with 162 to give in. "OK, we can do that picture." On the inside I am jumping up and down, on the outside I am trying to contain myself. I hand Stephanie the camera and hope she can snap a picture without any difficulty.

"Wow, you have been doing a lot of traveling," he says as we pose.

"Yes sir. I'm having a blast! I'm a big fan of your son."

Two big security guards join our circle giving Dr. Jeter a look as if to say, "Are you ready?" Then Stephanie hands me back my phone and pipes in, "Can I tell you a story about how your son got me fired from the Yankees?"

There are givers and takers. I like her, but she is a taker.

She proceeds to tell Dr. Jeter that she is now unemployed and homeless, because his son got her fired. I can tell that he is uncomfortable by his body language. I am hoping he doesn't think that we are together.

"That's horrible," he says. "I'm sorry to hear that." He just wants to get out of there.

I introduce myself to the two Yankees security guards during their brief interaction. I also tell them of the 162 mission and let them know that they would be seeing a lot of me. They look like they are straight out of *The Sopranos.*

I finally interrupt and tell her that they were waiting for him. Dr. Jeter gets swept away. She was definitely not finished.

"Can you believe he wouldn't give me a picture? How come he gave you one?"

We walk towards the gate.

"How do you know that it was even Jeter that got you fired?"

"Well, my friends at work started saying it was probably him."

"*Probably*? I don't think he would go out of his way to get you fired."

"Yeah, but I was just trying to be nice."

"Well, I think you should let it go."

She then asks to see Jeffrey Spaulding's card, which I still have in my hand, and she starts typing the guy's information into her cell. "Maybe they will give me a job," she reasons. Her mind works overtime seeing what she can gain from others. Maybe this is what I attracted since I hoped that she would lead me to the Yankees.

"Why don't you take me with you to all the games?"

I smile and don't answer. I'd rather have Marcinowski back.

I walk her back to the Ritz Carlton for the second straight night. I am doing a Yankee a huge favor whether he knows about it or not. She tells me that she is flying out at 7 a.m. Interesting. I guess two nights is enough for him.

I drop her off in the lobby and she gives me a big hug goodbye. I cannot help but wonder if she was attracted to me, but was just more enamored with being with a Yankee. We agreed to stay in touch and go to a game in the Bronx sometime.

Wednesday, July 6

It is 8:30 a.m. as I make my way over to the mall that is connected to the Yankee hotel. I get a tall coffee and decide to walk the mile or so. I make it to the lobby of the Ritz Carlton and am still buzzing over my meeting Dr. Jeter last night. I look around a little, but I do not see any Yankees. Half the season has already gone by and I haven't met one Yankee. They are going to have a hard time getting a restraining order against me!

I am circling the mall and looking in the different shops. My eyes go over to the Caribou Coffee and I spot the Yankees hitting coach, Kevin Long. I start to make my way over and take out a business card.

"Excuse me, Coach?" He is reading the paper and looks up with a smile. I hand him the card and introduce myself.

"I'm Kevin Long," he replies.

"I know who you are, Coach. I am on a journey to attend all 162 Yankees games this year. I'm a stand up comic and I'm hitting clubs along the way."

He relaxes a little. "Really? This is awesome. Are you performing any time soon?"

I explain that it has been difficult since most of the games are at night, but that I'm booked in Toronto in two weeks. That sounded lame.

"Do you think I can get a picture with you?"

"Sure."

I scramble to find another patron to snap a photo. K-Long looks like he may have just come back from a workout.

I wander around a little and check out the hotel again.

With Hitting Coach Kevin Long

This time I walk into the hotel's very fancy restaurant. I can't believe my eyes. I stop dead in my tracks and freeze. Derek Jeter and his dad both look up at me from their breakfast table. I smile briefly and backtrack quickly. I hightail it out of there. Dr. Jeter was nice enough less than 12 hours before, but they look like they are having a serious father/son chat.

That was my chance to meet The Captain. It might sound creepy, but I want our first real meeting to be cool. I do not want him to dislike me for interrupting his meal with his dad. Maybe his dad will tell him who I am and about the 162 Tour. I'm half mad at myself for not doing more, but half proud of myself for not acting like an idiot. I know that Jete cherishes his privacy and I want to meet him when the time is right.

I head back for an 11:30 phone appointment with Mike, Kim, and Jeff Olson. I have to pass Caribou Coffee again and peek over to see if K-Long is still at the same table. Wait just a minute. Seated with him is Yankee manager Joe Girardi! I keep walking and decide to catch my breath and gather my thoughts. It reminds me of how nervous I was when I first got into sales, making my first call 20 years ago. I talk myself into going to say hello.

As I approach, I take a quick detour and pay for a refill at the counter. K-Long answers his cell and I make my move. I can see my business card laying on the table.

"Hey Joe," I mutter.

He reaches out and shakes my hand. He has a nice, strong grip. Even as the manager, he is one of the strongest and most fit Yankees.

"How are you doing?" he asks.

His question throws me off, as I had my speech ready.

"I'm good, thanks. I was just talking to Kevin a little while ago. My name is Steve Melia. I'm the 162 Guy." I go onto to explain that I have attended all 84 games and only have 78 to go.

He flashes a big smile and considers what I've said. "Home and away?" I nod.

"That is amazing. What a fun time!" he says sincerely.

"You think that we could get a picture together?"

"Absolutely."

With Kevin on the phone, I solicit another patron. No one else seems to recognize him. Just as we line up, his phone rings. "Hold on a minute," he tells the caller.

We take a picture and shake hands goodbye.

Definitely another highlight of the trip. To everyone who asks, "Do the Yankees know what you are doing?" I can honestly say yes, they do. At least Girardi, Long, and Dr. Jeter do.

I recount my morning to Mike and Kim before we strategize about our call. Jeff is scheduled to be at our event in Orlando tomorrow. We are calling to discuss the event and to feel him out about his new company.

We have decided that Kim and Mike will stay and work Pre-Paid Legal and I will go to Jeff's new company. We have always believed that we have a unique circumstance since there are three of us. Even though I do not know anything about the product, company, or compensation, I know Jeff, and that is enough.

This shows you how loyalty can trump common sense sometimes.

Before we call him, I tell them that I have made a list of more than 400 people on the flight to Cleveland. Jeff answers and tells us that he plans on building his new company the right way. He makes it a point to tell us that he is building for the long term. He promises that so-called shysters who are usually attracted to start ups will not be welcomed in his company.

"I want in," I tell Jeff a few minutes into the call. We have been working together for 17 years and Jeff seems happy to have me onboard. We all agree that this has to stay top secret. Jeff has over $1 million per year coming in from PPL and would be jeopardizing that if he was caught recruiting an existing associate.

He won't give us any direction on what the product line is. Over the years, Jeff has routinely made a point of putting down the chance of start-up network marketing companies that offer a "me-too" product. This is a product that has tons of competition or that can be copied easily. He has given many, many speeches poking fun at every lotion and potion that comes along. He compares it to "money laundering amongst friends." I hope he knows what he is doing. We all really hope that he launches something unique. Jeff's enthusiasm is overwhelming.

When the call is over, I make four phone calls. The first two are to two big networkers that have a lot of respect for Olson. I am not allowed to use his name or say anything, so the call is more of me feeling them out. This is the first time in 17 years that I have decided to walk away and start over. I am scared and nervous. I make another call to a guy on my team who hasn't produced in quite some time. I know him better and spell out what I believe is the opportunity of a lifetime. He says that he is on board and will wait further instruction. "If you are in, I'm in," he says.

Kim and Mike are both just getting into Orlando for our summer retreat. They must be having some weird emotions. Rip Mason is flying in tomorrow. Associates from all over North America are beginning to descend on the beautiful Rosen Shingle Resort.

Meanwhile, the Bombers lose tonight as their comeback efforts fall a little short. Jeter starts it off in the ninth down two by blasting a double in the right field gap. The YES camera goes immediately to my sign as I hold it up and cross out the number four. 2,997 hits! My phone starts blowing up as I begin to receive text messages saying

they saw me on TV with my green sign.

Derek Jeter has four games at home against Tampa to make history before the All-Star break.

Thursday, July 7

I get home from Cleveland at 2 p.m., take a power nap, shower, and download my ticket. I'm out the door by 4:30 p.m. On my drive in, Michael Kaye is talking about the significance of Jeter's approaching accomplishment. He reads a quote from Hall of Famer George Brett. Brett says that he is amazed by Jeter and how he is able to do it in a market like New York. Brett is one of the 27 out of 17,000 that have ever played the game to reach the 3,000 milestone. Kaye is doing a nice job capturing the moment.

Then he interviews Vin Scully, the voice of the Dodgers since way before I was born. His voice is legendary and a pleasure to listen to. There are certain voices that take you back to your childhood and bring back many incredible memories. He, like everyone, has glowing things to say about Jeter. I am so excited driving to game 86 that I dial in and get in as the third caller.

"Steve, from Massapequa, you are on the MK show."

"Hey Mike, it's the 162 Guy. We spoke a few weeks ago. I'm the guy going to all the games."

"Oh, OK," he says with a sense of recognition.

"How was Cleveland?"

In marketing, I've learned that if you can get people to hear about something three times in 24 hours, you will get their attention. Over the last 36 hours, I met Jeter's dad, Kevin Long, and Joe Girardi. I've been on the YES network and been a caller on two ESPN New York shows.

"Mike, there is a real buzz around the Yankees," I continue. "When I was in Cleveland, I met Jeter's dad. He is a class act, just like his son. It's so exciting to be there for every at-bat. I just wish the focus would stay on how special a time this is for Jeter. He's such an important player to Yankees fans. I'm so tired of people questioning how good he still is and where he should bat in the lineup. Your show is doing a great job today focusing on his accomplishments. It's a time of celebration."

"Well, thanks Steve. That's a good point. Maybe the media is spending too much time on where to bat Jeter and how good he still is. Let's let him break the record, celebrate, and then we can talk about it. In Cleveland, every media seat was taken. There is a lot of anticipation for number 3,000."

My adrenaline is pumping now.

I'm at the game with Slug and his 6-year-old daughter, Lexi. I unroll my sign that is quite tattered after being constructed a month ago. A guy in the second row asks, "Were you in Cleveland? I saw you on TV last night."

"Yeah, I was on YES last night."

"Wow, did you go to all three games?" His friends start listening as well.

Slug pipes in, "He's going to all *162* games! He's crazy."

"What? That's amazing!" He introduces me to his friends. It feels like after 85 games and three months, I am gaining some momentum.

In the bottom of the first, the voice of Bob Sheppard rings throughout the stadium and all 47,787 rise to their feet. *Now batting, number 2, Derek Jeter.* The place goes wild. Sheppard passed away last season, but Jeter insists on the recording as his introduction. He's introduced him for nearly every home at bat since 1996.

This is his first at bat at home in 22 games since getting number 2,994. Even though ticket prices have gone up dramatically, it feels so good to be watching Jeter get this kind of reception at home. After experiencing the energy of his first at bat I am now delighted and relieved that he didn't do it in Cleveland.

Like I have been doing for every at bat, I unroll my sign. I stood out in Cleveland, but there are thousands of signs at the stadium. The crowd noise is deafening. *Der-ek Jet-er, Der-ek Jet-er.* This place is as loud as I can ever remember. It is as loud as the 2009 World Series.

In his first plate appearance, Jeter rips a double. The Stadium goes insane. Two away. His next three at bats are spectacles as the stadium continues to rock. Jeter goes hitless and the Yankees lose to the Rays 5-1.

Saturday, July 9

Always go to other people's funerals, otherwise they won't come to yours. — Yogi Berra

There is a memorial service for my cousin Diane's father, Ernie, at 10 a.m. Diane is married to my cousin Ray, who is a retired Nassau County cop. He retired young as he was shot on the job.

With such a rigorous schedule, I haven't been able to make many family gatherings. I drive by myself wearing a suit. I have my 162 jersey, glove, and neon green Captain's Countdown sign awaiting me in the Mustang. I get to see much of my family, including my aunt Maureen and my cousin Colleen.

Maureen's husband was my Uncle Tom who had passed in March. Uncle Tom used to play Wiffle Ball with me in his backyard every day and is a major reason that I'm such a fanatic. He was my dad's only brother and lived in the house next door to us in Bethpage, New York, growing up. This is the first time I've seen them since his passing.

The service is beautiful and I try not to look at my watch every 60 seconds. If I can leave there by 10:45, I can be in the Bronx parking by noon. I certainly don't want to break my streak of free parking. Most of my relatives know of my 162 journey and even the Mets fans wish me luck. I change in the church parking lot and speak into my navigation system, "Yankee Stadium."

By noon, I pull into my free spot. I am at least three quarters of a mile from the stadium. The weather on this 9th day of July is absolutely splendid as I liberally apply my sunscreen. I get two beers so I won't have to miss any of the action. Back in Orlando, my partners are running our summer event with an on eye on the Internet.

The middle of the first is like extra innings in the playoffs. No one leaves their seats. As Jeter takes his swings in the on-deck circle, the anticipation is bubbling over. Bob Sheppard's posthumous voice comes over the PA as it has thousands of times: *Now batting, number 2, Derek Jeter.* The stadium is rocking. *Der-ek Jet-ter* rings from every seat in the Bronx on this special afternoon.

It doesn't take long for DJ to rip number 2,999. The fans are delirious. All-out hysteria.

Bottom of the third, with one out. I hold up my sign,

while balancing my Flip camera and my phone's video cam. The stadium is electrified. Every fan is on their feet.

Der-ek Je-ter. Der-ek Je-ter.

The count goes quickly to 0 and 2. Jete works the count as he fouls off ball after ball. I have to consciously hold my eyes open and not look away. History is upon us. Jeter runs the count to 3 and 2. He fouls off three more. With every pitch comes "oohs" and "ahhs" from the capacity crowd. Finally, at 2:33 on Saturday, July 9th, 2011, Derek Sanderson Jeter connects with a 3-2 fastball from David Price.

I know it is a hit the second he connects. I'm not sure if it is the crowd reaction or the angle of the ball. The ball jumps off of the bat and is headed towards the gap. Another classic Jeter double is my first thought. My eyes stay with the ball. It keeps going and going until it lands safely in section 236, row 1, seat 21, into the hands of 20-year-old Christian Lopez. His life is about to change.

Number 3,000 is a home run!

Derek Jeter raises his right hand victoriously while pumping his fist as he moves briskly around the bases. History. DJ has become the 28th player in MLB history — and the only Yankee — to reach 3,000. He joins Wade Boggs as only the member to reach the milestone with a home run. The stadium gets louder. The DJ chant goes on and on. The entire bullpen empties and the pitchers run in to congratulate their captain. The entire Rays team led by Johnny Damon continues to stand and applaud in the visitor's dugout. Respect.

Derek Jeter.

As always, he did it big and he did it with class. My journey of a lifetime just got a big, fat, juicy, tasty, cherry on top. One for the good guys. One for the guy who never used a performance-enhancing drug. Jeter will always be remembered as a role model, a leader, and certainly a first-ballot Hall of Famer.

But he's not done. Jeter comes up again in the fifth to another standing ovation. The 37-year-old, who many in the media say is washed up, rips a double to the opposite field to go three for three. And when he comes up again in the sixth, want to guess what happened? He rips a single to right field going four for four. Simply amazing.

But he's not done. In the bottom of the eighth inning with first and second, and one out, the score is tied at four. Who do you want up? Derek Jeter, of course. As he has done 3,002 times before, Jeter uses the entire field. He connects and sends it right up the middle. The go-ahead run scores and the perfect day continues five for five. He has only done that three times before.

A historic day like today just affirms for me that the pursuit of this dream of mine is more than worth it.

Chapter Twelve

YOU CAN'T QUIT NOW

Monday July 11

I get off the plane in Orlando and I am greeted in the terminal by several of our associates who are flying home from our summer event. I get to the Rosen Shingle Resort and am bombarded with hugs and well-wishers. I head up with Mike to Kim's suite where we are going to have a quick meeting. My partners bring me up to speed.

Jeff Olson and Rip Mason were both there but not at the same time. Rip arrived Thursday and took off after his talk. Olson arrived a short time later. Rip came over to Kim's suite early in the weekend and met with my partners. He let it slip that Jeff's new product line was in skin care. He also rattled off 20 or 30 companies that were also in that industry and spoke of a competitive and limited market.

Mike's take:

> Rip Mason was on a mission. He certainly doesn't want to lose us.
> "I know you talked to Jeff," he acknowledged while he looked at Kim and me. We

looked right at each other. It's a good thing we weren't playing poker.

"Yeah," I said, "we spoke to him."

Rip looked down and shook his head. It was classic.

He looked back at us with a look of concern. "I told him," he offered, "that skin care is so tough.

"First of all, it would take three to five years to establish the company and to really build any sizable checks for the field leadership. And man, the competition is crazy. Besides the other network marketing companies like NuSkin, JAFRA, and dozens more, you've got the high-end stuff at Neiman Marcus and Nordstrom's, you've got Revlon and Elizabeth Arden, Vera Wong's, and the list goes on and on. There are easily over 100 lines."

I think Kim and I must have shook our heads in tandem. "Skin Care?" I thought, "Has Jeff lost his mind?"

I immediately had a picture of Steve giving somebody a facial and I almost spit out my beer.

This is the first time the three of us are together since hearing of Jeff's company and we are here to make some decisions. We convene on our super-sized balcony that overlooks the resort's pools. There are five of us. Joining the group is Alan Erdlee and his girlfriend, Colleen. Alan has referred to Mike as his best friend for years. Alan and Jeff have always been close as well.

The five of us discuss the possibility of working together in Jeff's new company. I am immediately turned off by the fact that Alan seems to know way more information than us. He also asks us not to discuss this

meeting with Renee or Jeff. He is being way too secretive
and I do not trust him.

We throw around some ideas, but the three of us
leave with a bad taste in our mouths. I help Kim out to her
car with all of her luggage and materials from the event. It
is sad and strange to spend such a little amount of time with
her. I watch her drive away to North Carolina.

Mike and I make it to Sebastian just as my dad
wakes up from his nap. He is happy to see me, but the grind
of daily living is wearing on him. He tells me that he's
proud of me and that he believes that I can do it now.

**Tuesday,
July 12**
I have
arranged
with Tim
Buckley
to do our
third story
live form
my dad's
kitchen.
My father
doesn't
understand
Skype and to him it must look like an episode from *The
Jetsons*. Mike and I prepare the set which includes the
Yankees flag being draped over the fridge.

I have my laptop on a chair, while Mike and my
dad are to my left at the kitchen table. My dad is watching
but having a hard time understanding what is happening.

"Where's the camera? Who is he talking to?" Mike politely keeps him quiet. Tim once again does a great job in gathering the info and editing a 3:09 piece.

> *WILMINGTON, NC (WWAY) -- Earlier this year, we told you about some Wilmington comics who were road-tripping to every New York Yankees game this year. Tonight marks the end of the All-Star break, the unofficial half-way point of the season.*
>
> *Can you think back to March? There was still a chill to the air, it definitely wasn't 100 degrees, and the baseball season was just starting. Seems like a long time ago right? That's when our two local comics hit the road on a quest to attend every Yankees game this season.*
>
> *Now that we're at the All-Star break, you'll be happy to know the dream is still alive, but you might notice a little something different since we last checked in with our comedic baseball team.*
>
> *"You know, I tell people they're going to have to buy the book to get the whole story," road-tripper Steve Melia said.*
>
> *Yes, the two Steves have been reduced to one. So what happened?*
>
> *"Steve Marcinowski wasn't a big baseball fan, and that was probably the biggest thing," Melia said. "Three to four hours a day of watching baseball is a lot. Two adult men, we were probably getting on each other's nerves a little bit too much, especially as comedians. We just decided that it was enough for Steve."*
>
> *But Melia's still going strong; flying solo to*

each game this season, and he hasn't missed a beat.

*"At this point, I'm at 88 games," Melia said.
"I tell ya, it's gotten past where it is weary, where it
is getting on me to now where it's just like pure joy
and pure fun."*

*Baseball wise, it's been another good season
for the Yanks with a certain special moment coming
just this past weekend, as Derek Jeter hit a home
run for his 3,000th hit.*

*"It was so exciting, and to just be in the
ballpark, and feel the energy, it was a magical
moment," Melia said. "Honestly, if the tour stopped
now for some reason — it's not going to — but
everything I could have wanted out of it, I got."*

*After Jeter's 3,000th hit, a lot has been made
of Christian Lopez, who caught the ball and gave
it up for free. Turns out, Steve would've done the
same thing.*

*"I actually put on my blog that I would give
the ball back to Jeter with no strings attached, and
then of course I had a list of strings that I wanted to
get," Melia said.*

*While he's still waiting for that elusive
meeting with Jeter, Melia has met Jeter's dad, and
even the Yankees' manager.*

*"I had met the hitting coach Kevin Long,
and I was just kind of circling the coffee shop like a
stalker, and Joe Girardi sat down with him," Melia
said. "I was so nervous. It was like I was in junior
high going to ask a girl out. That's how nervous I
was. I got my courage up, and I went up to him, and
he took his picture with me. I didn't even have to
ask twice. It was just great."*

So what's next for our road warrior?

"Right now we're at 74 games to go," he said. "It's sort of like being at a party that's a great party. It's like a four-hour party, and before you know it, you look at your watch and you go, 'Man, people are starting to leave, and the party's almost over.' I'm already starting to miss the experience."

Be sure to stay tuned to WWAY throughout the rest of the baseball season. We'll have more updates on Melia as he continues his now solo quest across the country.

Wednesday, July 13

We are sitting with my dad in the dialysis center saying our good-byes. This is the weakest and most out of it that I have seen him. He is doing his best to stay positive, but he is starting to give up on the fight. I am beginning to believe that this may be my last visit. As I have done many times before, I try to record visually what he looks like as I leave the room.

Mike and I get back in the car and head to Orlando International Airport. We talk about dad and how time freedom has given Mike the opportunity to do something great. He got to spend time and get closer with a dying parent. Priceless and rare.

We have an 11:00 appointment to call Kim on speakerphone and discuss our next business move.

Kim and Mike both review the weekend and the time they spent with both Mason and Olson. The rumors regarding Olson's new company are spreading and several of our associates are asking questions. Mike feels that if I go with Olson, it will cause immediate friction on the team. We would be both recruiting the same people and, in essence, competing. We have seen similar situations get ugly quickly.

We discuss all of the possible scenarios and the pros and cons of staying put or jumping ship. We look at track records, product categories, the age and health of those in management along with other factors. Mike, Kim, and I have been working together for a long time. A temporary breakup would certainly lead to a permanent one.

"Sometimes the student must leave the teacher." This is something Mike says during that conversation. The only real reason that I am considering joining Jeff is the loyalty factor. He has done a lot for me and my family. As we sit in Mike's Chrysler 300 cruising 70 mph north on I-95, we decide to have a vote. Will I stay or will I go? Mike votes that I stay with Pre-Paid Legal. Kim votes the same way. This make my decision easy as I do not get to vote.

The future of Melia Communications has been established. Skin care/anti-aging cream will not be my destiny. I am relieved. At 41, I do not want to spend the next 10-20 years talking about beauty marks and crow's feet.

Mike drops me off in Orlando and I call Renee Olson as a courtesy to let her know that I will not be joining. We play phone tag and never connect.

Thursday, July 14

I am flying into Toronto for a four game series. I have great seats thanks to the owners of St. Louis Ribs, home of our comedy show back in April. Just before first pitch, I make it down to the on-deck circle area with my neon green sign that reads "Congrats Derek Jeter -162 Guy." I call his name and receive his attention briefly. He looks at my sign and gives his customary head nod. Does he recognize me yet? Maybe, I'm definitely getting closer.

Game 89 is not a fun one. Bartolo Colon throws 42 pitches, is tagged for eight runs, and is pulled before even recording the game's third out. The Jays pound out 20 hits and win this one 16-7.

Friday, July 15

I am going to the game with a friend, Geri Soulliere. Geri is newly-minted grandmother and spends her days watching her new grandson. She doesn't look like a grandma, though, and in fact, dated my brother Mike for a few years.

We are grabbing a quick meal and some margaritas at one of Toronto's outdoor eateries. I look down to see my phone ringing and it is Jeff Olson. Although we are close, it is rare that he calls me. I step away and pick it up. He does most of the talking and lets me know that he understands that we are staying with PPL. He says that we have a lot to lose and wishes us well. He sounds stoic. It is obvious from the conversation that everything we discussed in front of Alan has made its way back to Jeff. Alan swore us to secrecy, but certainly did not hold himself to the same.

One of the things that turned me off and made my decision easier is the deceit and positioning that has taken place. We have built a much more significant business than Alan. It is not even close. Now Alan is doing whatever he can to try and jockey for position and it winds up driving me away altogether. Geri knows the cast of characters pretty well so I fill her in on the details. It is nice to have someone who understands the situation to be able to talk to.

Tuesday, July 19

It is just after 4 p.m. and Mike, his friend, Mollie, and I are starting our pre-game celebration at the Comfort Inn pool. I am on the phone with Kim, when I see that my dad is trying to call me. He doesn't make outgoing calls often and I hang up from Kim.

"Hello?"

"Hey Stevo, its Dad. How you doing, Pal?"

"I'm great. What's going on?" I step away from the table to hear him better.

"Listen, I am calling all of the kids. I've made the decision to stop my dialysis. Please do not try to talk me out of it. I have put a lot of thought into my decision."

Sadness begins to take over my entire body. I don't know the specifics, but I do know this means he won't have a lot of time left.

"I am sitting here with your sister and I just wanted you to know."

I was the one who persuaded Mary to go see him in Florida. I am already beginning to feel guilty. My dad continues on about how he has led a good life and my mind begins to wander and my eyes begin to tear up. The conversation doesn't last for more than three or four minutes. He once again reiterates that he doesn't want me to miss any Yankees games.

Mike is still sitting pool side when I return. I recall the conversation and we toast our 86-year-old dad, whom we call Pop. Mike appears to be in shock. I call Kim back and have a hard time fighting back tears as I tell her that my dad will be leaving us soon. Mike was stunned by the timing of it as well as how the news was delivered. In his words:

> *It was crazy to me that my dad told Steve and all the other kids before he told me. He had been preparing me for the possibility that he would quit dialysis. Still, I get the announcement second-hand from Steve, pool side. For me, it was totally weird. I was more stunned than anything in those first moments. For the rest of the day, my mind moved fast and slow at the same time.*

Mike is only staying for the first two of the four-game series and is returning to Sebastian tomorrow. I decide that I'll go with him and rent a car on my way back. It is four hours each way, so we'll have to leave by 9 a.m. I'm glad that I am with Mike when my dad called. It would have been more difficult for both of us if we were by ourselves.

Later that evening at Tropicana Field, we are joined by Ray Last and his wife, Wendi. They are big-time contributors to our foundation and big hitters in Pre-Paid Legal. We've known them for 15 years. Ray is with a big group and has just come over to say hi. He is there just two minutes when a Johnny Damon foul ball rips its way toward us.

From the time it left his bat, it couldn't have been more than a two second count before perfectly landing in my glove. It is my proudest and most athletic moment of 2011. Nick Swisher is only feet away and I hear some cheers. I take a bow in case the camera is watching.

There are several fans in front and behind me who all put forth what they consider a valiant effort. *You have to come prepared,* I think, as I pound my glove. It was amazing. I stood up and moved out into the aisle and the ball sailed right to me. Perfect timing.

A Yankees fan that I had been chatting with the night before comes over to tell me that we were just on TV. Then a guy a few rows over, who didn't even stand up, loudly offers his opinion.

"You should give that ball to a kid."

"Easy for you to say," I volley back.

He says something else that I can't make out.

"Hey, this is my 94th game of the year. I've worked hard to get this," I say loudly and in his direction. "If you want to give a kid a ball, *you* should try a little harder to get one."

Just a few days earlier, I watched a guy catch a ball in Toronto and the fans began chanting, "Give it to a kid." They did this over and over until he stood up and delivered it to the first kid he saw. Now there is a kid who won't understand working hard for something. He will always be looking for a handout.

The kids could wait. I have other plans for this ball.

Wednesday, July 20

My brother and I meet at the car at exactly 9 a.m. and we are both stocked with freshly-brewed Comfort Inn coffee in mini styrofoam cups.

My dad has dialysis today and he is usually pretty exhausted. Upon our arrival, we walk into the house to find him in his room with my two sisters by his side. My niece, Elizabeth, is there as well. We are very familiar with hospice as my mom passed away at a hospice center six years prior.

My dad calls over to his visiting nurse informing

her of his decision and within an hour a hospice volunteer is on hand to answer any questions. The five family members are scattered throughout my parents bedroom as the hospice volunteer and my dad begin to talk. My dad is seated in his recliner.

"I have decided that I am finished with dialysis and I want to start the process of getting ready for hospice."

My sisters are barely holding it together and Elizabeth has to leave the room. They are as close as any grandfather and granddaughter could be. My dad has his wits about him and deals with this — as he has with everything — with steely resolve and amazing courage.

He lays out what he has decided and listens intently as the woman details what his final days will be like. She describes how the body will begin to shut down. His hands shake as he speaks. He says that he wants to go to dialysis one last time to say goodbye to everyone there. He has been going there three times per week for more than five years now. He recalls a story of how a woman he says he didn't even think liked him cried when she heard that he was stopping dialysis.

Eileen is sitting closest to him, "You know, you can just go back and say goodbye. You don't have to go for a four-hour treatment, Dad."

"I know. I said I was coming back Friday. That's what I want to do."

I smile at the thought of him still being set in his ways. I make eye contact with Mike and he is smiling, too, and wiping his wet eyes. While this is a tough conversation, I am so glad I am here. This is a moment that I'll remember for a lifetime. We get to see our father calling his shots right down to the end.

All the while, the nurse walks through the physical

deterioration that takes place when a patient terminates dialysis. She says that for some it is a week or two and others have been known to live much longer. It is going to be at least two months until I can visit again. I do the math and believe that this will be my goodbye. Am I crazy? The thought of quitting the tour and spending the final days with him comes upon me.

My siblings gather in the kitchen and chat for a bit. My dad's room is empty, as he wanted to get some rest. I tell everyone that I am going in to say goodbye. I tell him that I love him and I support him 100 percent.

"I know that it has been really hard on you for six years. Especially this year," I whisper to him. He smiles and we both struggle to find the words.

"I am very proud of you. You can't quit now. We need the Melia name to be remembered for something big."

"I'll make you a deal," I counter. "If you make it to the end of the season, it will make a great story. If you make it to the 162nd game, Sept. 28th, I promise that my book will sell a million copies."

He smiles and agrees that would be nice. I pull out the ball from last night and give it to him.

"I got this ball last night. I want you to look at it everyday and know that I am thinking of you." I place it on his mantle.

I realize that I just made a real promise — possibly my last — to my father.

I reach down to his recliner and give his weak, bony body one more hug. We make eye contact and smile as I leave his bedroom.

The rest of the day I am in a fog.

Friday, July 22

I wake up at 4:30 a.m. and by 6:00 I am in the security line at the airport. I have not had any coffee and the group in front of me is being very rowdy. At first, I think that they are a softball team. There are a few older ones and some younger ones as well. There are seven in the group.

I hear one of the women say, "We better catch this flight, my son is supposed to play for the Yankees tonight."

My radar goes off.

"Your son plays for the Yankees?"

"Yes. He just got called up. He will be making his Major League debut."

Turns out I am in line behind Brandon Laird's family. His parents, grandparents, aunt and uncle, and his beautiful young girlfriend have made the trip from California. Brandon was called up on the 18th when Ramiro Pena was placed on the Disabled List. His entourage is traveling around waiting for his big moment. I thought I had logistical problems. Imagine booking seven flights to New York at the last minute!

Over the next hour, I sit with the Lairds. To me there is nothing cooler than watching parents bask in their children's glory. I wouldn't have guessed watching their childlike enthusiasm that their oldest son, Gerald, is already in the big leagues. Mr. Laird and I hit it off as he loves to

Me with Vicki and Gerald Laird, Sr.

talk about his sons. I visualize my own dad as I get lost in his stories.

He brags that 23-year-old Brandon led all minor leaguers last year with 105 RBI's and also clobbered 25 home runs. Gerald Sr. and I discuss everything from what its like to be a big league parent to beer prices in the stadiums. I tell them about my 162 journey. They think it is neat, but clearly not as neat as your son making his debut with the Yankees.

We get to Washington D.C. without incident and learn that our next flight is cancelled. The Lairds are freaking out. They are extra nervous because Girardi told them that Brandon will most likely play this weekend. I tell Gerald Sr. that I have Silver status with the airline and if he cannot get on a flight, he can have my seat. Imagine if my streak is broken because I gave my seat up to a dad of a Yankee making his major league debut!

I am pacing the airport and I notice a familiar face in line to board another flight. I recognize Greta Van Susteren from "On The Record" with Fox News. I am a closet tabloid news junkie and have spent hours glued to her programs. It takes me a few minutes to work up my nerve, but I put my jitters aside and make my way over.

"Greta?" She turns to me.

"My name is Steve Melia. I am a fan of your show. Can I share with you what I think would make a great news story? I am a comic attending all 162 New York Yankee games." I hand her my card. "I am just flying in from Tampa and will attend my 97th game of the season tonight."

She nods slowly and looks at my card. "I have been on some local news features, but no one has picked it up nationally yet. I saw you here and thought that it would make a great story."

She is cordial. "I'll check this out. Thanks."

Now that wasn't so hard, was it? Whether it ever turns into anything or not is irrelevant. The important thing is that I am out telling the story and I am facing my fears of awkward conversations.

I am upgraded to first class and take Kim's advice and write a letter to my dad. As I write the letter, tears fill my eyes and from time to time roll down my cheeks. I'm not sure if the guy next to me notices or not, but he keeps to himself even more.

Dear Dad,

Thanks for being the kind of man that we are all proud to call Dad, Grandpa, and Uncle Danny. To look over your accomplishments and the family and empire that you have built is amazing.

You are, and were, an incredible husband. We all loved mom so much and you have been so strong without her for the last few years. I love when you say, "I've had the best, you can keep the rest." It must have been difficult going on without her. Like many times in your life, you've displayed great courage.

I feel very fortunate and blessed to have been the youngest of your seven children, and the fact that I got to spend a great deal of time with you and mom during your retirement. I cherish those times on Sunset Dr. playing catch, our fishing contests, and our endless drives up and down I-95.

I'm almost ashamed to admit that I was often embarrassed when we first moved to Florida and the other kids would make fun of me and say things like, "Are you sure those aren't your grandparents?" I got over that quickly as others would soon realize how cool you both were and started to envy our close family.

All seven of your children and 21 grandchildren are very unique individuals and get along extremely well. I believe that this is a result of the individual attention and love that you and Mom gave all of us. We all had a unique relationship with both of you.

I also believe that this is a result of those wonderful vacations that we have every year. I hope we will continue them and I know that you'll be there in spirit.

The business that Mike, Kim, and I built is based on the same principles and lessons that we learned from you. The Melia Foundation will live on to help thousands of children thanks to you!

I know that a child's biggest need is to be loved and to be believed in by their parents. Although you have always been on the conservative side, you've always supported me and I've felt that you were proud of me. You wrote me a note in college that I still read often telling me that I could do anything that I put my mind to.

I have made many tough phone calls to you over the years (many made by the police or authorities from Vero Beach High School.) It meant a lot to me that you always stood by my side. You were not always happy with what I did, but you forgave me and helped me learn from my mistakes.

"Locks were made to keep honest people

*honest, not for criminals. You are not a criminal,"
you encouraged me.*

 *Maybe the hardest call was last year when I
called to tell you that my marriage was in trouble
and that Kim and I were separating. I know that
you were saddened and disappointed, but, as
always, you listened and were there for both of us.
I thanked you for understanding. You said, "I don't
understand, but I'll support you."*

 *I've always admired the example that
you've been as well. I can only remember one time
that you used bad language in front of me. When
I was 14, we were golfing with Uncle John and
you missed a putt. You screamed, "chicken ----."
You quickly realized that I was there and you were
suddenly more upset with cursing in front of me
than you were with missing your putt. That was
impressive and if I ever have children will aim to do
the same.*

 *You have passed on other qualities as well.
Your stubbornness is one of them. My stubbornness
has helped me not quit while others gave up. It
has helped me hang on during tough times. Like
you, I often like to be by myself and cherish my
privacy. Like you, though, I try to be very loyal to
my close group of friends and family.*

 *Some of my fondest memories are our trips
to Vegas and the cruises to the Bahamas. You taught
me the finer points of holding my liquor, gambling,
and money management.*

 *I remember vividly my little league career in
Sebastian. Whether I was on deck or at third base,
you and Mom were always in the bleachers smiling*

and rooting me on. While I'm sure that everyone believes that they have the best parents, I know for sure that I couldn't have been luckier or asked for more.

I'm glad that I had the chance to see you last week and say goodbye. Over the last few years I tried to visit as often as I could because I enjoyed seeing you, but also so you'd know how special you are to me and how much I love you.

With tears in my eyes and a heavy heart, Dad, I say thanks for being you, standing up for what's right, and for being such a loving family man. You'll never be far from my thoughts. I love you.

Your son,
Steve

Later at the game, the stadium thermometer has the temperature right at 100 sweltering degrees. This is the hottest game in the new stadium and the first triple-digit game since July 5, 1999.

There are several water fountains around the stadium and they are 20-30 fans deep. Fans are sitting with paper towels drying themselves off every few pitches. Yankee trainer Gene Monahan comes on the Yankees jumbotron encouraging the fans to stay hydrated.

After the seventh inning stretch, I notice an unfamiliar face and number moving towards the on-deck circle. The PA announcer blares, "Now pinch-hitting for Derek Jeter, number 60, Brandon Laird." Most of the fans barely look up from their conversations. The ones who do are mostly like, "Who is this guy?"

I answer the folks around me with what appears to be encyclopedic knowledge.

"Oh, that's Brandon Laird. This kid's a great prospect. He led the minors in RBI's last year. His brother, Gerald, plays for the Cardinals."

I think I may have impressed an old lady.

Laird's first Major League at bat is unofficial as he takes a base on balls. Imagine what it must be like to be on first base with Curtis Granderson up next in front of 46,000 people. Granderson walks next, as does Tex. With Laird on third, Cano hits a line drive to Matsui, which is enough for the speedy Laird to tag up and score his first major league run.

In the eighth, Laird comes up with Cervelli on second and Dickerson on first. He lines a single up the middle and now the rookie is batting .1000 and has added his first hit and RBI to his debut. A great night in New York for the Lairds!

Saturday, July 23

The papers make a big deal out of Brandon Laird making his MLB debut. I have a little time on my hands so I make a sign. The sign reads "Welcome to New York, Brandon Laird." I also tag it with "-162 Guy."

I get to my seat and look up at the scoreboard, and guess who is starting at third base? Brandon Laird. I position myself in the front row again and get my sign ready. The Yankees take the field.

Derek Jeter and Robinson Cano join Brandon Laird and offer a pre-game good luck. The three of them are located in the shortstop area like they do every game for the National Anthem. I am enthusiastically holding up my sign as Jeter looks into the crowd and spots it. He nudges Laird. Cano looks over as well. The three have a little chuckle as I'm sure Jeter said something like, "You made it. You have your own sign."

By this point, Jeter has seen many of my signs. Good branding should be consistent and I always use the same neon green color and always tag it with "-162 Guy."

In the bottom of the fourth, Laird comes up with the bases loaded and the Yanks down 2-1. Most of the crowd is still wondering who he is. The pitching coach visits the mound and the camera guy comes over and focuses on my sign. A second later I am on the jumbotron welcoming Laird to New York. A split second later, a little kid jumps next to me and sticks his sign in front of mine. I am ready to strangle him on national television. All year long I have been trying to get noticed and I spent a lot of time on my sign. I give the kid a dirty look as he disappears into the night.

Laird strikes out and leaves them loaded. The rookie's first start he goes 0 for 3 and leaves four on base.

Welcome to the bigs, kid.

Monday, July 24
Game 100

Most of my family are making plans to visit my dad now. I'm not sure what I'll do about the funeral. I hope that we can have it on a day off. I think through the different scenarios. I could go to a game, leave, and catch a late flight. I could then go to the funeral and get on a flight between 2:00-4:00 and go right to the stadium. No matter what, I'm going to every game this year. I promised my dad I would.

I make my sign tonight asking Michael Kaye and YES to put me on TV. I spend the day sending out my updated press release alerting the media that I am celebrating game 100. I begin to wonder why I never get emails from my website. I meet so many people and hand out so many cards, but never get any emails. Today I find out why. I call my web designer and she looks into it and something technical went wrong. She says there are a few dozens emails waiting to be delivered since March!

I am not freaked out, but excited that I have indeed generated some interest after all. There are a few from producers who are interested in the story. One email is from someone who calls himself the "Baseball PhD."

Dear Steve,

Baseball PhD produces a weekly podcast on Major League Baseball. We want to both interview you and help.

Our studio is in Cleveland, Ohio. We'd love to interview you in studio and take you to a game at Progressive Field.

The Yankees are in town July 4th. If you have no plans as of yet, Baseball PhD would be glad to take you to the game and plan a fun 4th of July for you. (I'm flying to San Francisco on July 5th).

Let us know. Your journey looks fun.

-Edward F. Kasputis
Creative Director
Baseball PhD

Wow! Again, I never think it helps to get upset. The reality it is that I missed that opportunity, but I'm sure we can come up with something else. I dial his number and apologize for just now getting in touch. Ed is happy to hear from me. I tell him that tonight is number 100 and he asks if we can do the interview in 10 minutes. It turns out to be a great interview and we agree to talk soon. (You can listen to it Baseballphd.net by clicking on their archives section and pulling up the August 5, 2011 episode.)

Next, I read an email from another die-hard Yankees fan.

> *Hey guys! Thanks to your video producer, I was able to come across this trek you are taking this summer. I am jealous beyond belief! I just wanted to send you guys a message and wish you luck, and let you know that I will be at Yankee Stadium on 4/2 and would love to buy you guys a drink. My buddy and I will be sitting in Grandstand Outfield Section 410. Good luck as you make your way to Opening Day.*
>
> *Brian Capozzi*
> **Founder and Editor of BronxBombersBeat.com*

I call Brian next and he is going to the game tonight and we agree to meet for a beer. Many of the other emails were from folks interested in our story or just wishing us well. It is just the shot of enthusiasm that I need to keep going.

I pick up my nephew, Shane, and we are off to number 100. The game is delayed for almost two hours. We meet with two new friends, Nadine Karnowske and Sarah Ptok at The Dugout. These gals are from Germany and

With my two new German friends

redefine the word *fanatic*. They cheer on the Yankees from thousands of miles away in Germany, and they decided to come to New York for the nine-game home stand.

Brian Capozzi and I are texting back and forth and finally meet behind Section 203. Brian is getting married soon and doesn't go to quite as many games. He also has a pretty good job and writes a blog called Bronx Bombers Beat. He sits with the Bleacher Creatures on occasion, but doesn't consider himself hard core. The Bleacher Creatures are a group of fans who are known for their strict allegiance to the Yankees and their merciless attitude to opposing fans.

It is rare to meet someone who is so genuinely happy for you living your dream. Brian is one of the people who are making this journey spectacular. That night, he tells me that I really need to meet Bald Vinny, the lead Bleacher Creature. Earlier in the season, I was intimidated to meet him. I felt like the Creatures would have a "So what? Who do you think you are?" attitude. Now that I have proven myself by attending the first 100 games, I feel like I am ready.

Wednesday, July 27
Tommy and Lucy head for Florida today to say goodbye to my dad. It is difficult to watch everyone else going that way and not being there.

I have been looking forward to this day for a few weeks. I am going to a bar after the day game where David Robertson is doing an event for the tornado victims in Alabama. There will be an auction and autograph session. I am bringing my "thermometer banner," which I haven't taken to a game since April 5th. I have filled it in to 101 games now.

Although I am tired, I have a lot of energy. I have been running a few times per week and am happy that I haven't gained a ton of weight. I may have gained five pounds since March 31st.

I sit with the Germans today as Seattle ace Felix Hernandez shuts down the Yankees to stop Seattle's franchise-record losing streak at 17. After the game, we agree to meet at the David Robertson fund raiser event. Robertson is the Yankees' ERA leader and a first-time All-Star. The Germans are jumping on the subway. I am driving and not looking forward to traffic or trying to find a place to park in Midtown.

I make my way down River and approach Billy's Sports Bar. Standing in front and manning his Bleacher Creature apparel booth is the infamous Bald Vinny. He finishes up with a customer and I introduce myself. With a big smile he tells me that someone told him about me.

"It's a grind isn't it? How are you holding up?"

"I'm good. Tired, but enjoying it."

"I did it in 2005. It was exhausting."

He asks me how I was getting tickets and offers me help with anything I need.

"Media contacts, tickets, anything at all, just ask. Anytime you want to sit with us, you're always welcome."

I make my way to the car my adrenaline is pumping at full capacity. I have been officially invited to do Roll

Bald Vinny and me

Call with the Creatures. I am jacked!

The event is at 7 p.m. at Foley's Bar on West 33rd St. The Germans are the very first to arrive and grab a table, which turns out to be a prime spot. David and his wife, Erin, are running the event with Steiner Sports Collectibles. There must be 400 fans there. When I make my way to the front, I roll out my banner and the Germans are giggling. They give me the idea to have them sign the banner. I wait in line with the rest of the fanatics.

I explain to the Robertsons that I am going to all the games. With that, I hear a voice say, "I've heard that story somewhere before." My new friend, Bald Vinny Milano, steps out from the back and shakes my hand. He and Nadine exchange pleasantries. It turns out that she has already met the man a few days ago.

The live auction starts and I am hoping to have a shot at winning a private lunch with the Robertsons. I increase the bidding from $200 to $250, but bow out as the bids continues over $1,000.

I also meet Erin Robertson who heads up the Robertson's foundation which is called the High Socks for Hope. I give her my card and explain that I am a comic and

I'd be happy to do a charity show for them.

Saturday, July 30
Let's Play two!

With Erin Robertson

Rich Shulman, one of my college fraternity buddies is flying up for the weekend from St. Augustine, FL. We attended Flagler College and he dated my roommate, Rahmi, who is now his wife. I consider them some of my closest friends.

I walk down The Grand Concourse with mixed emotions. I am elated that I am living a dream and have only two months left to go. I also feel very guilty and selfish with my dad lying on his deathbed. I dial Mike and he gives me an update. Surprisingly, my dad is doing pretty great. He has missed three of his dialysis appointments. His fourth will be Monday. It's been a week-and-a-half since I last saw him.

Old photo of the Melia Clan

Most of my brothers and sisters and their children are currently with him, or at least en route. It's like the Melia family vacation that never ends. I believe most find it great that they get to say goodbye and that my dad is at peace. I ask Tommy and Lucy to deliver my goodbye letter.

Although it is a sad occasion that brings everyone together, there is strength in numbers. I have been blessed tremendously with a huge, caring family and feel great about the fact that my dad is going out in style.

Back to baseball, I'm looking forward to seeing Rich. This double-header completes games 104 and 105. For Rich, it is game one and he almost sleeps through it. I talk to a few scalpers just for fun to see what the feel is today. I'll go two for $40 since it's such a nice day.

I stop in and say hello to Bald Vinny first. He is in front of Billy's Sports Bar.

"You need a ticket?" he asks with a huge smile and his dark sunglasses.

"Yeah. Actually, I need two." He whips out two.

"Here you go."

"Wow. Are these with you guys, in the bleachers?"

He smiles and nods. Dumb question. He *is* the heartbeat of Section 203!

"What do I owe you?" I ask. I'm so used to negotiating with people.

"Glad to help the cause."

"Really?"

He shakes my hand. "Enjoy the game."

I walk away and am blown away by his kind spirit. This is a highlight of the trip. Talk about dispelling all myths about New Yorkers. I am on my way to sit with the famous Bleacher Creatures!

What's more, though, I feel wanted. I feel like I have earned my way into true Yankees fandom. It didn't happen overnight. But it *is* happening. I fist pump several times as I make my way down River Ave.

Can I really be this excited four months in? I am.

The thrill of this trip is the rush of adrenaline I get everyday about something. It could be a great seat, a free beer, or seeing a kid light up when they catch a foul ball.

I now turn my attention to Rich being late. I almost feel disrespectful if we are not there for Roll Call. Roll Call is where the Bleacher Creatures chant the name of each starting fielder (except the pitcher and catcher), and continue to do so until there is acknowledgment from the players. Roll Call has become one of the trademarks of Yankee Stadium. When Rich gets there, he has his luggage and we head to the back to check it in at The Dugout. We have already missed Roll Call, so I say yes to Rich's request to grab a beer.

In between games, Rich and I make our way back to The Dugout to meet the Germans. We walk past The Hard Rock Cafe and I notice a Yankee favorite making his way through the crowd. Rich and I walk over to say hello to Mickey Rivers. Mick the Quick was the New York Yankees center fielder from 1976-1979. He earned World Series rings in '78 and '79.

"Hey, Mick," I say warmly.

"Hey, fellas, great game today!"

Without much prodding, he proceeds to tell us that he has to take off and miss the second game because of the kids.

"It is all about the kids. I still work with kids you know. I've got to get out of here and get to the kids."

We aren't sure what kids he is referring to, but it is cool meeting a true Yankees legend. We walk with him until we reach River Ave. and tell him that we'll see him later. It is great to see how friendly he is to the fans.

As an act of international goodwill, I comp the Germans to two bleacher seats. This will be their first game roughing it. I tell them that the game is a makeup and once an inning or two go by, we can move closer and sit wherever we want because the crowd will be light. They do not like to move from their assigned seats, though. I'm not sure if it is the German influence, but they do not like to break the rules.

The Yankees score 12 runs in the first inning. This is their biggest first inning in their 110-year history. Each Yankee starter records at least one hit and scores at least one run, with Robinson Cano getting two of each. Amazingly, the Yanks only have one home run out of their 10 hits.

We make it to the 7th inning before we bolt. I get a text from Sarah asking me what kind of a fan I am for leaving a game early. The exhausted kind.

"I'm going to go home and sleep," Girardi said after his team's 25-run, 35-hit, two-win day.

We are too, Joe.

Chapter Thirteen

GOOD NIGHT, BUDDY

I'm in Chicago and Mike calls and gives me his update on my dad. He thinks that today could be the day. He is very lucid and has a hard time keeping focus. Disoriented might be the right word. It has been almost two weeks since I've seen him. Mike puts me on the phone with him every time I call. Mostly I just say a quick hello, but hearing his voice is something that will soon not be available.

Dad read my letter a few days ago and brings it up.

"I read your letter. Thanks for thinking I am such a nice guy."

"I didn't say that," I joke.

"You inferred it." He argues back.

I feel the loneliest I have been on the tour. We are playing 21 road games this month. When I looked at the schedule back in February, I knew that this would be the most daunting stretch. Chicago, Boston, Kansas City, Minnesota, Baltimore, and back to Boston with a few stops back in New York. This is why they call it "the grind." I have a deep respect for the players. Especially those who have done it for over a decade.

Thursday, Aug. 4

Running into the Pre-Paid Legal provider attorney Frank Moscardini back in June pays off as he lines up two great tickets that I am able to pick up at Will Call. Frank is a partner at Evans, Loewenstein, Shimanovsky and Moscardini. They have been the provider firm for Pre-Paid Legal for more than two decades and I've had the good fortune to get to know Frank and his partner David Shimanovsky. These guys exemplify what is great about our legal system. They fight for their members every day and are very cause-driven. It is also great to see that they appreciate the field and go out of their way to score me great seats.

I spend a few hours gathering the materials and putting together my sign for tonight's starting pitcher Ivan Nova. He has been super, stellar and out of sight. My sign reads "SuperNova." The Yankees have six starters now competing for four playoff spots. Nova cements his claim for one of those spots tonight. Nova is brilliant and picks up win number 10, holding the White Sox to one run over 7 ⅔ innings and striking out a career-high 10. He leaves the game after 102 pitches and I proudly hold up my SuperNova sign. The Yankees have great momentum right now, having just swept the four-game series.

Friday, August 5

I arrive at O'Hare Airport on three hours of sleep. My exhaustion is matched only by my excitement as the Yanks and Red Sox are tied at the top of the AL East with a 68 and 42 record.

With 52 games left, they are hot at the right time. Fenway here we come!

My organizational skills are weakening as the season moves on. I head to Boston with no hotel, no transportation, and no tickets for the games. I have been talking to my dad everyday and once again yesterday his main topic was that he wanted me to complete my tour. "Don't worry about me, I don't want you to miss a game."

I keep playing out different scenarios about when he might pass. For instance, if he goes today or tomorrow then Monday would be the funeral. Next Monday is an off-day and Tuesday is a night game back in New York. So I could attend the funeral either Monday or Tuesday. If the funeral happens on Wednesday through Friday, I could go to a few innings the night before and fly out at night, attend the funeral, and make it back for the following night.

If someone didn't know the situation, I imagine this sounds very cold.

I land at Boston Logan for the first time in my life and make my way to a desk with a sign that reads Hotel Information. I quickly realize why it isn't named Courtesy Desk. I wait patiently for my turn and than approach the desk.

"I'm looking for something close to Fenway, as I don't have a car."

"You're looking at 350 bucks a night."

He doesn't even look anything up.

"Are you sure? I was on hotels.com a few hours ago

and there was a lot of stuff available."

"You should have grabbed it. Everything's sold out. I can get you in the Hilton for $350 a night."

"Can you just humor me and see if there is anything else available?"

"I just told you, the entire city is sold out."

$350 per night? As Bob Uecker would say, "Juuuust a bit outside" … of the 162 Guy's budget.

I walk away and silently pledge my revenge on this guy. I feel lonely, tired, and frustrated. I force a smile as I consider calling Mrs. Marcinowski and asking if she can pick me up and put me up for the weekend.

I walk over and grab my suitcase. It is only 8:30 a.m. as I sit on a bench and get on the Internet. Hotels.com leads me to an Extended Stay in Waltham, which is a good 30 minutes away. I get a room for $99 a night. I call them up and find that there is a Charlie stop (train) a few minutes from the hotel that I can take into Fenway.

When I get there, they are friendly enough and allow me to check in early. They hand me my towels and inform me that there is no maid service and that these are my towels for the weekend. I enter the room and am greeted with a foul stench that will stay with me long past game 162. The hotel seems to be full of low income families that have moved in temporarily. I notice a dirty sock on the floor in the corner. I don't bother to do anything about it.

The hotel is in the middle of nowhere and I spend the day catching up on my sleep and watching movies. I go to StubHub and pay $150 for tonight's game.

I get to Fenway just as they begin letting fans in and move towards the right field bleachers.

I don't bring my glove tonight because I may go out

and hit the bars afterwards and I don't want to be made fun of. I inch closer to watch the pitchers warm up towards the end of batting practice.

I am standing behind the bullpen to the right of a little Red Sox fan named Jake. He is about 10. He has never gotten a ball. He is friendly, polite, and adorable even for a Boston fan. Mark Texeira is up at the plate. He belts a line drive that bounces deep in the outfield and jumps into the stands to my right. With a beer in my left hand, I reach over and grab it barehanded.

My hand went directly in front of the guy's glove to my right. It happened so quickly. I immediately turn to Jake and present him the ball. He is so excited that he thanks me and runs to tell his parents.

That is the last swing of batting practice and the Yankees depart the field. The guy with the glove is sulking.

"Sorry bro," I offer.

"You're not sorry." He is angry. He is close to 50, but pouting like he's 5. He is right. I'm not sorry.

"Dude, it is batting practice. I am totally allowed to reach for a ball."

"It was right at me."

I begin to walk away and a group of Red Sox fans sitting behind me call me over and acknowledge my act of kindness.

"That was hilarious, man. You reached right in front of that guy, made a great catch, and then gave it to a kid."

"Classic," a friend agrees.

"What does 162 mean on your jersey?"

"I am going to all of the Yankees games. Home and away. Tonight is 111."

"For a Yankee's fan, you're pretty cool."

Saturday, August 6
Giving it Up

Mike thinks that today is definitely the day for my dad. He continues to flow in and out of consciousness. He is calling out for my mom.

I get to Fenway early enough for batting practice today and bring my glove. It is 85 degrees and a little cloudy. I position myself behind the bullpen again. CC Sabathia is beginning to warm up. The players shagging the balls in batting practice are usually the pitchers. Freddy Garcia is always right in the middle of the action. There are plenty of kids around me today.

Freddy just misses a ball that bounces and lies against the wall. He looks up and pitches it into the crowd. It bounces off the ground before ricocheting right into my over-sized glove. I am going to keep this one for myself.

A little Yankees fan of about 8 is standing next to me with his glove. "Can I hold it?" he asks with big brown eyes staring up at me. He is adorable. What am I supposed to do, say no?

"Okay, you can hold it." I stress the word *hold*.

We continue to talk as he plays catch with himself. A few balls come close but nothing right at us. I begin to feel for him.

"I'll tell you what," I say. "If I get another one, I'll give it to you."

The Yankees retreat to the clubhouse. Freddy turns again and throws it into the stands about five feet over my head. I reach as high as I can with my beer resting comfortably by my feet. I come down with my third ball in two days!

I keep my promise and switch balls with the kid. He thanks me and runs off into the night. It is probably good that he was holding the first one, because I'm sure I would have dropped the second one if I had one in my glove already.

It's about 45 minutes before the Fox Game of the Week. I brought a sandwich with me from the outside and am looking for a place to sit and eat. In Fenway, there are picnic tables located behind the outfield bleachers. They are packed. I am a little intimidated to just pull up a chair and sit with Sox fans. I notice there are a few seats open at a table.

"You mind if I sit here?" I ask a mother and her son who are both dressed head-to-toe in Red Sox gear. She smiles and welcomes me. I put my glove and ball on the table in front of me, while I eat my sandwich. A few minutes later, the woman's husband arrives with their daughter, who is in a wheelchair. She is maybe 10 and severely handicapped.

They began to feed her. The mom unwraps the burger and holds it up for her to take small bites. The father waits patiently and holds up her soda. She chokes on it after each sip. I do my best to observe without staring. The little brother is sitting quietly eating his burger and not receiving much attention. A simple task like eating lunch is not so simple for this family. The entire family must be so consumed with their daughter's care. She is so innocent and has a precious smile.

My eyes began to tear up as the last year of my life flashes in front of me. My thoughts go to my dad, who is surrounded by his loved ones while slowly slipping away from this life. I think about some of the things that I wrote in my letter. They jump to Kim and how we decided to call it quits a year ago, almost to the day. I think about the orphans in Guatemala and how blessed they are to have

Kim visit there five times in the last year.

I glance at my glove that is holding my new American League baseball with fresh scuff marks. I think about giving it to this precious girl and I know that it's the right thing to do. I haven't said a word since I sat down. I finish my sandwich and prepare to leave. I feel a little awkward as I stand up, clean off my spot, and approach the girl in the wheel chair.

"Hi, I got this batting practice ball and I can't fit it in my luggage. Would you like it?"

She smiles, but is confused as to the proper etiquette. She glances to her parents quickly, never losing her smile.

"Say 'thank you,'" they advise.

"Thank you."

"You're welcome. Just remember, not all Yankees fans are jerks."

I smile and walk away as the father thanks me.

That felt great. Really great. I'm glad that there is a sea of Red Sox fans around, because that is the only thing holding me back from crying. Maybe I got those three balls in two days because I could brighten a few kids' days with them. Maybe baseball games should be more about celebrating the goodness in us and less about the violence, cursing, and fighting between fans. 112 games in and I'm getting delirious.

Sunday, August 7

In the bottom of the 10th of a wild back-and-forth game, and with the bullpen depleted, Girardi puts Phil Hughes into the game. Phil was scheduled to start Tuesday against the Angels. Big Papi hits a ground-rule double and is replaced by a pinch runner. Hughes intentionally walks Carl Crawford and elects to pitch to Josh Reddick. Reddick is the hero tonight as he rips a single winning the series

Yankees vs. Red Sox, with Favs and Josh

and sole possession of first place. The game ends at 12:20 a.m. going four hours and 15 minutes.

I was happy to share this game with my friend Aaron Favolise (Favs) from Wilmington and his friend, Josh. It certainly is nice to have some human companionship. It is funny that you can be surrounded by 40,000 fans every night and still feel lonely.

Favs tell me that he expected me to look like shit.

"After four months of going to more than 100 games, living out of a suitcase, and drinking beer the way you do, you look great."

I am in a great mood even though my team lost. I recommend every Yankees fan make their way to Fenway. This is baseball at its best.

Monday, August 8

The Extended Stays save money by not providing shampoo in the room. Today I wash my hair with a mini bar of soap and vow to never stay here again. I check out of The Extended Stay and I am thrilled that I won't be extending my stay.

On my flight home I decide to begin exercising immediately. I can't recall the last time I worked out. This is my longest streak of not having worked out in 10 years. I also commit to turn up my plea for publicity. I only have two months to go and I have not gotten a real bite. Was I wrong about this being really cool?

I pick up the phone and debate calling Jeff Spaulding with MLB, whom I met back in Cleveland. He produced the Derek Jeter special *3K* that premiered on HBO two weeks ago. It was a great piece and probably gave the fans more access to Jeter than any previous interview. It's out of my comfort zone to call him. But there is only one way to get rid of the fear. Make the call. I dial and he answers.

"This is Jeff."

"Jeff, it's Steve Melia. We met in Cleveland,when you were filming Jeter's quest for 3,000. I'm the guy going to 162 Yankees games."

He is hesitant. "How are you?"

"I'm great. First of all, everyone is buzzing about *3K*. I'm not sure how much you had to do with it, but it is awesome."

"I produced it," he says with confidence.

"Wow, well it was great! Hey, the reason I'm calling today is to follow up on my journey. I want to see if HBO or MLB wants to do a story on me."

"It's been done. Like you told me last month, the Yankees did a reality show a few years ago."

I am immediately crushed, but don't want him to know it. I have been to 113 games in a row and am not giving up that easily.

"Well, the difference with my story is that I'm the one who's financed the entire thing. No one has ever done that before."

He doesn't bite. "The season is starting to wind down and we are looking to do stories about baseball and not focus so much on the fans."

I want to leave on a positive note and at least keep the door open.

"Well, I'll be sure to keep you updated on my progress over the next 49 games. If you change your mind, let me know."

I hate rejection, but it fuels me. I resolve that the world will hear my story.

Tuesday, August 9

Today begins a stretch of 30 games in 30 days. This would be a marathon experience if I was just starting now and had not done 113 already. I need to be ready physically. I start the day by running three miles and doing 150 pushups. I feel better.

I get a call today from FDNY's Jerry Wren. He has four tickets to tonight's game. The weather is looking suspect and he is up in the air. He calls me again at 6:15 as I am getting close to his house in Queens. We meet on the side of the road and he gives me three tickets and keeps one for himself in case the weather holds up. "Sell the other two and get yourself a steak sandwich," he instructs. He has been one of my brother Danny's best friends for years and his generosity is appreciated. It must be nice to have the luxury of deciding if you want to attend a game.

I go from having no tickets to having two extras. I walk around the ticket area shouting, "Who needs two?"

With the rain coming down it is a buyer's market. Sitting on a bench is a young Asian man. It is after 7:00 and the game has started. He sees me holding up two fingers.

"How much?"

"They are bleacher tickets. Face value, $15."

"The game has already started." This kid knows how to negotiate. "Would you take $5?"

"Give me $10 and you got a deal."

"$5 or $10 what's the difference? What else are you going to do? You'll eat those tickets."

"No I won't, I am about to walk over and give them to the bartenders at The Dugout."

We are at a standstill. We begin talking and I learn that we are both pretty fanatical Yankees fans. The young fanatic's name is Vincent, and he can't be more than 20. He comes to every home game and never has a ticket. "I get in most of the time," he boasts. "Somewhere between free and $10."

We agree on $8. Neither one of us has change. Vincent agrees to buy me a beer inside. I give him a ticket and we agree to meet in our seats. I walk over to The Dugout where Louis the General Manager is and hand him the extra ticket.

"Do whatever you want with it," I say. "Sell it or give it to one bartenders." He tells me to come back for a free beer later.

In the stadium, Vincent and I exchange our love for the Yankees. Vincent is 19, lives in Brooklyn, and takes the subway into Yankee Stadium every home game. Every game without a ticket? Now *that* is fanatical! He usually sits with his friends in the last row of the bleachers against the back wall in Section 202 under the mural of "The Boss," George Steinbrenner. An inning later, we walk over to the beer stand and he doesn't mind buying his new friend a $12 Yuengling. I guess I won that negotiation.

At various points of the trip, I have been getting referred to as The Yankees' biggest fan. I don't like that title. I never wanted it to be a competition. Who is to say how big a fan Vincent, Bald Vinny, or the Germans are? We are all doing what we can within our means to support our team.

I did pretty well tonight. I got a free ticket, a free beer from Vincent, and a promise for a free beer from Louis. I spent $12 on a beer and $5 on dinner. I parked for free, and Mary and Steve paid for my tolls. I return to my rent-free pad in Massapequa.

I am starting to figure this out.

Wednesday, August 10

It's a gorgeous night in New York and I am looking for a good deal on tickets. I see a guy wandering around and we make eye contact.

"What do you have?"

He's got a prime ticket in the fourth row of section 110. He immediately points out the face value of $110. "Make me an offer," he says.

"As much I'd like to, I don't want to insult you. That ticket is out of my range."

"Just make me an offer." This guy must have read my manual. Never be the first to say a price.

I, however, ignore my own advice.

Exception: If you make the first offer, lowball it.

"I can go $20," I tell him.

"$20? Come on. You can do at least $30."

I take a break from the negotiation and give him my 162 card. The father of five is blown away and now I can tell that he wants me to sit with him. We agree on $25.

I give him $25 and he gloats, "I just got these for

free five minutes ago. I was waiting in line and some guy hands them to me. Can you believe that? Then I get $25 from you!" He thinks this is hilarious. He calls his wife to tell her the great news. She tells him to give me my money back. Overruled. He turns to me on our way to our seats,

"Do you like beer?"

Is the Pope Catholic?

"I love beer!" I exclaim, and for the second time this week I have met a really cool cat whom I enjoy watching the game with. Turns out that Joe works for Homeland Security and finds the whole concept of my 162 Tour fascinating. His enthusiasm is immediately suspended as he orders two Yuenglings and the cost is $24.

Welcome to Yankee Stadium.

Monday, August 15

I am up at 4:30 a.m. and Tommy drops me off at LaGuardia by 6:30 a.m. I don't know how I would have managed without their free lodging and limousine services. I have a seven-game road trip to Kansas City and Minnesota. I am staying with Ross and Cindy Chantrell in KC. They are nice enough to offer me to crash while in town. I'll rent a car for three days and I'll save $1,000 on hotels this week. Not bad.

I will be doing a PPL lunch on Wednesday in KC, and Friday in Minneapolis. On Saturday, I will also be doing a sales training in Minneapolis.

I arrive at the Chantrells. Ross is in Arizona doing some PPL seminars. Their home is buzzing as it is their daughter's first week of school. They own a promotional and apparel company called Freedom Team that has been servicing PPL associates since the mid-'90s. Cindy is a little on edge as they have a huge inventory of PPL merchandise on hand and word on the street is that Mid-Ocean is changing the name of the company in a few weeks at our convention. This means the Chantrells need to toss out all of their inventory and start fresh. Like many top PPL associates they are concerned about their futures.

Although we have known each other for over a decade, this is the most personal time I have spent with the Chantrells. Cindy is a great example of Midwestern charm and hospitality. She's just a great person. Turns out she's ready to let loose tonight and I chuckle as she asks me to drive.

"I'm thinking of having a few beers tonight," she confesses. That is Midwestern for "Let's get drunk."

We buy two tickets at the counter for $12 each. By the third inning I realize that we are on pace to drink a beer an inning. Cindy and I jump seats the entire game, moving closer each time.

Despite a 5-3 Yankees loss, the evening was great — made greater by having enjoyable company.

Thursday, August 18

My mind moves to Minnesota. I am looking forward to seeing the new stadium. I've been to Minnesota once before when I went to the last game ever to be played at the Metrodome. It was game three of the 2009 ALDS. Andy Pettitte pitched a gem and completed the sweep of the Division series.

This trip will be four nights with Steve Baker. Steve is yet another Pre-Paid Legal success story.

He was born in London and has now lived in the U.S. for 20-plus years. He was a house painter earning

$10 an hour. He switched careers in his late 30s and has been making a six figure income selling access to the legal system.

For years, the incident that defined our relationship was born in Cancun, Mexico. PPL does an all-expense-paid vacation every June for their top performers. That year they were paying for 800 couples at the all-inclusive Moon Palace. Baker was drinking tequila all day. He is a huge soccer fan and was all jacked up watching The World Cup. I don't think either of us could tell you what the argument was about, but we were both intoxicated and words eventually led to fists.

Everything happened so quickly. He tackled me over the bar and several people joined in attempting to pull us apart. I have only been in one real fight as an adult and neither of us landed a punch. So, I've never been punched or punched anyone with a goal to inflict pain. I think he could have really belted me if he wanted to. He is much

bigger than me and definitely a lot tougher. The rest of the week in Cancun was awkward as we avoided each other like the plague.

We didn't talk for several years. We gradually made up since that incident six years ago. Today, I consider him a close friend I genuinely like and respect him tremendously. He's also an extremely talented producer — number one over the last several years, in fact

— on our team. Naturally, I try to stay on his good side! I will be staying with Baker for four nights and he is loaning me his pickup truck while I'm in town.

He and Kevin McDaniels — a talented photographer and a Pre-Paid Legal Millionaire Club member — take me fishing. Not exactly up my alley since I refuse to even bait my own hook. Then, the first fish that I catch is smaller than the worm that I use to catch it. At 3 p.m., I insist that we cut bait (sorry, I couldn't resist) and head back in. Baker gives me the keys to his pickup truck and I am off to The Mall of America. The train runs from there to the stadium. I learn that the train is based on the honor system. No one is there to collect tickets and no one does it on the train, either. It is $2 each way. This would never work in New York.

I scalp a ticket for $20 and I am into the stadium for the start of a four-game series. I have now officially visited every American League park.

Friday, August 19

Baker hands me a plate with scrambled eggs and toast and I comment that "we have come a long way." Steve and Kevin are in charge of the events this weekend. We make our way to the hotel both dressed in our business suits. A nice crowd of 40 joins us as we put on a convincing and powerful business presentation.

No one realizes more than me that it is PPL that butters my bread. I am happy to do presentations whenever I can. I haven't referenced it much, but it's the constant cash flow that is making this trip possible. Like Tim Ferris referred to in his book, you must have a steady and predictable cash flow to pull something like this off.

Monday, August 22

After a successful time in Minnesota, it's time to move on. Baker drops me off at the airport. I have five weeks to go. Although I am run down, it was a great week for the 162 Tour. My only real expenses were my airfare and my car rental. I saved a ton of money on this trip thanks to Baker and the Chantrells. It is a long travel day and I'm happy that there is no baseball.

I get home to an empty house. Tommy and Lucy are in full gear for the 2011 World Police and Fire Games.

> *The New York City Police Department, The New York City Fire Department, The Port Authority Police Department, and the New York City Department of Corrections are inviting you to experience our City and participate in the most memorable World Police & Fire Games ever. Spread throughout the five Boroughs, the city that never sleeps will be the setting for the world's largest multi-sport, Olympic style event. As many as 20,000 full time firefighters and law enforcement personnel from 70 different countries are expected to compete in 65 sports.*

He has spent nearly two years working on this huge project. As many as 20,000 athletes are descending on New York City. There is one unexpected visitor.

Her name is Irene.

Thursday, August 25

The Daily News is calling Hurricane Irene "The

Monster."

Today is my dad's 87th birthday. It's amazing that he is here to see it. The report from Florida is that he is holding strong. He has been off of dialysis for five weeks and his kidneys are working overtime.

Even though Tommy has been in the people-saving business for a few decades, he has no experience with Hurricanes. He walks into the backyard and begins surveying the situation. I can tell that he doesn't know what he's doing as he starts weighing the convenience factor of putting heavy objects into storage.

At my strong recommendation, we begin to move everything into the garage. Everything from the grill to the patio set is moved in just a few focused minutes. We remove the heavy and cumbersome AC unit from a window which is both dangerous and exhausting. We get a ladder and clean out his gutters in a few furious moments.

At the stadium, it is a light crowd as the Bombers begin to get crushed. The A's are up 7-1 after the third inning. Phil Hughes is rocked to the tune of six runs on seven hits in 2 ⅔ innings. The Yanks look sluggish as I walk around the stadium contemplating when would be a good time to head for Baltimore. It's not fun sitting in the rain getting swept at home by the lowly A's.

Russell Martin hits a solo home run in the fifth to close the gap to 7-2.

I am getting restless and move to Section 104 in right field. Robinson Cano is up with the bases loaded and one out in the fifth. Cano lifts his 22nd home run just over my head and lands eight rows behind me. 7-6. Looks like I'll be in the Bronx for a while.

An inning later, Russell Martin is up with the bases loaded. He slices one to the opposite field that lands in the front row, two seats to my left. 10-7. Two grand slams in one game!

New York bats around in three consecutive innings beginning in the fifth, sending 31 men to the plate and scoring 14 runs over those three frames. The score is now 16-7. It's time to go. I have a long drive and a longer weekend in front of me.

It is 5 p.m. and the height of congestion in New York traffic. I turn on the radio and John Sterling is going crazy. The Yankees have hit their third grand slam of the day setting a new MLB record. I *almost* saw history again. As much as I hate leaving early, I am glad to be heading south on I-95. The final score is Yankees 22-9. The Yankees came up to the plate 16 times with the bases loaded.

I hit the rest stop around 7 p.m. on the New Jersey Turnpike. This is not the first time I have been here on this tour, but I still walk around looking for something healthy to eat and a place to charge my cell phone for a few minutes.

I am not pleased with my food choice once again and sit with all of the other unhealthy customers. I eat my fast food slowly (doesn't that defeat the purpose?) and hope to charge up my phone.

I check my email and notice that I received one from a fellow comic I worked with in Charleston, SC, just before the season.

> *Dear 162 Guy,*
>
> *You are the Cal Ripken Jr. of sitting in the seats! I have been following on Facebook and am blown away that you are still at it.*
>
> *One of my favorite players of all time is Ripken. He was steady and dependable. There's*

*something really inspiring and empowering about
that. Win or lose, he was gonna show up. Steve —
you inspire the same feeling.*

*How are you staying healthy? Eating on
the road is rough on the gut. All it takes is one
Applebee's, Golden Coral, or McDonald's in
the middle of nowhere to turn a road trip into a
nightmare.*

*I remember when the162 thing popped up
in my Facebook newsfeed and I thought it was
really cool. I have to say that I was envious. I never
thought you'd pull it off. I figured it would be like
going underwater and seeing how long you could
hold your breath. I thought you'd come up gasping
for air about 60 games in.*

*What about all the things that go wrong with
travel? I remember thinking that around game 40.
All of that traveling and you mean to tell me that
something like a flat tire didn't send the whole 162
thing down in flames? What about a flight delay or
something? I wouldn't call myself a pessimist. I'd
say much more of a realist. The realist in me said
that something would go wrong somewhere along
the line.*

*In the wake of strikes and steroids, baseball
needs all the good stories it can get. This is one of
those good ones!*

Good luck in your quest to do all 162!
Your friend,
Myles Hutto

Hearing from folks like Myles is like putting gas
in my tank. It will keep me going for a while. I hope he's

wrong about something going wrong. As exhausted as I am, I have a surge of adrenaline necessary to drive the three remaining hours. That, and a large coffee to go!

In Florida, the hurricane has now passed my dad's with no damage, outside of a little rain.

Kim is a different story in Wilmington. She hasn't been through a hurricane either and it is hitting tonight. I wish I could be there to help. She moved in the patio furniture and is hoping for the best. I miss her every day.

There are four games scheduled this weekend. The make-up game of April 22 is being made up as part of a Saturday doubleheader. Irene is due to hit Saturday night. Hmmm. At 10:30 p.m. I arrive back to the home of the Bradshaws in Pasadena, MD.

Friday, August 26

At 4 p.m. there is an emergency Pre-Paid Legal conference call. Rip Mason, Jeff Olson, and every top leader is invited to be on the call. Rip gets right to the point and announces that Jeff has decided to move on and will not be at the Dallas convention in a few weeks. Brian Carruthers — one of our top field associates and member of the Corporate Marketing Team — encourages everyone to stay focused and downplays any impact this will have on the company. Jeff will be missed. He has been my mentor for 17 years and best friend for many.

Sometimes the student must leave the teacher.

Behind the scenes, Brian is encouraging Ben and I to stay sober tonight and be ready to handle the incoming calls. He is pretty intense and warns us that our futures are on the line.

The weather is rainy and windy all day. Girardi

declares publicly that they should have tried to get in a doubleheader since the games tomorrow will be rained out. Girardi knows that there will be a lot of traveling over the final five weeks and doesn't welcome a return trip to Baltimore.

I am wearing a rain poncho as we head into Camden Yards for the third and final series of the year. The Bradshaws and Nicole are kind enough to accompany me to the game. It is student night and Lauren and Nicole come back from the box office with four $5 tickets. Nicely played.

Less than two minutes into the game, the umps suspend play and the fans scatter for cover. The wind continues to howl and the downpour is relentless. In the sixth inning, they announce that tomorrow's doubleheader has been postponed.

This is where it starts to get interesting.

One of the games will be made up on Sunday night as part of a day/night doubleheader. The other game will be made up on September 8 at 1 p.m. I sit in the rain and try to mentally reconfigure my travel plans.

"We didn't agree to play Sept. 8th," Girardi said. "They scheduled it, we didn't agree with it, and I really don't understand it. We're going to fight it. It just doesn't make sense."

Girardi is not the only one having a problem with that date. The September 8th game is really throwing me for a loop. It is only a week-and-a-half away and I've bought all of my plane tickets for that trip. Luckily, I bought all one-ways in case of a situation like this.

September 8 is also the first night of our PPL convention. This is the Thursday night that kicks off the festivities and we are hosting the kickoff party. With the new owners officially being at the helm for the first time at this convention, and with a possible name-change/rebrand on the horizon, this is definitely one not to miss.

I sit in uncertainty as the Bombers continue to get bombed in the rain. AJ Burnett looks as bad as I can remember. I am booing and hissing along with the other Yankee fans as he gets bombed. He was bad in Chicago three weeks ago, he was awful in Minnesota last week, and he is downright brutal tonight. They wind up losing 12-5.

Saturday, August 27

Its Super Saturday time again. I will be sharing the duties today with the man himself, Brian Carruthers. I have known Brian for 15 years and have never seen him not engaged in the building process. He is the hardest working person I've ever met. Because of the inclement weather, he has declared today "relaxed wardrobe day." Most associates usually wear suits, so this is a nice treat. I opt for my 162 jersey, jeans, and sneakers. The only thing missing is my fanny pack. What was I thinking?

I walk into the seminar room and am greeted warmly by most. Brian, however, looks like he has other things on his mind. As I begin to set up for my presentation, Brian shrugs his head inviting me to join him backstage. With hundreds of participants in the hall waiting outside, Brian is as direct as always.

"There are rumors that you are with Jeff."

I smile and say nothing.

"I have to know before you get on that stage."

"I can appreciate that. The truth is that I looked and thought about it when he called us two months ago. I considered leaving before I knew details. I am not going anywhere."

He looks into my eyes and checks my body language like Robert DeNiro in *Meet the Parents*.

After a few uncomfortable seconds, I guess I pass the test.

"OK, I have your word, right?"

"You can trust me. I'll do a good job for you today."

With the successful event finished, it's time to bunker down and stay inside. The rain continues all day. Irene hits around 11 p.m. and most of Maryland loses power. I am glad to be at the Bradshaws with a month to go in the season. They have plenty of beer, food, and, best of all, are great company. I would be going crazy if I were in a hotel … especially if it lost power. The wind and rain pound the house all night as our guard dog, Pablo, hides under a bed.

Sunday, August 28th

I awake and tip-toe around as my hosts like to sleep in. I am overjoyed as they announce that they want to go to the 1 p.m. game today. With no electricity at his bachelor mansion, Brian Carruthers opts to join us for game one of the double-header. Also joining us is a 21-year-old Pre-Paid Legal associate named Curtis Honeycutt. They arrive separately and everyone shares their hurricane stories. Curtis is star-struck in being able to hang out with Brian and I. He insists on calling us Mr. Carruthers and Mr. Melia. I prefer he didn't, while Brian appreciates the respect.

As quickly as the city shut down, it comes back alive. The drive to Camden Yards is full of fallen branches, inoperable stop lights, and welcome rays of sunshine. I am truly amazed that only a few hours ago a hurricane blasted through here. Games 130 and 131, here I come! I work my magic as we get five tickets for $30. Scalping today is like taking candy from a baby. (I've never understood that saying. Babies *love* candy and they'll scream if you take their candy! Maybe the saying should be "It's like taking spinach from a baby." Unless that baby is Popeye.) I am also amazed by the number of fans who are coming out for an afternoon of baseball. The scoreboard would read 28,000, but there are probably more like 15,000 fans. Impressive, still.

Ben uses his connections to get us on the club level. We are in the second level in the very first row. We settle into our seats and Brian, one of the richest people I know, breaks down and announces that he is going to buy me a beer. As he sits next to me, he is full of questions as it just hits him that I'm going to every game.

"When you first told me about this I thought it was a stupid idea," he announces. "But being here with you and seeing how excited you are is really neat."

We make small talk with the usher and he tells us that we are in the area that gets the most foul balls. We are about halfway between home plate and first base. With that, a ball whizzes by our heads and barely grazes the top of my glove.

"I can't believe you missed that!" teases Brian. "You go through all of the hassle of carrying your glove to every game and you missed it!" He is laughing hysterically.

In the fourth inning, however, Mark Texeira is batting lefty and rips a foul that quickly makes a bee-line toward us and is stopped abruptly by Curtis' left bicep. With 129½ games under my belt, I react quicker than everyone else and pick the ball up as it rolls by his feet. He is rubbing his arm and looks like he wants to cry as the ball leaves a huge red mark. Moment of decision. I decide to keep it.

"Man, I have been trying all year to get foul balls! This is only my second real live ball." I'm pumped. Curtis flashes a smile and tells me that he wants me to have the ball.

Uh, thanks, but you really don't have a choice.

Monday, August 29

After the game ends tonight, my navigation system informs me that the 403-mile trip should take 7:22. My friends in pinstripes are still in the locker room and will fly over me at any minute. I get coffee and fast food at one of the rest stops along the I-95 corridor. My plan is to drive until I'm too tired and then get a hotel. My lack of planning is actually liberating as I'll just get a hotel wherever I please.

My thoughts wander to Tommy as the World Police and Fire Games have become a logistical nightmare. They have thousands of athletes who have traveled from all over the world to compete. Two years of work to be trumped by a hurricane named Irene. Women!

With midnight approaching, I make it to the New Jersey Turnpike. It almost makes sense to go sleep back in Long Island, but I'll lose an hour or two of driving time. I decide to keep going. I drive past New York City at 1:30 a.m. I'm wide awake but getting restless. I think how strange it is that Marcinowski has been gone now for almost three months. If he were still here, we could drive through the night and crash at his parents' place. I'm sure he would have learned to drive a stick-shift by now.

I'm ready to stop, but a decent hotel in New York City, if available, would be $300-plus. I make my way into Connecticut, and around 2:45 a.m. start seeing signs for Boston. I'm headed to the Renaissance Waterfront in downtown Boston. There is no way that I'm going to get there at 5:30 a.m. and pay for an extra night. So I begin to look for a hotel off my highway 91. My goal is $60, but I'll go $100.

I see a sign for Hampton Inn a few minutes before 3 a.m., turn on my blinker, and make my way to the exit ramp. I am excited to crawl into bed. I pull up and prepare to negotiate.

The lady raises her eyebrows as I walk in draped in my Yankees apparel. I tell her I want to see the best deal I can get on a room, considering it's so late. She actually laughs. Welcome to New England.

"We're sold out, honey. In fact, every hotel is sold out. There's a power outage — you're not going to find a hotel *anywhere* around here."

I mumble something in disbelief as I slowly walk back to the Mustang. I begin to drive away, but suddenly change my mind and pull into a spot in the back of the parking lot. I notice a semi truck. If he can sleep in there, then I can sleep in the Mustang. I'll sleep for a few hours and then make my way to Boston. I have a pillow and my Yankees blanket in the back seat. I crack the windows less than an inch and pull my seat back as far as it will go. I laugh to myself as I have saved an entire night's lodging. I quickly fade away.

BANG. BANG. BANG.

Someone is knocking loudly on my window. A flashlight is being aimed directly at my eyes. I try to focus and comprehend what's going on.

"Open up. Police!"

"Who is it? What do you want?"

"Connecticut State Police. What are you doing?"

I reach over and push the button to put my window down. I try to gain my composure as it is never good to answer questions when awoken from a dead sleep. I can see that there are two officers on my driver's side window. The dashboard light reads 4:01 a.m.

"What are you doing out here?"

"The hotel was sold out. I couldn't drive anymore, so I pulled in for a nap."

"What are you doing here from North Carolina?" The older of the two officers is doing all of the interrogating.

"I'm going to every Yankees game." I'm not sure why I tell him this. "We played in Baltimore last night and we are playing the Red Sox tonight. I'm doing all 162."

"Really? Are you serious?" asks the younger and friendlier of the two cops. The veteran has no interest and wants to keep things moving along.

"There've been a few cars that have been broken into. You know anything about that?"

I shake my head no.

"You didn't hear anything. Glass breaking?"

"No sir, I have been here sleeping for an hour."

"It's strange that you didn't hear anything?"

"It would be stranger if I broke into a car and then went to sleep in the same parking lot."

"You have a laptop?"

"Yes."

"Can you prove that it's yours?"

"Sure. It's in the trunk." I get out and move toward the back of the car.

The younger officer revisits 162. "So, are you really going to every Yankee game?"

"Home and away," I yawn and stretch.

I open the trunk and retrieve my laptop. I pop it open. My screensaver is the picture of me and Joe Girardi.

The questions now turn sarcastic rather than accusatory in nature.

"Why would you want to follow the Yankees."

"What are you a Red Sox fan?" I jab back.

The younger cop finds this funny. I spend the next few minutes explaining that I'm a comic and I'm on the 162 comedy tour. I conclude our meeting by asking if it is illegal for me to sleep in my car in the parking lot. They explain that it isn't, but warn me to be careful. I settle back into the Mustang, lock the doors, and smile that Girardi sort of got me out of trouble.

I attempt to go back to sleep, but am now very uncomfortable with the Hampton Inn parking lot, so I opt to find another. Thirty minutes later, I pull into a Courtyard Marriott and drive to the back of the lot. It is almost 5 a.m. and I'm not going to pay $100 to sleep for a few more hours. This parking lot looks much safer and is very well lit.

I knew the tour would come with sacrifices, but I never envisioned sleeping in my car. If Pre-Paid Legal associates could see me now. Before I pass out again, I check my navigation to find that I'm only 90 minutes from Beantown. Only 30 games to go in 30 days.

Tuesday, August 30

After roughing it in the car, I pull into my new digs this morning in Boston. It is nice to be staying at a luxurious hotel. I got a great deal on this place at $169 per night. Marcinowski-less living! It would be funny if I just showed up to their house with my big red suitcase and announced, "I *told* you they play in Boston three times!" Nobody in that house believed me.

After a nice nap, I take public transportation to Fenway. This is my seventh game at Fenway and I am beginning to know my way around. I catch the Yankees batting practice and once again come away with a souvenir ball. This makes number 10. At Fenway, the ushers do not check your ticket upon entering the section. This makes it easier for me to scout seats.

Just as the game is set to begin, I spot four seats only 10 rows behind the Yankees dugout. About 20 feet away, I notice that famous Yankees fan Rudy Giuliani is in the house.

In the second inning, the folks whose seat I'm currently occupying arrive. I am in the aisle seat and rise to let them through. The young man sitting next to me hands me a ticket telling me that their fourth person couldn't make it and that I'm welcome to stay in his seat. I am touched. Red Sox fans being nice to a Yankees fan! I return the gesture by handing him my batting practice ball. Easy come easy go.

For the last 10 years, Fenway plays Neil Diamond's "Sweet Caroline" over the PA System during the bottom of the 8th inning. I don't like singing along with 37,772 Red Sox fans, but it is hard to help myself.

Hands, touchin' hands
Reachin' out
Touchin' me
Touchin' you

Sweet Caroline
Good times never seemed so good
I've been inclined
To believe they never would
But now I look at the night
And it don't seem so lonely
We fill it up with only two
And when I hurt
Hurtin' runs off my shoulders
How can I hurt when I'm with you
Warm, touchin' warm
Reachin' out
Touchin' me
Touchin' you
Sweet Caroline

I smile and thank myself for having the courage to live out a dream.

Wednesday, August 31

It is the Jimmy Fund week. Since its founding in 1948, the Jimmy Fund has supported the fight against cancer in children and adults at Boston's Dana-Farber Cancer Institute, helping to raise the chances of survival for cancer patients around the world. The Red Sox use this series to raise money for the worthwhile foundation. I am in a great mood and decide to donate, but don't want to buy any Red Sox gear. I walk up to a booth located in the outfield concessions and hand a $100 bill to the lady.

"Don't you want to buy anything?"

I tell her my dilemma. She talks me into taking two red hats with the number 9 on them. Ted Williams' number.

I agree and move on.

After the game, I quickly hightail it back to the hotel and decide that it's time to look for the Yankees again. I shower, change out of my fanatic clothes, and catch a cab to the Ritz Carlton. I am delighted as I enter the lobby bar and see many of the Yankees. I nestle to the bar and order an $8 beer.

At one table I see Freddie Garcia seated with Francisco Cervelli and their wives. Seated at some tables in the back is the YES Network crew with Michael Kaye, Kimberly Jones, and Ken Singleton. Singleton is seated with Boston Celtics coach Doc Rivers.

But my attention is focused immediately to my right, in the couch area, where Jorge Posada is seated next to Derek Jeter. Mr. November, as Jeter is known, is joined by Mr. October, Reggie Jackson. Also present are the Yankee bodyguards I met back in Cleveland.

I begin chatting it up with three other bar patrons from the Ritz who are almost as star-struck as I am. I am telling my 162 story to anyone who will listen.

"Don't they know you by now?" I am asked.

"That's a good question. You'd think so, 134 games in. But I try to respect their privacy. We run in different circles. I'm in survival mode."

I continue to say everything but the magic words: "Yes, they know me."

Lame. This is the same way I would act around girls that I liked in high school. It didn't work for me then, either.

I ponder back to my promise to WWAY's Tim Buckley: *"I guarantee I'll be friends with Derek Jeter by the end of the season."*

I am there a good two hours as the crowd begins to dwindle. The Yankees stars have a few beautiful women in their circle on the couch. I read earlier this week that Jeter and his fiance, Minka Kelly broke up.

Singleton and Rivers start to leave and make their way over to the Yankees captain. Jeter stands up and he and Rivers shake hands. I can tell by their words and body language that this is the first time they've ever met. It is interesting to watch one famous person meet another.

They have a very chatty conversation. Rivers congratulates him on his career and number 3,000. Jeter congratulates him on sweeping the Knicks and acknowledges their tough loss to Miami. He asks about his son who is a freshman at Duke and a highly-touted basketball star.

They finish up, and I'm guessing Rivers doesn't know one Yankee from the next. As he walks by my barstool, I turn and have some fun.

"What do you say, Doc?" He stops with Singleton closely behind and extends his hand. He's not sure if he knows me.

"How have you been?" he asks.

"Good, good. Everything's great. You doing OK?"

If there was any more conversation I don't remember it.

A minute later Jeter stands up and begins his good nights. Two females are happy to collect a hug, but disappointed they're not getting an invitation to his room. He is a true gentleman as he walks away.

This is my chance. He is coming right at me.

I turn, smile, and blurt out, "Have a good night DJ."

"Good night, buddy."

This might not seem like much to anyone reading it, but to me it is awesome. The Captain and I are like The Waltons saying good night to each other.

Derek Jeter called me "buddy." What? That's right! He also wished me a good night. Which it certainly has become!

I pay my tab and head back to the Renaissance. Doc and DJ, all in one night. I'm on fire.

28 to go.

Chapter Fourteen

SHUT THE
FRONT DOOR

This is a day that I have been looking forward to for a very long time. I am going to a game with Mark Michaud. Mark is a PPL associate from Maine and is taking the train in this afternoon. Every Yankees fan has a few friends who are Red Sox fans that they have a love/hate relationship with. Mark is mine.

We met in Cancun, Mexico, on a company trip in June of 2003. I happened to sit next to him at a bar. He was wearing a Garciapara jersey. We became instant friends as we traded jabs about one another's teams. Since then, we have been busting each other's chops.

He shows up at the Renaissance decked out in his Boston garb. I recount the story of how Jeter and I said good night to each other. He shakes his head.

"Have you tried to tell the Yankees what you doing?"

I answer sarcastically, as I often do with Mark, "Wow, Mark. What a great idea. What do you suggest? Should I just email them? Call 1-800 Yankees? Hmm, tell

With Red Sox die-hard Mark Michaud

the Yankees what I'm doing."

"If it were the Red Sox, I guarantee that they would have recognized you by now. You don't have to be so defensive. I just can't believe that they haven't recognized you at all. Nothing."

"Dude, they are a billion dollar corporation."

"Still."

"Well, I met Joe Girardi. He knows what I'm doing. He's the Yankees. Kevin Long. Dr. Jeter. So, yes, they know what I'm doing. They all acknowledged that it is really cool."

"Not even a letter?"

He is getting under my skin now. I pull out one of my Ted Williams caps and toss it at Mark.

"I don't know why I'm this nice to you."

He is sincerely appreciative that I would give him anything with the Red Sox on it.

"Don't be mad at me. I just think that the Yankees should recognize you, that's all."

I make my way to Fenway for maybe the final time of 2011.

I quickly realize that I am way more familiar with

Fenway than one of their "hard core" fans. We go without a ticket for Mark and he is freaking out.

"How are we going to sit together? How much will we have to pay? What if I can't get in?"

"Relax, bro. I do this a lot."

We're in the heat of a pennant race between the best rivalry in baseball, and I am still able to buy Mark a ticket from a scalper for $50. We make our way in and move right to my new favorite spot. We are in the first row behind the Yankee dugout as the Yankees warm up.

Derek Jeter walks by and I holler," Let's go, DJ!" He looks over, makes eye contact, and gives me a nod. I'm not sure who is more impressed, Mark or me.

"You saw that?"

"If I went to 135 games, he'd know me, too!"

Mr. Positive.

The tension in the air is thick tonight as there's a playoff feel to this game. The Yanks don't waste any time getting off to a 1-0 lead on Robinson Cano's 38th double of the year scoring Granderson. Burnett is on his game tonight. He only gives up a walk and a hit going into the bottom of the fourth.

Adrian Gonzalez leads off with a ground-rule double. Dustin Pedroia gives the Red Sox a 2-1 lead with his career-high 18th homer of the year. Burnett gets yanked in the sixth after a allowing a Pedrioa hit and a Big Papi walk. With one out, Boone Logan comes in and strikes out Carl Crawford on four pitches. Crawford is met with a whole lot of boos from the Fenway crowd.

By the top of the 7th, Boston is leading 2-1. Andruw Jones starts the rally by working a one out, 14-pitch walk from former Yankee Alfredo Aceves. Jesus Montero, making his major league debut, reaches base for the first time as a pitch grazes the front of his jersey.

Martin then tags a full-count fastball from Bard, belting a double into the gap in right-center, giving the Yanks a 3-2 edge. Eric Chavez follows with a pinch-hit RBI single to right field, knocking in New York's fourth run. Yankees baseball!

Mark and I are having a blast at the game tonight in one of the most exciting games of the year. The Yanks bring in Soriano and Robertson to handle the 7th and 8th. Mo gives Jed Lowrie a rare free pass. Rivera takes out the next two Sox batters — a fly ball and a strikeout, respectively. He walks Jacob Ellsbury. Two on and two out. Marco Scutaro singles on a soft liner to right and the Sox hold Lowrie at third. I'm shocked that he wasn't running with two outs.

This is a picture from our rock star seats. Jesus Montero (63) lines up for his first National Anthem as a Yankee

Bases loaded, and up comes the MLB-leading hitter, Adrian Gonzalez, who's batting .343.

The crowd is now standing and no one bothers to sit after every pitch. To me, this is what the tour is about. Moments like this don't come every night, but I savor them when they do come. Win or lose, I love it!

Gonzo fouls one right over our heads off the third base line. Mariano lays a cutter on the outside corner for strike three as Gonzalez protests with the home plate umpire. Game over. Yankees win just their fourth of 15 against Boston. The Red Sox lead is back to a half game as the Yanks take two out of three in the biggest series of the year.

Friday, September 2

I am gliding through the streets of Boston during a morning jog as I watch all the nine-to-fivers going into work. I feel like that song ("9 to 5") is about my tour. I feel alive and want to scream to the world, "Pick a dream and live it!"

Sunday September 4th

Today is my great niece Desiree's christening on Long Island. With such a tight schedule, I've have been AWOL from most family events. I pull in for the after-party. Tons of my nieces and nephews are there. It was my great niece Chiara's 6th birthday party last week. Chiara

is Mike's oldest grandchild. I grab my Mark Texeira foul ball from last weekend in Baltimore and write a note to her on it. It is amazing how people young and old love foul balls. I'm saving a ton of money on presents this year! She lights up when I give it to her.

"This is from a real game," I tell her.

"Thanks, 'Oh, jeesh man.'"

That is what she calls me, because she says that I say "Oh, jeesh" a lot, which I do.

Her sister Jemma can't stop eating long enough to snap a picture.

Tuesday, September 6
"It gets late early out there" - Yogi Berra

After a comical series of weather-related starts and stops, this game, which started at 11:07 p.m., has officially made it into tomorrow. With the Yanks now winning 5-3 in the 8th, it is shortly before 2 a.m. It's time to go. I make my way to the gate. I am driving to my brother Danny's tonight in Rockville Center, a part of Long Island that is a little closer than normal. He is supposed to wake me up at 5:30 a.m. (only a few hours from now!) for the FDNY celebrity breakfast.

Before the game started, I dozed off in my Mustang and when I woke up, the dashboard electronics flashed and then everything went dead. Uh-oh. I realize that my lights have been on for an hour-and-a-half while I slept. I try and start the car. Nothing. Should I do something now or come back and see if the three hour break will recharge it? I decide to shut it down and deal with it later.

Well, now it's "later" and as I'm walking to my car I remember the situation I'm in. Crap. I hope the Mustang starts. I try to remember if I have jumper cables. I'm pretty sure I don't. What was I thinking putting this off?

I walk in the drizzle and say a little prayer as I finally put my key in the ignition. Nothing. Important lesson: Never put off until tomorrow what you can do today. It is now tomorrow. Anyone who knows anything about cars probably saw this coming four hours ago. I sit in the Mustang and dial AAA. Because I have a California phone number, they route me to California. That takes five minutes. AAA then patches me through to North Carolina where I have my membership. *Then* they try to patch me through to New York. I wait on hold again for five minutes.

It's 2:15 a.m. and I walk towards the stadium to see if I can get a jump. I have never witnessed the streets this empty. I consider leaving my car here and taking the train. How would I get to my brother's from the station, though? The trains only run every few hours now. I see a taxi cab driver walking and looking for a customer. I have exactly $30 on me.

"Hey man, do you have any jumper cables."

He doesn't, but is kind enough to hail one of his friends who does. I jump in and we go right to my car.

"I'll give you $20 if we can start it." Hopefully this will be just a cheap lesson.

He begins to attach the cables from his taxi to my car. He signals for me to help put them on, but it only takes a moment for him to realize that I have no idea what I'm doing. I jump in the car and try to crank it. Nothing.

"OK, jump in," he says calmly as he explains that we need a bigger booster. "My brother has one at his shop."

I succumb to his advice and jump into the cab. I look down at his clock as he speeds through the empty streets of the Bronx. It's 2:35 a.m. I am too exhausted to be scared. Game 140. I smile and sigh. He is whipping in and out of neighborhoods like the Coney Island Cyclone, flying down streets that I have never seen before and, hopefully, will never see again.

A minute later, we pull into a garage that appears to be open. Wow, a 24-hour garage in the middle of the Bronx. You do not get this kind of excitement sitting at home watching TV! He tells me to get out as we enter this warehouse. His brother looks angry at first, but my driver says a quick hello and grabs a big booster. We are there less than a minute.

At 2:50 a.m., with the car now fully charged, I give

the cabbie the 30 bucks I had and thank him.

"You saved me big time tonight," I yell as the Mustang peels away.

If he only knew. Game 141 is now only 10 hours away.

Wednesday, September 7

I hear a light rap at he door.

"You up?"

Exactly two hours of sleep. I'd like to say I jump up, but it's more like I slide out gradually. In the shower I go over my comic baseball material. Danny told me I *may* be performing and that I should prepare five minutes worth of material just in case.

> *"One positive result of the tour is that I am praying a lot more than before; Every time AJ Burnett pitches. I think that it is why we have gotten so much rain. Even God is thinking, 'I can only do so much!'*
>
> *I am a big Yankees fan, even my cat is named Jeter. We had a little scare recently. We found out that Jeter has herpes. We are still looking for the pussy that did it. One of my neighbors overheard this and was confused and didn't know that I was talking about my cat. 'I thought A-Rod was the one banging out Madonna.'*
>
> *You have to be careful of deceptive advertising when you buy tickets. I bought these tickets that were supposed to be an all-inclusive deal. When I get there, it is the boring-est group you've ever seen. Nobody is partying. So, I'm like,*

'Where are all the free drinks?'
With that, security comes over and tells me
'Sir, you are in the alcohol-free section.' I know, that
is what I am trying to do ... get my free alcohol.' I
show him my ticket, and point. Alcohol dash Free.
Where's the confusion? Apparently alcohol-free and
free alcohol not the same thing.

As I rinse my hair, I pray that they leave me off the agenda today and that they don't want me to do comedy.

At 6 a.m. with a cup of java in hand, we pull out of my brother's driveway. I am going to the stadium for game 141 after breakfast, so we take separate cars. My brother's nickname is Hyper Dan. He likes things to move along at a brisk rate. Danny is 13 years my elder. Every summer growing up, I would visit New York for a few weeks. I'll always appreciate the time and effort that Danny took to hang out with me as he brought me to many baseball games. Unfortunately, they were mostly Met games.

We stop along the way and pick up two other fire chiefs. It is a few days before the 10-year anniversary of 9/11. As high ranking officers, these guys have seen and been through a lot and I am humbled to be spending the morning with them. It's another highlight of the trip. The Yankees are great, but I don't believe that anyone in pinstripes would argue that the FDNY are the real heroes around here.

When we arrive to the breakfast, my brother introduces me to one of the other fire chiefs. He is the nicest guy. We joke around a little, and Danny is great at telling the 162 story.

"Hey Chief, listen to what my brother is doing. He has been to every single Yankees game all year. Home and away."

"Get out of here! You there last night?"

I smile and nod.

"That's amazing. See that guy over there?" He points to an impeccably dressed man. "That's Jeff Wilpon, owner of the New York Mets. Want to meet him?"

He takes us over.

"Hey Jeff, This is Chief Melia and his brother, Steve. This guy is a Yankees fan, but listen to what he is doing; he has been to every game this year. Home and away."

Wilpon lets it sink in. "The Mets need some fans like you."

Mr. Wilpon is super nice. I tell him how much that I enjoyed Citi Field.

The rest of the morning is quite emotional and is filled with celebrity speakers recalling their thoughts and sentiments on 9/11. We hear one tearful story after the next about how 9/11 affected them and how much they appreciate the FDNY and all emergency responders. It is an intimate crowd and we all hang on every word. I feel so lucky to be here. There is not a dry eye in the place.

With Mike Francesca from WFAN Radio

Mike Francesca is one of the speakers. Mike is the afternoon voice on WFAN, the world's first 24-hour all-sports radio station. His introduction says that he has been in broadcasting for 30 years and touts him as being the most recognized figure in New York sports journalism. When the official part of the event ends, I break out my camera and shoot over first to meet Mike. He is a key person that I've wanted to get to meet. This will make the call much easier when I launch the 162 book. We snap a picture.

Danny and I continue to make it through the crowd and snap as many photos as we can.

I look down at my watch. It is 10 a.m. Game 141 is less than three hours away.

I do not have a ticket for today and make my way over to Bald Vinny. Like most days, he sees me and points, "You need one, Steve?" I nod and hold up one finger. He hands over a bleacher ticket and I hand him $15.

Since meeting Bald Vinny in late July, I have come to be one of his biggest fans. I have watched him bend over backwards to make the fan experience at Yankee stadium a great one. The Creatures may have the reputation of being rough around the edges, but this is not an accurate description of their leader, Vinny Milano. There is an old proverb that says *Always leave the pile bigger than you found it.* This more accurately describes him.

I have known Vinny for less than two months and he certainly has made my journey more enjoyable. I am too new to the group to be considered a real Creature. Many nights I would show up and feel like an outsider as the Creatures were celebrating a certain theme. This was not their intention in any cold way. They have just earned entry into this exclusive club one game at a time. One Friday night, all Creatures were wearing Hawaiian shirts. As much as I enjoy the environment, this is a group that had been together a long time and you don't just demand your way in.

For the first time I have the opportunity to ask Bald Vinny about his attending all 162 games and his version on YES's *The Ultimate Fan*. Vinny was newly married at the time and it wasn't his best financial move.

"We didn't actually work for the Yankees," he recalls, "but a third-party production company that produced the show. I went broke that year. I got paid $500 per week, plus expenses. They paid for flight, hotels, tickets, and gas. They gave us $40 a day on the road and $20 at home for food and whatever. When you are in airports, hotels, and ballparks, that $40 does not go very far.

"If It was physically possible to drive, we drove. We drove from Kansas City to Minnesota. We drove out to Detroit. Getting along with three other people in a car like that — while I'm thinking of my young family at home — was not fun."

"We wound up staying mostly at Holiday Inn Selects and places that were much more affordable."

I smile to myself as I realize the irony of my asking all the questions that I have been getting since late March. Meeting Bald Vinny is indeed a highlight of my trip. Getting to spend the day chatting with him is priceless. I wind up doing all of my T-shirt shopping through him and I encourage all those going to games with me to do the same. Like any good host, he makes me feel at home in Da Bronx.

Thursday, September 8
New York to Baltimore to Dallas to San Diego to Anaheim to Seattle to Toronto

Today is a day that I have been keeping an eye on all year. Tonight is the one PPL event that I was hoping to attend in Dallas, Texas. There are meetings all day that I will now miss thanks to the Baltimore Orioles' decision to not play the Friday doubleheader due to Hurricane Irene's little visit a few weeks ago.

MidOcean Partners will be laying out the new company name, logos, and marketing materials. This is an important meeting for my partners and I. I wake up 5 a.m. and still need to pack for my 11-day odyssey that will see me visit Baltimore, Dallas, San Diego, Anaheim, Seattle and Toronto. I pack everything from business suits to bathing suits.

I sit on the New York City-bound train and I go over in my head what can go right or wrong today. My plan is to be on the 9:35 a.m. Amtrak arriving in Baltimore at 12:13 p.m. I got a last minute ticket for $100. The game is scheduled to begin at 1:00 p.m., but there is a 60 percent chance of rain. The likelihood of rain increases as the day goes on.

Then, I have a flight to Dallas at 4:55 which arrives at 7:15 p.m. There is a black-tie dinner that starts at 7:00 for the top 500 executives in the company and their dates. Mike and Kim are among the keynote speakers and this is a huge honor. I will do whatever it takes, outside of missing a game, to be there.

I will have to leave Camden Yards at 3 p.m. sharp. If the game is delayed for more than two hours, I will have to miss my flight and go directly to California. There is only one more day off the entire season, Sept. 15, next Thursday. If we do not play today, we will have to fly from Seattle to Baltimore after the night game on Sept. 14. This would mean canceling the flight to Toronto that cost me $500. It also would mean I would need a Seattle to Baltimore ticket and a Baltimore to Toronto ticket. This can add up quickly. What is my criteria for being at every game? As long as I see one pitch, I was at the game.

The other thing that can go wrong is that there is a problem with the flight from Baltimore to Dallas. I could play it safe and just fly to Anaheim, but what fun would that be?

This is my first time on the Amtrak from New York to Baltimore and it is awesome. They have wireless internet and very comfortable seats. I spend the time journaling and planning for the next few weeks. I am also constantly checking the weather.

At 12:45, the Amtrak train arrives 30 minutes late to Baltimore. I drag Big Red to the exit and look for a taxi stand. I need to dump my bag at a local bar and find a ticket.

Sliders Bar and Grille is one of the bars directly across the street from Camden Yards. I arrange for the same cab driver to pick me up in the exact spot at 3:15. I step out and walk inside the bar that is usually packed. Today I am the only customer. They happily take my bag and I stop for their $2 special Natty Bo. I'm thirsty and drink my first beer of the day in about 60 seconds. My adrenaline is pumping as I am in the midst of the craziest travel day of the year.

At 1:10 p.m., I get my ticket scanned for the 142nd time this year. I am delighted to hear the PA announcer talking. As I make my way to the outfield section, I can see that Derek Jeter is up to bat. This has worked out beautifully. I know exactly where I want to sit and confidently stride down to a seat directly behind home plate on the Yankees dugout side. The sun is shining over the few thousand fans in attendance.

Camden Yards is often referred to as Yankee

Stadium South when the Yankees are in town. Today, there aren't too many who've made the trip from the Big Apple.

One of my friends, Randy Parker, who lives in Auburn, CA, has been following my tour on Facebook. He is a high level umpire in high school and college and he has been egging me on to get ejected from a game. Well, this would be the day to do it. I have reasoned all season that if you are going to get tossed, do it in a stadium that you won't be visiting again this year. I have to leave early anyway. Heck, even Girardi has been tossed twice.

I am sitting in the second row enjoying every minute. The Yanks score three in the second and it looks like we are going to roll today. After the bottom of the second I approach the Yankees dugout.

"Kevin Long? K-Long?" The batting coach turns around and acknowledges me.

"Game 142, man. I've made 'em all."

He smiles and nods his approval.

"Today was a tough one logistically, but I'll see you in LA."

"That's awesome," he remarks as he gives me a thumbs up and processes the information. This is probably the fourth time that I have reminded him of my journey.

The Orioles catcher visits the mound for a quick chat. My body needs a stretch as I have been up since 5 a.m. This week has been exhausting and I stand and move around. We have not had a day off since the hurricane two weeks ago. I reach into my jeans and check my cell.

An inning earlier there was a friendly usher who was standing guard. His replacement, a crotchety old man in his 60s, barks, "Sit down." I look over and he is indeed talking to me.

"I'm stretching. I'll sit back down in just a second.

I'm not blocking anybody," I say as I turn to look behind me.

"I said sit down," he demands more forcefully this time.

"The catcher is on the pitcher's mound. It is a time out! I'll sit in a second, when I'm ready."

Now I'm not sitting only because he told me to sit. As I finally sit, he rushes over.

"Let me see your ticket."

Most of the people in my section have snuck down from other seats. "I don't have one here," I mumble.

He starts calling on his walkie-talkie for backup. I get up and leave. He is yelling after me. I can hear him yelling someone else's name. It is a good thing that the Orioles hire really old ushers as I quickly walk away from the altercation.

Ejected would be great, arrested would be tragic. With the Yankees up 4-3 after six innings, I leave Camden Yards for the final time in 2011.

20 to go. I sort of wanted to get ejected just to have a fun story, but I was too much of a chicken. I hear Marcinowski's Boston accent, "Don't engage, Melia."

When I get to BWI, I learn that my flight is delayed. We finally board at 5:30 p.m. and it will be close. I sit in an aisle seat with a pretty big guy in the middle. He is extremely nervous and quickly informs me that this is first time flying. He's in his mid-twenties.

"What are you going to Dallas for?" I inquire. "It must really be important if you are willing to fly."

"I'm going to a business conference."

"Let me guess, Pre-Paid Legal?"

"How did you know?!" he asks.

"Steve Melia'" as I extend my hand.

He shows a hint of recognition, "Marcus Cherry. I've heard of you," he says as he looks down at my gold PPL ring. "Wait, you are one of the Melias!"

We spend the next few hours talking about life, business, and my 162 Tour. I am keeping a close eye on the time. Marcus is a mess taking off and he is even worse as we prepare to land. His knuckles are gripping both arm rests. I have a favor to ask him, but I decide to wait until we land, because he is hyperventilating.

We land at 8:15, an hour late.

"Marcus, can you do me a huge favor?" I ask. Now, keep in mind that this guy has never flown, been to a baggage claim area, or been to a foreign city. His eyes are open wide.

"My partners are speaking momentarily," I continue, "and I have to take off as soon as I get off this plane. I need you to get my suitcase and meet me at my party later at the Hyatt downtown."

He agrees. He is staying at a different hotel, but accepts my challenge. I peel off a $20 bill for his trouble and thank him repeatedly. I describe my big red suitcase and hope for the best. I make it off of the plane and sprint through the airport.

As I enter the taxi, I say what every adrenaline junkie dreams of saying one day: "Hyatt Regency Downtown ... and step on it!" Kim texts me that they are about to be introduced in minutes. I can still make it. The Hyatt is a 25-minute drive. I tell the driver that if he can get me there by 8:50 p.m. there is a great tip in it for him.

I smile in the back seat as I think how important taxi drivers have been to me this week. It is less than 48 hours ago that I was wandering around the Bronx looking for a jump.

He gets me there quickly and I'm immediately off to the races trying to find the banquet. A few folks recognize me and start cheering, "Steve Melia — 162 Guy!" It is hard to believe, but I am actually famous to a lot of these people.

I enter the ballroom and Frank and Theresa Aucoin, who are hosting the event, are on stage introducing my partners. The timing couldn't have worked out better.

"Please bring to the stage, the dynamic Mike and Kim Melia."

The crowd gives them a standing ovation. Just as everyone is sitting, I make my way to the head table and sit next to the CEO Rip Mason and President Alan Fearnley.

"We have been waiting for you," Rip says with a smile.

I shake his hand and reply, "I got here as fast I could."

Kim sees me as they make it to the stage. Mike doesn't notice me for a while. They are both dressed to the nines. They give a 15-minute talk on partnership. They are both electrifying speakers. Towards the end they reference me and bring me up to the stage.

I ask the crowd, "Who has been to a game with me this year?" A slew of hands go up. I briefly describe my day and how great it has been to live out a dream this year. I thank Mike and Kim for being the best partners a guy could ask for.

The dinner breaks

a few minutes later and I get to see a lot of friends. Our party is under way and we head over. Like usual it is loud, dark, and crowded. I spend the night catching up with old friends.

Friday, September 9

The new company is unveiled at American Airlines Arena. The name of our new company is LegalShield. Rip and Alan paint a prosperous future and show a few new company videos. Our new marketing slogan is "Worry less - Live More." I am happy to have made a brief stop in Dallas, but I have something to finish.

142 down and 20 to go. The Yankees are holding a 2 ½-game lead over the Red Sox who hold a 7 ½-game lead over Tampa with less than three weeks to go.

I really took a big chance flying out so late, but I wanted to see the launch of LegalShield. My 1:50 flight gets into San Diego at 4:10 p.m. From there, I still have an hour drive to Anaheim.

Julie Eaton picks me up in San Diego and is going to the game with me. In addition to taking in the baseball game together, we both have something else in common: We are both watching our fathers live out their final days.

Julie is very concerned that we will have a hard time getting tickets. We walk up to the main area by the huge Angels hat. It's difficult for two people to walk and scalp, so I have her wait there.

The first ticket I get for $10. Supply and demand. There are always more people who come with extra tickets than people that show up with no tickets. The second ticket is comped by a gentlemen who is a season ticket holder. Even before I told him about me going to every game, he offered it for free. Some people actually like to do nice things. I give him a card and tell him that he just made the book. I am back in less than five minutes.

The Yankees are playing in their third city in three days and, unfortunately, the outcome is the same. The Yanks are shut down by Jared Weaver who is having a fantastic year. He throws three-hit ball for eight innings and gets the win 2-1. The Yankees bats are tired tonight.

Tuesday, September 13

I wake to the young voices of Aidan and Conor

Dunn and briefly have to figure out where the heck I am. I am in the guest bedroom of my friend Kevin and Cecilia Dunn. I am taking up most of his kids' play area with my fold-out bed doubling as the couch. The kids are off from school today because of a teacher's strike.

On the verge of another historic day with the Dunns

I met Kevin in 1999. When he overheard me and Mike talking at the bar, he immediately locked in to Mike's New York accent, and had only one question for him: "Yankees or Mets?" When Mike said, "Yankees, of course!" Kevin knew that he had made two new friends for life.

We spend the morning with the kids and drop them off at a friend's house. Kevin is another example of a stay-at-home dad (thanks to LegalShield) who gets to make his own schedule. This week, his schedule is filled with Yankees baseball. In his own words:

> *During Steve's trip, my little Toyota Corolla went over 200,000 miles and Steve leaned over and got a picture of it. I guess that's how my family has chosen to live – make decisions now that will bring your dreams closer. Maybe I should drive a nicer, newer car, but driving this old, reliable car makes dreams more possible, and more quickly. I've always been willing to sacrifice the present in favor of the future.*
>
> *Steve's visit, however, reminds me about a powerful ally that I've been ignoring for years: Urgency. As I look in the mirror every night after getting back from the games, I realize that without urgency, there is no end in sight to sacrifice. After witnessing the painful death of my dad at a young age, I eventually developed a coping mechanism where I am always basically happy. Steve reminds me that the purpose of adversity, of the great struggles in life, are not just to forge you into a better person, but to create an incredible lifestyle. For the juice to be worth the squeeze in life, you have to get to the juice part at some point. I have an urgency in my life that I have not felt in years, specifically thanks to Steve.*

On this night, Kevin gets to witness two significant milestones:

1) I am lucky enough to get my 11th ball of the

year. Well, it's more of a sympathy ball, actually. The guy who caught the ball was looking around and I must have looked like the kid who wanted it the most. He must have noticed my oversized glove and my enormous smile. He turns to me and says, "Here you go, kid." It makes no difference how I get them. I appreciate all of them the same.

2) Mariano Rivera joins Trevor Hoffman as the only pitcher to record 600 saves. It couldn't have happened to a nicer, more talented guy than #42. And Kevin was there to witness it with me. Very cool.

Wednesday, September 14

Back at the Dunns, I begin to pack up for my trip to Canada. 148 down and 14 to go. Over the last few weeks I have reflected a lot on the season. I must admit, I am a little disappointed that the Yankees and the press didn't pick up on the 162 Tour. I keep telling myself that I am doing this for me and no one else. I don't need anyone to acknowledge my accomplishment for it be special. I remember the funeral story. What do I care what other people think?

I am laying in the fold-up bed going through my cell phone. I click on my messages to see if I have any new ones. A Facebook message pops up from August 8. It is from Tara Cannistraci of the New York Yankees. For some reason, it delivered to my phone only and not my regular Facebook account.

Steve, I lost your card. Hope your tour is going well. I wanted to see if we can set up an interview.

"Kevin!" I scream as I run into the kitchen. "We did it! The Yankees want an interview, baby! They Facebooked me over a month ago." I quickly begin writing back.

Tara, I just saw your message from last month. I am still going strong and would love to meet up with you.

Wow, they were ready to interview me a month ago. Well it certainly makes things more exciting going down to the last minute! Mark Michaud's words are ringing in my ear from two weeks ago: "They haven't even acknowledged you?"

I am so jacked I can barely sleep.

Thursday, September 15

Today is the last off-day of the season. I reach for my phone and see that I already have a message. "Steve, it's Tara. Glad to hear that you are still on track. I'll be in Toronto this weekend, maybe we can do something there."

I rush into the kitchen where Kevin and Cecilia are serving pancakes to the boys. Aiden and Conor must think that I'm just a big kid seeing my excitement.

"I heard back from the Yankees already."

"That was fast." Kevin gives me a high five and two large pancakes.

Kevin's words best describe my time in Seattle:

I had a blast going to the games with Steve, but it became about more than just the games. There is something magical about watching a man pursue his passion, living his dreams at such a young age. Steve's pursuit of 162 has really influenced me. Being so close to his pursuit, having him stay with us, has brought my dreams into sharper focus.

It is obvious that Steve has paid the price and, therefore, gets to reap the benefits. Every single person, upon hearing of the legend of the 162 Guy, has asked one question: how did he afford to do it? Well, as mentioned previously, Steve has put in his time and grown a very successful business. Watching that makes it easier for me to pay the price. It helps me put my life into great perspective, watching it stretch out from my childhood with my dad, into the future with my two sons, Aidan and Conor. They are still young, so thank God I have time left to hopefully influence them the way my dad did for me. What better example to give them than showing how hard work pays off in living your dreams? Over the last few months, I have definitely worked harder, dreamed bigger, and felt more connected to the path of my life.

Steve is a bit of a folk hero around my house. Thanks to the power of indoctrination of the youth, my boys are Yankees fans as well. They both play baseball, and they were blown away that Steve got to go to every single game. Steve amazingly has caught 11 balls on the 162 Tour, and he gave one of them to Aidan and Conor. The inscription reads, "Aidan + Conor, Live Your Dreams! – 162 Guy, Steve Melia".

The boys love that baseball, and it sits by the door where they look at it every time they come in and out of their room. It is a physical reminder that

*thoughts are things, and that living your dreams is
the inevitable result of your philosophy, attitude,
and activity. My family owes a debt of gratitude
to Steve Melia for touching our lives, especially
those three days in September. While his visit only
lasts a few days, it has had a lasting and incredibly
positive impact on our family.*

Saturday, September 17

Toronto. I wake up and quickly get ready for my
first Super Saturday with LegalShield. I get on the subway
wearing my suit at 9 a.m. My longtime friend, Darryl
Campbell, picks me up at the subway and drills me with the
regular questions. Darryl is a retired high-ranking cop in
Toronto, where he served for nearly 30 years.

The event, hosted by Rob and Charlene Mackenzie,
is packed with hundreds of associates. Rob and Charlene
are the first Millionaire Club members that our company
created in Canada, and they are just fantastic people. I am
scheduled to give a 20-minute talk at 11:30 a.m. and then
get quickly escorted back to the subway. I arrive and realize
most of the associates are wearing their new LegalShield
T-shirts. I shake my head. I should have worn my 162
jersey.

Just after noon, I get a ride from Jose Barros back
to the subway. Jose and I go back a few years and he is nice
enough to get me there quickly. My phone rings and I let
it go to voicemail. I notice that it is a 917 area code, which
is a cell phone area code from New York City. I have the
same thought that I have had hundreds of times this season.
Only this time I'm right.

My thought is that the New York Yankees are

calling me to talk. I check my voicemail and it is from Tara Cannistraci. Tara wants to interview me today at The Rodgers Center! I text her back right away. She tells me to text her when I get to the game. Today is game 150. This is the day that I've been waiting for.

Dilemma!

I am wearing my suit and I still have to go to my hotel, change clothes, and then get back on the subway to go the game. I decide to go straight to the game wearing my suit. As the subway goes from stop to stop, I keep re-evaluating my decision. I certainly don't want Tara to think that I am late for every game. I need to get there. But I also don't want to look like a dork.

Whenever I see someone at a game with a suit on, I always think of how uncomfortable they must be. Here's this guy who goes to every game and he is wearing a suit in 80-degree weather. Weirdo. Thankfully, I change my mind and get off at my hotel's stop. I resign myself to the fact that I'm going to be late to the game, but it beats looking like an idiot.

It's 1:00 p.m. as I get to the Town Inn and Suites. I rip off my suit and don't bother hanging up my clothes. First pitch is in seven minutes. I throw on my 162 jersey and a pair of shorts. I feel like Superman when I put the jersey on. I get this surge of rocket juice.

On the train, my heart is pounding quickly and I am sweating like crazy. I look out the window and see a reflection of myself. I think about all I've been through over the last six months. With my sunglasses to conceal it, I tear up as I realize that my dream is coming true. On my way to game 150, I am filled with a sense of accomplishment. I'm proud for not quitting.

I get off at Union Station and maneuver my way

through the crowd like OJ Simpson in a Hertz commercial. I keep the pace for several minutes. I soon realize that it is a lot longer to the Rodgers Center than I thought. My sprint turns into a slow jog and then eventually a fast walk. I wipe the sweat away and I start to look for a ticket. Those who have been to a game with me know I never get a ticket from the first scalper I see. Call it superstition.

I find a scalper who agrees on $15. I give him a 162 business card, quickly tell him of my mission, and continue towards the gate. Just as I scan my ticket, I receive a text from Tara asking me where I am. I tell her that my ticket is in the upper deck and that it is pretty far up and that we may want to meet somewhere else. I almost never sit in my assigned seat, anyway. She says that my seat will be perfect as they need a quiet area to tape. We agree to meet in Section 532, Row 15, Seat 7. I hit the bathroom and grab a cold Stella Artois. I am dancing with excitement.

At 1:52, Tara and her crew arrive. They seem as excited to meet me as I am to meet them. They are intrigued as we review a list of questions. I think about how many times I have answered the same questions. I feel more prepped than Obama during his campaign debates (the 2008 ones!). Tara explains that we are going to wait until the bottom of the 2nd begins. It is much louder during the breaks because of the music.

She opens the interview and introduces me as a hard core Yankees fan who is at my 150th game of the year. She starts firing away with questions about what inspired me, what are some of my favorite moments of the year, what was my favorite stadium, and many others. The interview continues for maybe 10 minutes as Tara asks what some of the biggest challenges were. I talk about all of the rain games and she is especially touched when I tell her about my dad.

It is a good thing Colon is getting rocked because it definitely prolonged the interview. Colon threw 30 pitches and Toronto scored four runs on four hits and a walk.

As we finish, the producer hands me a ticket. "On behalf of the New York Yankees, we would like to upgrade you." The ticket is for Section 118, Row 9. I am jacked and will not be returning to my upper level seats any time soon.

Well, that was the moment I have been dreaming about since February. I am excited to see where the Yankees want me to sit. I get to Section 118 and begin walking towards the field. I keep walking and realize I'm in the second row directly behind the Yankees dugout. I feel like a rock star!

When I get to my upgraded seat, it's already the fifth inning. Although the Bombers are losing, I am beyond excited. I enthusiastically cheer on my team and think how fitting it would be if we come back and win.

With the Yanks down 6-1, it's not very likely, but just as I think that, Curtis Granderson rips one that bounces into the seats for a ground-ruled double. Mark Texeira makes it interesting with an RBI single. Tex moves to second on an error and to third on a wild pitch. Cano gets plunked as Blue Jay starter Henderson Alvarez is beginning to unravel.

A-Rod steps up to the plate with the score now 6-2 and goes on to do what he's done more than 600 times in his career. He rockets the first pitch fastball over the left field wall to bring the score to 6-5. This is one of the best swings I have seen all season. These seats are great. I feel like I'm part of the Yankees organization. Welcome back, Alex.

Derek Jeter opens up the 7th with a single, and Granderson steps in. The count quickly goes to 2-2 before Curtis fouls off the next seven in a row. On the 12th pitch

Shut the Front Door

of this gutsy at-bat, he sends number 40 into the seats. 7-6 Yanks! I exchange high fives with the guy in front of me.

That is all the offense we would see today. Rafael Soriano comes in the game in the eighth and is filthy in striking out the side.

Mo comes in, and with just 15 pitches, ties the all-time record for saves. Mariano is amazing. I have so much respect and admiration for the way that he handles himself. I am as happy for him as I am for myself for being there. I believe he truly cares about the fans and appreciates us.

Game 150 will go down as one of my favorite moments ever. The Yankees fans are hovering around the dugout and we don't want it to end.

I meet the enthusiastic fan who was seated in front of me with whom I had earlier exchanged high fives. His name is Chad Snyder and he's from Sydney, Australia. I learn quickly that he flew in for the series and is then on his way to Yankee Stadium. I tell him about 162 and he is blown away. After knowing me for less than three minutes, he offers me a ticket to the Sunday game. (Face value $210.) I accept.

"Wanna go for a beer, mate?" he asks me. Uh, is the sky blue?

Chad and I walk outside in search of a post-game bar to celebrate. We get much luckier as we see a huge party right in front of us. It is Oktoberfest. I am really glad I didn't wear my suit. Chad and I spend the next 10 hours hanging out. Meeting Chad is truly one of the highlights of the 162 Tour. He is one of the coolest, most generous people I have ever met. He is also a total extrovert and we precede to meet what seems like hundreds of people. As the night goes on, we can't walk by anyone without a big hello to Chad. He looks a lot like Matthew McConaughey and the ladies absolutely adore him.

"In the Action" with Aussie Chad Snyder

Sunday, September 18

I thank Chad continually for the best seats of 2011. We are in a section called "In The Action" seats. They are a row of leather VIP seats that jet out from the first base line.

Eric Chavez is playing first base today as the Yankees are starting an unusual lineup. We have had a tough last few weeks and today is the day that everybody gets a rest. The final out is recorded in the bottom of the first. Chavez turns around as we stand up and ask for the ball. I have my glove outstretched like a first-basemen. "What do you say, Chavez?" He tosses the ball our way, and number 12 lands softly in my glove. I immediately turn and hand it to Chad. "This is yours, bro." He tries to say no, but I insist.

"Dude, I'd be up in the nosebleeds today. This is your ball." He takes it and we are both jacked. This is my 12th ball of the year. It helps to have seats like this every day.

My phone vibrates and I notice that I have a text from Tara. This weekend keeps getting better.

Hi Steve, I know that you are with friends today, but we have an extra ticket behind the dugout if you want to stop by Section 118, Row 9, Seat 3.

Are you serious? Decisions, decisions! In the third inning, I venture off to visit my new friends with the

306

Yankees. I leave my VIP seats and find Tara and the gang enjoying the game behind the dugout. They are as nice as can be. They do not have an agenda; they just want to visit with me. They tell me that they are going to put together a video from the interview and put it on the Yankees website.

Tara also says that they would like to do an interview with me live at Yankee Stadium during the last home game of the year against the Red Sox, next Sunday, Sept. 25. Gulp. In all of dreaming and fantasizing, my imagination didn't come up with this one: Introduced to the Yankees fans live in front of Boston during the last regular season home game. Shut the front door!

The four of us banter back and forth for a few innings before I make my way back to Chad. He is driving to Rochester after the Sunday game and volunteers to take me to the airport. We have spent nearly the last 24 hours together and are both sad to see it end.

We pull up to the Toronto airport. We shake hands goodbye and he hands me his ball. I politely decline and hand it back. He is the one person I've met whose enthusiasm trumps mine. Two balls in two games. I have a feeling we would be seeing each other very soon.

Chapter Fifteen

162!

Monday, September 19

    I pull up to LaGuardia at 11 a.m. on my way to the stadium for the 1:05 game. I am meeting my brother Mike and The Breeze at The Dugout at 12:30. At 11:03 a.m. Chad steps into the baggage claim area as we exchange a man hug. I've know him for 43 hours and it's like we have been mates for decades.

    As we drive into the Bronx, I get a text from Tara Cannistraci. The Yankees want to know where I am sitting as they want more footage. My ritual of late is to start the game with the Bleacher Creatures for Roll Call. We will then be moving to our seats in 227. Chad is super excited to be at the stadium and do Roll Call. This is his first time at the new Yankee Stadium and he is looking forward to the entire experience.

    We make our way into Section 203. Chad looks around like a kid in Toys R Us for the first time.

    Tara told me that the camera would be on us in Section 203 whether we see it or not. I introduce The Breeze and Chad to Bald Vinny and let him know that we are on camera.

"Well, we better make some noise, there is no one here today," he observes. Day-game makeups are always a much lighter crowd, especially when the subway stops running, which was the case today after a pipe broke in the subway and shut things down.

Chad, The Breeze, and I do Roll Call with the Bleacher Creatures as the cameras roll. We then make our way to our other seats. The cameraman shows up in the top of the second. His job for the day is to get good shots of us. He moves around and films from every conceivable angle. The fans around us have no idea who we are or what we are doing. Mike, who was stuck on the subway, finally arrives and sits next to me as Chad and The Breeze are behind us. I think that is the best chance of everyone getting on camera. I politely remind Mike eight or nine times that we are being taped and to put down his beer. The Breeze isn't really into being on camera and is constantly trying to avoid it.

The Yankees are up 6-4. Mo had a day off yesterday. We want to get a closer glimpse of history.

In the seventh inning, I ask the cameraman if he has enough footage because we want to move over to our other seats. He makes a call and then tells us they have enough. We shake hands and thank him. The four of us have just enough time to get a round of beers. Chad breaks out a $50 and treats. We move to the section directly next to the Yankee's bullpen.

In the bottom of the eighth, Mariano Rivera begins to stretch and throw lightly. The crowd starts to gather and there is a huge buzz. Austin Romine is the bullpen catcher. After hearing his name being called over and over with an Australian accent, he turns and flips Chad Mo's warm-up ball. Chad has now gotten a ball in three straight games.

The crowd is smaller than usual, but it is great

that Mo is doing this one at home. "Enter Sandman," the Metallica anthem, begins blaring, and Mo trots out on his way to history.

Thirteen pitches later there is a new all-time saves leader with 602.

We cheer, jump around, and exchange high fives with anyone in reach. Chad is so pumped that he can hardly speak. The Breeze is as cool as ever. Mike screams like someone who has just won the lottery.

To me, memories are as valuable as anything. Games 150-152 put an exclamation point at the end of a great season. Many times during my six-month journey I felt alone and wondered if I was a little crazy for attending all 162 games. I am now more elated than ever for following the fulfillment of a dream. I think back to Dr. Tom's advice, "People often regret things they never do, but rarely regret things that they do." So true. No regrets.

I am living the dream.

Tuesday, September 20

I am just pulling into the Bronx on the Grand Concourse. Tara texts,

I'm looking at you on the big screen.

I don't know what that means, but I come to find out that the video is complete and they are playing it during batting practice. Wow, more than I ever dreamed! I quickly forego all of my pre-game rituals and head right into the stadium. I walk through the gates and I think I hear a father say to his son, "There he is, the 162 Guy."

I turn, but am not sure if it was my imagination.

Another fan stops me and asks me if I was the one going to all the games. I nod and smile. I keep moving. I make my way over to see Greg standing in his usual place in front of 134.

"There he is," he says in his most welcoming voice. "You're a star!" I give him a big high five. "They played a really long video of you on the jumbo screen. I knew I recognized the voice. I'm looking all around and I look up and see this giant likeness of you. We did it!"

With Cedric, one of the great Yankees employees

I enjoy a brief moment with Greg. As I think back over the season, I recognize that Greg has been a huge part of my journey. He supplied a sense of normalcy and congratulated me every day for doing something special. I'll always fondly recall our daily chats as he brightened my day, every day. To me, Greg exemplifies the importance of a great employee. Be friendly to your customers and make them feel important. Especially the really good ones!

I follow my normal path by the Mohegan Sports Bar and up to the bleachers. I see Cedric in his normal spot. He says hello in his Australian accent. We exchange our daily fist pump. We are Facebook friends and he also mentions the interview in Toronto. I keep moving.

"Mr. 162!" yell a group of beer drinkers. I hold up my Yuengling and toast them. I wish Marcinowski were here to witness this. He would be smiling from ear to ear. Even though he is not here to celebrate, he's here in spirit. We will always share a bond of attending 57 games in a row. If it weren't for him, I wouldn't have made it this far.

Chad was kind enough to give me his tickets for tonight and tomorrow. I tried to talk him into staying, but he had to head back home. I get to Section 203 right before Roll Call. They played my video before most of the Creatures piled in, so they are unaware of my new celebrity status. Roll call has now become the favorite part of my day. These are the hard core fans who come every night and leave their problems at home. As usual, I do Roll Call and then move on to my other seats after the first inning.

I make my way to my "broken nose" seats at Yankee Stadium. Section 110, Row 2, Seat 1. With my 162 jersey on, I am easy to recognize. This is all part of the master plan. Fans are constantly coming down to say hello and ask if I'm the 162 Guy. Pretty cool. Eight to go. My mission is 95 percent accomplished.

Wednesday, September 21

Today is the fourth day/night double-header of the year. The Breeze has taken off all day to attend. The Bombers' magic number for making the playoffs is one. The magic number for winning the East is just three. Any Yankee win or Boston loss and we are in the playoffs. Any combination adding up to three and we win the division.

I get another text from Tara.

There are two tickets waiting for you in the press box, 2nd level. BTW We will run your SuperFan video in between games today. I know you'll be here!

Again, I find words difficult to express my
adulation. The Superfan is superjacked! I think back to the
game in Cleveland 2 ½ months earlier where I was dubbed
Superfan. I liked it then and still do.

Game one is over by 4:00 and the stadium is clear
by 4:45. The rain is now coming down pretty heavily.
I want to get back inside ASAP to see the video. I have
one ticket for tonight, but need to get another one for
The Breeze. I think he is having fun. He told me that his
favorite part was watching me scalp tickets. Before the
season, The Breeze and I hung out almost everyday for a
month last September. It was at a time that I really needed
a friend and he was there for me. You never know who and
when the next friend to enter your life will be.

We are meeting Laura and Jill who have a ticket for
me, but won't be here until 6:30. So if we all want to see
the Superfan video, I must buy a ticket for myself as well.
Because the game is an hour-and-a-half away, the scalpers
aren't budging off the $20 ticket price. I try to explain that
I'm the Superfan and they will be playing a video of me
on the jumbotron. The scalpers don't seem to care. I peel
off $40 and we make our way into Yankee Stadium. It's
emptiest I have seen it all year. The more famous that I get,
the more expensive these games become.

The rain is coming down steadily and we make
our way over to Section 134 into our wet seats. We sit just
past the left field wall in the second row. A few minutes
later, with maybe a few dozen people watching, I see Tara
Cannistraci and myself on the big screen. I feel like we are
at a private screening. The video lasts 7:08. The footage
from Monday's game is edited in, as they show action
shots with Mike, Chad, and The Breeze. I look around
the illustrious and famous house that Jeter built. It is sure

lonely, cold, and wet at the top.

The thin crowd doesn't dampen my enthusiasm or how proud I am of my accomplishment.

I think back to the most-asked question I have gotten all year: "Do the

Mike and me on the jumbotron; too bad hardly anyone else was there to see it

Yankees know about you?" Apparently they do. Watching my video on the jumbotron will go down as one of the coolest things I have ever experienced. By the time the Superfan video is over, it is pouring.

We meet Laura and Jill at The Dugout. It becomes clear that this game isn't starting on time.

Accompanied with a Red Sox loss, the Yankees win game two and clinch the American League East.

Saturday, Sept. 24
Yankees FanFest

If you share a good idea long enough, it will fall on the right ears! - Jim Rohn

The game is at 4 p.m. today. WCBS Radio is sponsoring Yankees FanFest at Pier 86, adjacent to the Intrepid Sea, Air, & Space Museum.

I drive in early and pull-up to the West Side Highway at 10:45. There are four former Yankees that will be in attendance signing autographs. Bill "Moose" Skowron, Goose Gossage, Dwight Gooden, and John Flaherty. Flaherty is one of the YES Network play-by-play announcers. With six games to go, my goal is to meet him and get on TV this week.

The weather is overcast and in the 50s. There are thousands of fans in attendance. There are batting cages, games, and rides for the little ones. There is one really huge line for autographs. There is a stage with a band warming up. A man goes up to the mic and introduces himself as Steve Scott, one of the voices of WCBS radio. He introduces the band and walks off stage.

I follow him with my eyes as he goes behind the curtain to a makeshift backstage area. I abandon my place in the autograph line to see if I can make any headway. Scott is talking with someone as I wait until he finishes up. I am now backstage.

"Hi, my name is Steve Melia. I want to introduce myself. I have attended all 156 games this year, home and away."

He looks at me to see if he heard me correctly.

"Wow. Steve Scott, CBS Radio."

"The Yankees picked up on my story and did a seven-minute video that they have on their website. Here's my card. I wanted to see if you guys wanted to interview me this week as I finish up all 162."

"Let me run this by my producers. Thanks for saying hello." He seems like he processed it. He was really listening and not just blowing me off.

I leave the backstage area and walk around the event. I hand out several more cards and introduce myself to anyone who looks official.

I still have plenty time before the start of game 157.

All year I have been hearing about The MLB FanCave.
The idea of the Cave is to have two guys in the middle of
Manhattan watch every MLB game and tweet about it.
They will have watched more than 2,500 games by the end
of the year. Their cave is set up like a living room and the
ultimate bachelor's pad. Their mission is OK, I guess. They
have MLB behind them doing all of the promotion and are
getting paid $250,000 for the season. They must be there 12
hours a day.

I feel like I need to go and see it. Tara Cannistraci
had given me a number of someone at MLB who could
introduce me to them, but it is a Saturday and they don't
answer. I am attending all 162 Yankees games at my own
expense and am doing all of the promotion by myself.
They have also been doing a ton of cool things with players
stopping by all of the time. I think it would be cool to have
the 162 Guy in the Cave.

I drive over. I try to get their attention, as I can see
them inside. There are no tours today and I'm sure that I
look like every other fan walking around outside trying to
get their attention.

They have a camera set up so you can get a free
souvenir picture at the cave. I get my picture taken and
decide to move on with the day.

My media blitz continues and I am starting to
generate interest. I get a Facebook response from my friend,
Hailey Winslow, who is a reporter in Jacksonville, FL, at
WJXT. We became friends when she worked for WWAY in
Wilmington. I told her that I'd be in Florida this week.

*Steve, r u coming thru jacksonville? maybe we
could do a story on you - u nut. (252) xxx-xxxx.
hope all is well.*

I call Hailey right away. She hints that a morning show appearance might be possible. She doesn't know a lot about baseball, but says that she'll run it by her producers. I hear that a lot.

Sunday, September 25

Friday night's game was rained out and today we will play the last two regular season home games of the year. A lot has happened in the last week. It was one week ago that Tara mentioned that they wanted to interview me today live at Yankee Stadium. I can't remember anyone ever being interviewed live at the stadium during a game. With everything going on, we haven't revisited the conversation.

Tara has done a lot for me this week and I don't want to push my luck. I sit at the kitchen table with Tom, Lucy, Mary, and Burger whom are visiting. Burger is going to game one of the double-header.

I email Tara asking about the 90-second interview. I am very nervous. On the way into the city, I hear back from her. We are a go for the final game which starts at 6:30 p.m. Gulp. As Burger and I drive into the city, he has a bright idea that I should spend my 90 seconds doing comedy, since I am a comedian. Interesting thought. I am not 100 percent committed to it being a good idea, but we spend the drive in preparing a "top five" list. Ten would take too long for the 90-second spot.

Top five signs that you have been to
159 games this year

5. *I no longer think $12 is unreasonable to pay for a beer.*

4. I just landed a Preparation H endorsement.

*3. I no longer view the Bleacher Creatures as that
   fanatical.*

*2. I now think that hotdogs and Cracker Jacks are
   two of the major food groups.*

*1. The six-month restraining order against Derek
Jeter is almost up.*

I call Tara and tell her our idea to do some comedy.
She tells me that she will have to run it by her producer.
Hmmm. I think that is her way of saying no. The Yankees
have a different plan. We will go live after the third out in
the third inning.
She will ask me
three questions.
1) What
inspired you?
2) What was
your favorite
moment of the
year? 3) Will
you be going to
Tampa for the
final three?

Three Steves; with Burger and Slug

We meet
Slug at The Dugout for game one. Both Burger and Slug
have only planned on staying for the first game. I try to talk
both of them into staying. My sister, Mary, is picking up
Burger as soon as game one ends. Slug talks his wife Tina
into letting him stay for game two.

Slug and I meet my friend Marisa Hansell at The
Dugout. Marisa is a good friend and we have been through
a lot together. I'm glad she is here for the final home game.

I do my best to avoid beer and stay as sober as possible for game two. Slug offers to take me out to dinner. We opt for the convenience of the Court Deli. Have I mentioned that I am really nervous?

For Boston, this game means everything. A win will put them a game up. A loss would even them with Tampa. For Girardi and his Yanks, the playoffs start Friday.

I have witnessed many wild games between these two and tonight is near the top of the list.

The Yanks draw first blood in the bottom of the first. With two men on, Tex rockets one that hits the top of the wall and bounces back into play. He goes to third on the throw home and scores on Jason Varitek's overthrow back to third. Yanks up 3-0. I am counting the outs until my big moment.

I am sitting in Section 203, Row 12, in back of four Red Sox fans. Tara Cannistraci is on my left and my friends are on her left. Tara has been here for an inning and we have practiced three times. She is very reassuring. The cameraman is ready and waiting in the aisle. Tara warns the Boston fans that if they get any bright ideas, they will be going home early tonight.

The Yankees are sending up Cano, Tex, and Swish. *Please make this a very long inning!*

Cano lifts a lazy ball into center on just the second pitch. Texeira has a lengthy at bat as he sees eight pitches and earns a walk. Swisher comes to the plate. On Nick's second pitch, he hits a hard grounder to Pedroia, who tosses it to Scutaro, who fires it to Gonzales for the second and third outs. It's a close play and many fans are booing the call.

Tara springs into action. "Okay, Stand up. This is it."

The bleacher creatures are loudly protesting the call at first base. Tara and I are live on the jumbotron.

Tara: (talking over the fans): "Hi Yankees fans. This is Tara Cannistraci. With me is a Yankees fan who has attended every New York Yankees game this season, home, and away. Tonight is his 159th game of the year."

The Yankees fans begin to cheer and many are giving me a standing ovation. I touch my heart and begin to pound it as the fans continue to acknowledge my accomplishment.

Steve: "Thank you. It has been incredible to watch the greatest sports franchise in history play every day. Even more incredible was to watch them alongside the greatest fans in the world, Yankees fans."

The fans to continue to cheer and applaud. I look up to see myself on the big screen and let the feeling soak in. The Yankees are on the field and are looking up to watch.

Tara: "What inspired you to do something so fanatical?"

Steve: "I first got the idea seeing Bald Vinny on the Ultimate Yankee Fan a few years ago and I just decided to go for it. It has been amazing."

Tara: "You have been able to witness some amazing moments in Yankees history this year. What has been your favorite?"

Steve: "There have been so many. The best part has been coming to the ballpark everyday.

I'd have to say the best was July 9th watching The Captain have an incredible afternoon hitting numbers 3,000, 3,001, 3,002, and 3,003."

The fans cheer louder with every number that I mention.

Tara: "So, will you be able to make it to Tampa to close out all 162?"

Steve: "Absolutely. I have my plane ticket for tomorrow morning. Ready to go!"

Tara: "Congratulations!"

Bald Vinny is the first to come over and give me a fist pump. I look back and see Vincent smiling and cheering. Slug and I leave our seats for my first beer of the game. As we walk up the aisle, I receive many congrats from my fellow fans. My 15 minutes of fame is here and I'm savoring every minute of it.

I keep going back in my mind to September 1st in the Boston Renaissance talking to Mark Michaud: "It blows my mind that the Yankees haven't acknowledged you."

Tara texts me.

John Sterling just talked about our interview on the radio.

John Sterling and Susan Waldman

John Sterling: *They just interviewed a fan, Susan can attest, they interviewed a fan, a young man, a nice looking young gentlemen, who has been to 159 Yankees games this year, including this one. Every game. How he can afford it, I don't know. How he can get to all of these places, I don't know.*
Susan Waldman: *Airplanes, cars, hotels.*
John Sterling: *Carl Crawford takes a strike. Tara Cannistraci interviewed him and her final question was, "Well, will we see you in Tampa tomorrow? Here's the 0-1. It's grounded foul. "Can we expect to see you in Tampa tomorrow?" "Oh of course,"*

He laughs. It's gonna take all I have in my body to get to Tampa. (laughs.)
Susan Waldman *(Laughs): Well, isn't it a little expensive?*
John Sterling *: I would think that it would be very expensive.*
Susan Waldman: *Airplanes aren't cheap ... You used to get a shuttle from New York to Boston for $12. It's not $12 anymore. (Laughs)*
John Sterling: *No, no. And then hotels, rental cars, etc., etc., Anyway, that guy's gotta be congratulated, gee.*

Game two ends five hours and 11 minutes after it began in a grueling 14-inning slugfest that ended up in a Boston victory. Slug and I are already moving as we want to beat the fans out of the stadium. We say a quick goodbye as he heads for the subway back to Connecticut.

I reach for my keys and realize that I gave them to Slug hours ago to hold for me.

Gulp.

My flight leaves in a few hours. I call his cell and get no answer. I try again and again and again as I make my way to the subway. Fans are saying hi to me, but I am laser focused on getting my keys. Finally, he answers. A few minutes later I see his smiling face and he hands me my keys. Catastrophe averted. 159 down and three to go. Chump change.

Monday, September 26

I have a 7:29 a.m. flight from JFK to Tampa. I am in line and I notice that Brian Capozzi has just checked in on

Facebook at JFK. He is on his honeymoon. I text him and we agree to meet.

A few minutes later I'm standing with Brian and his glowing bride. They were just married over the weekend and are on the way to Puerto Rico. Brian is the one who introduced me to Bald Vinny. He is super excited about his honeymoon and his trip to Puerto Rico. I made it this far by feeding off of the energy of other fans. I'll always be grateful to Brian and others like him who made the 162 Tour so enjoyable.

Once we touch down in Tampa, I splurge and upgrade to a convertible. I cruise over to the beach in St. Petersburg with the top down. I pull into the Thunderbird Motel and get a call back from Hailey Winslow from WJXT. They are interested in talking to me about doing the morning show on Thursday morning. It will be a stretch driving the five hours over to Jacksonville.

I spend the day at the beach soaking in the rays. By the time game time approaches, it is raining like crazy as I make my way to Tropicana Stadium. It is pouring so hard that I forego any pre-game festivities. I pull into the stadium lot and ask, "How much?"

The lady, covered head-to-toe in rain gear, quickly waves me through. "Just come in and park."

You would never see that in New York.

All the fans are staying in their cars. I sit in my rental for a few minutes and can't take it anymore. I go for it. I step into the monsoon and begin my fast jog in. It is like I am running in quicksand. The closer I get to the entrance, the deeper the water gets. It goes from being ankle deep to knee level. I am still 50 yards away and it feels like one of those reports you see on CNN when people are evacuating their homes. I finally make it through and my sneakers and jeans are drenched up to my waist.

I laugh at myself as I unfold my dry ticket and enter game 160. Only the diehards are out tonight.

Nevertheless, I endure. Two to go!

Tuesday, September 27

I am on the road to visit my dad. Mike really wanted to be here for the series but couldn't leave his side. It has been nine weeks since I last made this drive.

I put the dial on ESPN. It isn't long before I am on hold waiting to speak. Dan Sileo is the host of the 6-9 a.m. shift.

"Steve you're on air."

"Thanks, Dan. I have been listening to the show about the games last night. I'm a Yankees fan and I have been to all 160 games this year.

"You have been live to every game?"

"Yes, I have."

"Are you rich or something?"

"I do OK. I have a business that I can work from the road."

"Wow, every fan's dream. What did you want to say?"

"There is a lot of talk about who the Yankees want to play and how hard they are trying. Priority one is to make sure that everyone is healthy. Priority two is to make sure that everyone is fresh and ready to play Friday night. The Yankees aren't scared to play anyone. I personally want to beat Boston in front of the world. It is such an intense rivalry. I'd love to play them in the ALCS."

"Well it certainly is getting exciting. Have fun at the game tonight."

By 9:30, I am halfway across the state, but still picking up 620 WDAE. Ron and Ian are on the air now. They are talking about how few people showed up for the game last night. I dial back in.

"Hey fellas. I am the guy going to all 162 Yankee games. I called in back in July."

"How's it going? I remember you."

"It's been a blast. The weather was insane last night. I'm sure that there will be a bigger crowd tonight."

"So this trip must have cost you a fortune?"

"Not as much as you'd think. I have been on a strict budget."

"I know what it costs to go to one game. I usually spend a few hundred dollars. I'd venture to say you spent well over $100,000."

Ian then speaks up, "No, way more. I would guess $250,000 with all of the travel."

I laugh.

"You are both way off. I haven't added everything up, but I'm guessing between 50 and 60K."

"No way."

We go back and forth about the trip and they are very engaging. A few minutes later, the hater calls start coming in.

"I've been listening to the station all morning. That blowhard Yankees fan has called in twice. Who cares? Is it that hard to root for a team that buys their championships?"

Another caller: "Tell that Yankee fan to go back to New York. This show is supposed to be about the Rays. I'm tired of these fans coming down here."

Ron stands up for me. "I think it's neat that the guy went to every game. He worked hard and this is what he wants to do. What's the problem?"

Another caller chimes in. "The problem is that he has to call in and brag about it. I hate the Yankees. Anyone can win with that payroll."

It is amazing, but they just keep calling in. I definitely generated some conversation. Part of me is mad and defensive, while my marketing side realizes this is great publicity!

I arrive in Sebastian just before 11 a.m. I pull into the local Publix grocery store. Publix is where I had my first job as a bag boy more than 25 years ago. I am in the Deli line ordering a sandwich when my phone buzzes. The girl looks annoyed as I step back. It is a 212 area code.

"Steve Melia."

"Steve, it's Steve Scott from CBS radio. How was the game last night?"

"It was great, thanks!"

"Listen, I spoke with my producers and we'd like to interview you."

A huge smile comes across my face.

"Just so you know, we checked you out. We can't just take the word of everyone we meet at FanFest. It seems like you have a great story to tell."

He asks me a few logistical questions and we agree to the interview tomorrow at 11 a.m.

"We could do it right now," he says, "but I'm superstitious. I want to make sure that we do it on the day of 162. So what are your plans for today, enjoying the beach?"

I tell him about my dad and that one of the interesting things about the journey has been that life doesn't stop.

He is very empathetic and doesn't rush me off of the phone. We say goodbye and agree to talk tomorrow.

I now have *Newsday and* CBS radio tomorrow. Strong! I gather my sandwich from the deli and make my way to the checkout as I hear an all-too-familiar voice.

My brother Mike is in line scanning his items. I go over and put my sandwich with his items. He pays for it and we walk out together. I share my great news with him. Mike is happy to see me as he has been going stir crazy. He has barely left the house over the last few weeks. The visitors have all gone home and he has been waiting it out mostly by himself. Mike is coming back from his daily excursion to the gym. It is the only hour of the day he gets away.

My dad is lying in bed and is down to skin and bones. He gives me a big smile, as he didn't know that I was coming. Mike feels it is better to surprise him than to disappoint him. He is barely eating or drinking anything.

I sit in his room and talk to him for a few. He is very tired and has a hard time staying awake. It is very sobering being here. He isn't able to get up by himself and Mike has taken on all of the caregiver responsibilities. Every time my dad needs anything, he asks for Mike. They are as close as any two people I've ever seen. Mike and I have both created freedom in our lives. I chose to attend 162 games in a season. Mike chose to spend my dad's last months, days, and now minutes by his side. My older brother is my dad's hero now and the rest of family probably concurs.

Shortly before 2 p.m., I say goodbye to my 87-year-old father. I know that I'll be back soon. I just don't know how soon. I get back in my convertible and head back to St. Petersburg. I am very grateful that I am able to see him and equally grateful that he got to see me finish out the season.

I am definitely taking a chance being four hours away from a game that starts in five hours. I have no wiggle room. I pick up my friend, Virginia, from the Tampa airport just after 6 p.m. She has flown down for the last two games. She really encouraged the tour back in February and wants to be here for the celebration.

I walk in and scan my ticket. I'm down to one, baby!

Tonight is a lot like last night. The Tampa fans are getting excited and there is a playoff feel all around the city.

The fans are living and dying with every pitch in such a close race. It is fun to watch the energy and to enjoy the game without having a negative reaction. Normally I would be freaking out. Tonight, I can sit back and enjoy an incredible Wild Card race. Tampa holds on and wins 5-3. Boston barely holds on, nipping the Orioles 8-7. Boston and Tampa remain tied with one to go.

Wednesday, September 28

Game 162!

I am up early. Well, if you consider 9 a.m. early. I grab a cup of coffee and take a quick walk on the beach. I go over the season in my head. Two comics down to one guy. I haven't done a set since July in Toronto. The movie is temporarily out of the equation.

With everything said and done I am happy and proud of myself. I am also eternally grateful for all of my friends and fans who helped along the way. There is a certain satisfaction to accomplishing something that many said would never happen. I am grateful to myself for sticking it out.

At 10 a.m. sharp, my phone rings. It's Neil Best from *Newsday*. We proceed to chat for the next 20-plus minutes. Neil is a great interviewer and seems truly interested in the story and what makes me tick. I am used to the normal questions and he adds in a few as well. I thoroughly enjoy the experience.

At 11 a.m., Steve Scott from WCBS calls.

"How's your dad doing?" was the first thing he asked me. Wow, even though we only spoke for a few minutes yesterday, I believe that we connected. I find him to be a true gentlemen. Steve tells me that they plan on airing the interview during drive time today.

At 2:07 p.m., my story hits the wire. The interview plays during drive time for millions of New Yorkers.

> *NEW YORK (WCBS 880) - Imagine going to every Yankees game this season. Not just home games. Home and away. All 162 of them!*
>
> *Steve Melia has done just that. Melia is in Florida today, for the Yankees' 162nd and final regular season game, and he's seen each and every one of them.*
>
> *Melia says he decided this past spring to try to make it to every game.*
>
> *"I've worked real hard," he told WCBS 880's Steve Scott. "I'm 41 years old. I've had a business since I was 24. I just felt like if I didn't do it now, I'd probably never do it."*
>
> *He says he laid out the whole schedule at the beginning of the year, deciding which games he would drive to and which ones would require a plane ticket.*
>
> *Then, there are rain-outs and makeup games.*
>
> *"Logistically, it was kind of a nightmare," he says. "I didn't get any special deals from the*

airlines or hotels."

Surprisingly, he says he never really came close to missing a game. He missed just one flight, in California, and that was on an off-day, so he was able to re-schedule without missing a game.

His favorite road city? Boston, just for the atmosphere.

His least favorite road city? Wrigley Field in Chicago – not so much the stadium, he says, but the fans.

"They were very unruly," he says.

And, his favorite moment of the season? July 9th – the day Derek Jeter went 5-for-5 and hit a home run for his 3,000th career hit.

So, how much has all this cost him? Melia says people have guessed anywhere from $100,000 to $250,000.

But, he says it's actually lower than that, closer to $60,000.

"I've been on a budget," he says. "I never paid for parking. I pack a lot of sandwiches and bring bottles of water into the stadium."

Will he follow the Yankees into the post-season?

"Absolutely," he says. "I looked at how much money I had left for the trip. You know, it's a great story ... but, I think it'll be an even better if the Yankees can go all the way and win the World Series. That's what I'm hoping for, and that's what I'm betting on."

Steve Melia has documented his season-long odyssey on his website – 162yankeegames.com.

I am trying to get outside and get some sun, but WJXT wants to do a pre-interview for the show Friday morning. I spend 20 minutes on the phone with the producer. I go out to the pool and at least get my vitamin D for the day. When I get back, the story has broken. It is being Tweeted all over the place. Every sports website is re-posting the story. It all happened just like that.

Would the story have broken if I didn't push it? I doubt it. Serendipitous account; I met Tara. Tara and the Yankees produce video. I meet Steve Scott. Steve likes story and puts it on CBS radio. I also made the *Newsday* story that will hit tomorrow happen by emailing Neil Best all year.

I am having a party at 4 p.m. at Ferns. I have a few people from out of town meeting me for game 162. My college roommate, TJ Vranicar, called me a week ago and invited me into his company's suite tonight. He said I can bring anyone I want. Free game tickets and all-we-can-eat and drink. Sounds like a great way to close it out.

Mike's friend, Mollie, is town for the party as well and offers to be designated driver for the night. We arrive at Fern's Sports bar across the street from Tropicana Field. There are a lot of people I wish were here. Mike, Kim, and even Marcinowski, just to name a few.

It was a long journey. Barring any major catastrophes I am home free. No fights, no arrests, no anything. Behave and walk through that gate.

My friends begin to arrive. Paul Strazzula is a buddy from high school. He's happy to be there and celebrate and he's ready to have a good time. Gary Coccaro is there, too. He's Mike's buddy from high school and he's been to a bunch of games with us over the years. He and his friends buy me a beer. My good friend Chip Humphrey is there with his college-aged son, David.

It is great hanging out in the gorgeous weather, and the drinks certainly are flowing. But there is a baseball game to see. I hand off the

Enjoying Game 162 with high school buddy Paul Strazzula

video camera as we get closer. There is no way for this not to be anti-climatic. Six months of living out of a suitcase and being a complete lunatic comes down to a simple ticket scan. I've had 33 flights, spent 53 nights in hotels, slept in 23 different people's houses, logged 40,000 miles traveling to 15 cities. Whew!

My friends cheer as I explain to the non-interested ticket scanner that I just broke a world record for attending all 162 games in one season.

BEEP, BEEP. The laser scans the bar code on my ticket and history is made. I am in. I did it. Let the celebration begin!

My new world record is spreading around the suite and I am becoming quite the minor celebrity.

This is the first time I've seen my roommate TJ since college and he appears to be doing well. Thanks to him and his company, I'm able to celebrate 162 in style. My fan club shows their appreciation to TJ by eating and drinking everything in site.

The last place Orioles are playing the Red Sox and strike back with a two-run blast by JJ Hardy to give the Rays fans a little life. 2-1 Orioles. Our suite has two televisions. We watch both games at the same time.

In the top of the fourth, Boston ties the game on a balk, making it 2-2. They grab the lead in the top of the fifth on a Dustin Pedroia home run.

In our game, the Yanks add solo runs in the fourth and fifth and now lead 7-0. The Yanks use seven pitchers to record seven shutout innings. I am doing my best to stay humble and not rub it in to the Rays fans at all. I am making my way around the suite and congratulating them on a good season and a heroic attempt at a comeback. So close.

I begin to dream about a New York/Boston ALCS. Tickets will be expensive, but it will be great for the book.

I am not sure how many Rays fans left early, but I'm sure they will regret it for a very long time. With the Yankees leading 7-0 in the middle of the 8th, the improbable happens. Johnny Damon singles. Ben Zobrist doubles. Casey Kotchman walks to load the bases. This is when things start to get crazy. Luis Ayala is the ninth Yankees pitcher and he comes in to walk Sam Fuld and force in the Rays first run. He then hits Sean Rodriguez, sending home another run. BJ Upton hits a deep sacrifice fly scoring Kotchman. Yankees 7-3. Hmmm.

The fans are not only coming alive, but they think they're going to win. Evan Longoria steps in. He only needs one pitch, a 91 mph fastball, that lands in the left field stands for his 30th of the season, sending the crowd into complete hysteria.

Yankees 7-6.

With the other game on a rain delay, everyone is on edge. My entourage and I leave the suite and head for closer seats. We want to feel the energy as much as possible. We get to some seats behind the Yankees dugout for the bottom of the ninth.

Cory Wade comes in to pitch. He retires the first two batters on eight pitches as the Rays dream of a comeback begins to quickly fade. Joe Madden pinch hits Dan Johnson. Johnson only has one home run all year. The Sox, Orioles, and the entire baseball world watch as he becomes an unlikely hero drilling a 2-2 change-up just inside the right field foul pole.

The game is incredibly tied 7-7. What an amazing comeback. Scott Proctor comes in to record the final out and game 162 is going into extra innings.

Meanwhile, everyone in the stadium is keeping an eye on the Red Sox/Orioles game at Camden Yards. In the bottom of the 9th, Red Sox closer Jonathon Papelbon enters the game. He is a deadly 77-0 when leading after eight innings. But no one seemed to tell that to the last place Orioles. He strikes out Adam Jones and Mark Reynolds easily, for what looks like a sure thing. Rays fans are whispering updates from their smartphones, before the scoreboard can catch up.

Chris Davis doubles on his first pitch. Nolan Reimold hits a ground-rule double to tie the game. Robert Andino is up next. He rips one to left that Crawford has a chance to catch but hits off of his glove and drops in to score the winning run. Baltimore wins it 4-3. The Red Sox blow the game and perhaps the biggest September lead in playoff history. They'll only have to wait moments to find out their post-season fate, pending what happens here tonight.

Back here, with the game tied in extra innings, Evan Longoria steps in with one out. Knowing that the Orioles had just won, Longoria launches a 3-2 pitch just over the left field wall. With one swing, he sends his team to the playoffs and the Red Sox home licking their wounds. Final score: Tampa 8, Yankees 7.

Though the Yanks didn't win, this was the perfect ending to 162 games. I was happy to be part of such a gutsy Rays comeback and such a monumental Red Sox collapse.

But on a personal level, this night didn't merely belong to the Yankees and the Devil Rays. It belonged to a kid who had an impossible dream and the support structure to see it come to pass.

Chapter Sixteen

THE DASH

Thursday, Sept. 29

We did it! I almost can't believe it. The whole thing seems surreal to me.

I am so thankful to everyone who has been a part of my incredible odyssey. The goal was simple. I really wanted to attend every game in one year. I had been talking myself in and out of it for several years. This year I talked myself into it and never looked back.

My friends and family were so supportive and so congratulatory after the fact.

> *Thanks again Melia. That night will go down as one*
> *of the best night's of my life.*
> *Paul Strazzula.*

I received many, many congratulatory messages from as far away as Scott in Scotland to Chad in Australia. I Googled myself right before I left and I made it onto the Red Sox website. They actually wrote a story about me. Take that, Mark Michaud! I can hear his New England accent: "The Yankees haven't acknowledged you? Seriously?!"

I guess the best revenge is winning. The Red Sox completed the worst collapse in Major League Baseball history. A 9 ½ game lead. I remember back to something said on the Boston Sports Radio show: "These game are hard to watch, because they do not really matter."

They all mattered. Every one. All 162.

And now, the publicity that eluded me for so long over the past six months is suddenly upon me like an avalanche! At a little before 1:30, I see that I have a message on my phone. It's a 212 area code. New York City, baby!

"Steve, It's Peter Vicini with Fox's Good Day New York."

Oh my gosh! I quickly circle around and try to control my breathing.

"We want to see about getting you on the show tomorrow, in one fashion or the other." He leaves his email and number. "Nice talking to you, Steve," He signs off.

I can't believe it. I listen three more times. I over-analyze it. "In one form or the other?" There is no way I can make it. Can I do it Saturday? Can I fly in after the Jacksonville show? Maybe I can Skype in. Maybe I can do it Monday and then fly to Detroit.

I call him and continue to remind myself: Stay calm and embrace the moment.

"Peter, it's Steve Melia."

"Hey Steve, congratulations on doing all of the games. We'd like to have you on the show tomorrow. Where are you now?"

"I'm still in Florida. I am booked to do a morning show in Jacksonville tomorrow. What time is the show?"

"We go from 7-9 a.m." That rules out flying back for both.

"Maybe I can call in or Skype in?"

He hesitates before responding. "We could do something like that. Probably not as effective, though." His enthusiasm is wavering.

"Peter, I'm new to this. Your show is a much bigger deal. What is the etiquette if I already told the other guys yes?"

"That's up to you. Your decision."

"How did you hear about me?"

"You are in the papers, bud. Your story is hot."

Yes! My story is hot! My biggest fear is that I would do this and no one would care. *Your story is hot* keeps running through my head.

I briefly run through my options. "Peter, how about I call you back in a little bit. At the very least I can Skype in from Florida."

I hang up. I do not think it at the time, but, indeed, this is a great problem to have! Two morning shows want me live on the first day of the playoffs! I dial my brother Mike for some quick advice. I run him through my choices.

"Are you kidding me? Get back to New York! This is what you've been working for." The call lasts less than two minutes, but the advice I'll remember forever.

I call WJXT with my tail between my legs. I speak candidly with John and explain the situation to him. I lay it all out on the line and I apologize profusely. Amazingly, he understands and is gracious enough to allow me to call into the show tomorrow instead of being there live. I call Peter back in New York and tell him I'll be there.

Problem solved! Peter tells me I can Skype into Florida and do the WJXT interview from the Green

Room. I am only an hour outside of the Orlando airport. I call JetBlue and, for the third time this week, change my flight. I tell the customer service rep that I am writing a book about my travels and would hate to include all of the JetBlue fees in my book. Maybe she could help me out. I'm not sure what happened, but this one only cost me $50. Sometimes blackmail works!

Kim is flying in for the playoffs. I was going to pick her up tomorrow in New Jersey and now she has to make alternate plans. Burger is in town and agrees to pick her up from the airport. I invite them both to meet me at the Fox studio in the morning.

Friday, September 30
As You Sow, So Shall You Reap

My alarm goes off, but I am already awake and have hardly slept. I'm way too excited.

I wear my 162 jersey and bring my glove on set. I asked Tommy if I should wear my glove and he said, "No way!" I ignore his advice and bring it anyway. This is a fun story, so I should have fun, right?

When I first started doing stand up, Kim, who went to every show, would always say, "When you make it to Letterman, I'm getting into the Green Room." She and Burger are definitely on my A-list no matter what. They have both been a huge part of my life and the 162 journey.

I make it to Fox and set up my laptop in the lobby. Within a few minutes, my entourage arrives. It is great to have them there. Celebrating victories is so much sweeter with your loved ones around. We are moved to the Green Room and I set up my laptop for my Skype interview.

At 7:15 I am on with WJXT doing a run-through.

Kim and Burger are checking out the digs.

We are moved to hair and makeup. There is a wall leading from the Green Room to the set that is signed by many of the guests throughout the years. I find a Sharpie and add a little note from the 162 Guy.

The three of us are escorted onto the set. Straight ahead are Greg Kelly and Heather Nauert. Greg flashes a huge smile and waves at the sight of us. We sit and fraternize with a producer about 40 feet from the dynamic duo. To our left is the couch where the interview will take place. I'm glad I did the WJXT piece first because I am totally warmed up.

It would be hard to throw me a question that I'm not ready for. They have given me an outline of the interview, but I am too excited to read it. It is hard to decipher and my attention span is way too short. I am doing my best to soak up and enjoy the experience.

I have this thing that I do, that I always think someone or something is going to surprise me. I suppose it's like a defense mechanism, so I won't look silly. For instance, every time I get off of a flight, I quickly scan the crowd to see if someone is going to yell out "Surprise!" I have been doing this on my birthday for years.

The one I am watching out for today is a special surprise appearance by the Yankees Captain, Derek Jeter. As I am being ushered around the studio, I am secretly looking for signs of #2. I sort of figure that there is no way since the playoffs start tonight. I certainly wouldn't want to be the reason that Jeter is tired.

In my mind though, the possibility exists.

I'm sitting on the couch between the two hosts.

"So who's your favorite Yankee?"

"That's tough. I love em all. If I could only pick one, it's The Captain."

"We understand that you have had a goal to meet him this season. Have you had a chance to meet him or hang out with him on the road?"

I begin to answer. "We run in different circles. I usually stay in ... "

With that, from behind a curtain, wearing a beautiful pin-striped suit, is the man himself. Derek Jeter. He flashes a big smile and you can't wipe mine off. He comes over to the couch and sits right next to me.

Greg Kelly: "What do you think about your biggest fan?"

DJ: "To me, it's all about the fans. Steve has done something very special. It's a long season. Heck, I didn't even go to every game this year."

We all laugh.

He pulls out an envelope from his left breast pocket. "On behalf of the Yankees, we'd like to invite you to come visit us in the clubhouse before the game. We'd also like you to sit next to Giuliani tonight. Here's four tickets. Have fun."

Back to reality.

The producer taps me, "OK, let's get you to the couch."

It is a commercial break as I get moved to the couch. Greg and Heather make their way over and I stand to greet them. I introduce Burger and Kim. I specifically introduce Kim as my ex-wife hoping that it will steer any questions away from that subject. Greg is wearing a beautifully tailored pin-striped suit and Heather is wearing an attractive red dress. They both sit to my right. Greg quickly scans the outline and sees enough to get the gist. They are both very welcoming and make me feel comfortable. They seem as excited as me.

We get the 10 second cue from the producer. We have cameras and monitors set up right in front of us. Here we go.

Greg: Most people like going to a baseball game every now and then. There are some die-hards that are lucky enough to have season tickets, maybe. Our next guest did something incredible, however. He went to every single Yankees game this season, home games, and away games, 162 of them. This video, is I believe, he is packing his car for his incredible odyssey. The guy who did this…

Heather: Are you kidding?

Greg: His name is Steve Melia. He is 41 years old. He's from North Carolina. He's on our couch right now to tell us why you did this incredible thing. Welcome, sir.

Steve: Thank you, thanks.

Heather: Steve, you are originally from Long Island.

Steve: I am.

Heather: Obviously, a huge Yankees fan. Your car there looks like you are packing up to go of to college. Really? 162 games, how did you do this?

Steve: You know what, I saw the schedule at the beginning of the year. I've had this desire for about three years. Every year I say that I'm going to do it. I knew that I wasn't getting any younger and just physically if I ever was going to do make it, I knew that I had to do it now.

Greg: Lots of people have the desire, but the ability

to do this, this cost serious money and time ... your job ... what do you do?"

Steve: I have a business called LegalShield. I am an independent associate. It's like a franchise. I have a couple of partners that have given me the liberty to take a few months off. It's just been great.

Greg: My goodness gracious. Where do we start? OK, how much did this all cost?

Steve: I haven't added everything up, but it's in the 50-60K range.

Heather: That's just in expenses. Not including the money you lost by not working.

Steve: Right, that's just for what it costs in airfare, hotels, tickets, gas, rental cars.

Greg: Was it worth it?

Steve: Absolutely. It was so much fun. I tell you, the best part about it was everyday I'd go to the ballpark whether I'm on the transit or driving, the adrenaline rush, I get it still everyday.

They have been flashing pictures and video of the trip on the screen.

Heather: Tell us about some of the pictures that we are seeing. We just saw a picture of you and Joe Girardi.

Steve: Yep, this picture is some friends from Cincinnati.

Greg: So the Yankees knew about this crazy guy who's stalking the team.

Steve: There is a fine line between stalking and just being a fan. So I'm not sure what they thought of it. I met Girardi once, he thought that it was pretty cool.

Heather: So, what are you doing along the way? Are you staying in hotels? Are you calling up strangers saying, "Hey, can I crash on your couch?"

Steve: [laughs] I have a pretty good social network from the business that I am involved in. When you really break it down, it's not that difficult. You are looking at 14 cities. And then you start asking, "Do I have friends in Toronto? Do I have friends in Seattle?" I spent 51 nights in hotels. I stayed in 23 different people's houses. I caught 33 flights.

Greg: Did you catch any foul balls?

Steve: I did. I got 12 all together. Two live balls and 10 batting practice and such.

Greg: [Laughing at my last answer] You're single right? You're are a bachelor?

Whoa, I wasn't expecting that question. It certainly wasn't on the script. I begin to nod my head as I think what to say.

Steve: Yes.

I say it very hesitantly and for some reason everyone is laughing.

Greg: OK, 'cause otherwise … Didn't you have a buddy that bailed out at one point? What happened?

Steve: Well, he probably would't tell it that way. He lasted 57 games. He is a comedian and so am I. So the idea was that we would hit stand-up comedy shows in every city. At first, it was working out great. We were doing gigs almost every night. It finally became too much. The tickets were expensive and I'd look over and he'd be playing Scrabble during the game.

Greg: He was bored. [laughing]

Steve: Yeah, he was bored. Bored out of his mind. Which, I don't blame him. So after 57 games, we had a rough trip on the West Coast.

Greg: Whoa, whoa. What made it rough?

Steve: Well, just two guys traveling together, in a

On the Fox set with Kim and Greg Kelly

hotel all of the time.

Greg: This is a movie! This is a movie! We have got to make this into a movie!

Me: I'll play myself if you want. [Everyone is laughing].

Heather: Now, what would you say to the ladies? You're a single guy.

I thought I was prepared for any possible questions.

Heather: What would you say to the ladies if you are going to go out on a date with them and you are trying to explain your fanaticism about baseball?

Steve: Yeah, I don't think that most people would really understand it.

Heather: So, you are resigned to staying a bachelor, then?

I just smile and hope they will change the subject. I feel like Jeter trying to duck relationship questions from Barbara Walters.

Greg: So, you going to the playoffs?

Steve: Absolutely, I can't wait, I'm so jacked for tonight.

Greg: So what about next season? Watch it on TV?

Steve: I don't know. I tried for 30 days to get a sponsors this year. I tried every airline, hotel, beer company. They all said, "Maybe next year, we have our things going for this year." So, if I could get a sponsor or someone would back me, I do it again in a second. I had a blast.

Heather: Well, maybe.

Greg: Steve, you have a website that you'd like to plug?

Steve: Sure. It's 162yankeegames.com.

Greg: 162yankeegames.com. We will put a link on our website. Congratulations, Steve Melia. Unbelievable. This is really cool.

Steve: Thanks, Greg. Thanks, Heather.

Heather: You're living the fantasy that Greg wants to live.

The interview lasted 4:07. They were both awesome and their enthusiasm was contagious.

At the break we all stand up and make our way to Kim and Burger. They both agree that it went really well.

When we hit the street it is just 8:30 a.m. Kim and I walk into a little cafe and grab a spot in the corner and Burger takes off. We immediately start posting pictures on Facebook. My phone is blowing up with people who saw the show. Everyone thought that it was great. Some reference all of the single/bachelor plugs.

One lady is staring at me as she waits in line for coffee. I look up and smile.

"Were you just on TV a few minutes ago?"

"That was him," Kim responds.

My cell notifies me that I have a new email.

> ***From:*** Tellez, Al <<u>atellez@cbs.com</u>>
> ***Subject:*** *Steve please call WCBS TV 212 -xxx-xxxx*
> ***Date:*** *September 30, 2011 9:46:52 AM*
> ***To:*** <u>*melia@162yankeegames.com*</u>

Email reads: "Ask For Al Tellez. We want to do an on-cam interview ..."

That is all I need to see.

"Is Al there?" Things are moving now.

"Where are you? We want to send a crew over ASAP."

I look around the cafe. They are already tired of our act and it is a little crowded in here.

"How about I come to you?" We agree and he hands me over to Chris Scagglione, the producer. We need to make it across town and are deciding whether to leave the car or get in it.

CBS calls again with a change of plans. They think that Yankee Stadium would work better. We agree on 12:30 in front of the Press area. Kim and I jump in the Mustang. The Funnymobile could drive to the stadium by itself!

At 11:40, we are pulling into the best spot I've had all year. As we are making our way to the Court Deli, several New Yorkers recognize me. "Weren't you on TV this morning?" At noon, Kim and I get a table at the Court Deli. She places the orders while I step outside and talk on our team conference call. When I'm done, I hand her the phone and she does the same.

We wolf down our sandwiches and make our way to the stadium. This is Kim's first visit to the Bronx since the 2009 World Series Game Six win. I note several points of interest such as where I buy my water, where Stevie the scalper hangs out, and where Bald Vinny sets up shop. I am getting texts and emails like crazy about the Good Day New York piece. Everybody loved it.

A familiar face walks up to shake my hand. It is Danny Hansbury from Yankees customer service. I stop by and see him occasionally, but haven't seen him in a few months now.

"Hey man," the enthusiastic Yankees employee greets me. "My girlfriend calls me into the living room this morning. 'Do you know this guy? He went to every game!' Congrats on Good Day New York."

"Thanks, it has been wild."

"Are you good for tickets tonight?"

"Yes, we should be. Thank you."

Danny was very nice to me during the season and I'm glad that I had a chance to see him again. It is nice to celebrate with those who made the journey more enjoyable.

By 12:45, the CBS interview is underway. They are going to play this as the lead at 5 p.m. The reporter is just learning my story and attempting to come up with some questions on the spot. A few minutes later, Kim joins me in the shot as he wants to get a shot of us heading into the stadium. We cross the street about 10 times in order to get the right shot. We are with CBS for at least a half hour.

The cameraman is extremely jubilant about my accomplishments. "It's been great to meet you two. Everyday, I get dragged around this city reporting about crime, drugs, and murder. It gets to you after doing this 25 years. It's refreshing to meet someone who did something positive. Someone who is out there living the dream. You are an inspiration."

I am touched. "Thank you. I just hope that the Yankees can win the World Series. It will make this a better story."

"You did your thing," he argues. "Nothing else needs to happen. You should be proud of yourself for seeing it through."

We say goodbye and I walk away reinvigorated.

Kim is not only a good sport, but is helping me stay focused and grounded. I am thrilled she is here to see all of this. She and Mike made a lot of sacrifices for me to be able to do this all year.

We leave the Mustang in its rockstar parking spot on River and head for the subway.

At 2:30, we meet my niece, Dani, on the street and walk into a sushi place for a late lunch.

"Uncle Steve, your interview was awesome."

"You ask your boss who the crazy one is now!"

"He still thinks you're crazy."

Kim and Dani are very tight and I'm glad they can stay that way. I have agreed to meet my brother, Danny, at Cafe 31 Sports Bar and Grill. I really want to see the CBS piece at 5 p.m. The game doesn't start tonight until 8:20.

We grab a taxi and get dropped off. There is a group of Yankees fans gathered at the bar.

One of my brother's long time friends, Kevin Egan, is meeting us. I can hear them talking about me and my brother Danny. I haven't seen Kevin since my brother's wedding more than 25 years ago. I go up to the alpha male of the group.

"Kevin Egan?"

"Hey. It's Dan's little brother." He signals to all of his friends. "This is the guy I've been telling you about."

I get introduced all around and do the same with Kim and Dani. A few minutes, later Hyper Dan arrives. Even though he is really a Mets fan, he's excited to be going to the playoffs. Kevin and his business partner are buying drinks for everyone and the word is spreading about the 162 Guy.

A group of guys come over. "Hey, we overheard your conversation, congrats."

"I heard John Sterling talking about you the other night."

"Really? That's cool." I hadn't heard the broadcast, so I ask him a bunch of questions.

It is getting lose to 5 p.m. and Kevin arranges to have all of the TVs put on CBS and the volume turned up.

A few seconds after 5:00, my face is on the largest regional news program in the world, CBS New York. The bar is going wild at seeing my face. Everyone quiets down to hear the TV. When it is over everyone cheers. This is fun.

I have a message on my phone. It is a photographer from *Newsday*. We are scheduled to meet in front of the Press Office at 7 p.m. I meet the photographer and we begin to set up a few shots. As he is snapping picture after picture, I notice Kim talking to a guy with a pad. She is pointing at me and I hear her say "That's his 162 jersey." After a few minutes, the photographer says that he has enough and we shake hands and say goodbye.

Kim and her new friend are waiting.

"This is the guy that you want to interview. Steve, meet Mike Feeney from *The Daily News*.

"You've really have been to every game?"

"All 162."

I hand him my card.

He begins to fire off questions. "What do you do for a living? Where are you from? What inspired you? What was your biggest obstacle. Are you worried about any other teams beating the Yankees?"

I probably would be a lot further along if Kim had been with me all year. He has my cell number and says he might want to meet up during the game for a picture.

It is so crowded in the Stadium that it is almost not fun. People are pushing their way through crowds and the beer lines are outrageous. Danny is great to sit with as he is introducing me to everyone in the area.

"Do you recognize this guy? He's the 162 Guy. He's been all over the TV today. He's been to every game!"

I always kid him about being cheap, but he is no cheapskate when it comes to buying beer at a game that he gets into for free.

The grounds crew runs on the field as the players retreat to the clubhouse. The all-too-familiar tarp is put on the field. The four of us make our way to the third level which has a bar that is outside and inside. Mike Feeney, *The Daily News* reporter texts me.

We like your story for tomorrow. Can we meet to get a picture?

We make our way through the crowd and snap some photos. The game is postponed.

Saturday, October 1

I go out and buy a *New York Daily News*. I start in the back with Sports section. Terry Francona was fired as the Red Sox manager. Wow. I don't see my story anywhere. Oh, well.

A few hours later I am casually reading the *The Daily News* beginning now with the front page. When I open it, page 3 catches my eye.

"Fanatic at Game 163 of '11 Season." Good gravy! The well-written article delves into all the specifics about my story. In other news, a high ranking Al-Qaeda terrorist was killed … and that was on page 5!

I'm on fire now!

One thing that I kept bragging about during the interviews is that I made it the entire season without paying for parking, getting a parking ticket, or having my car broken into. New Yorkers seem to be most impressed by the free parking in the Bronx.

We walk outside of Luke's on 7th Ave. and 15th Street only to find that I have indeed jinxed myself. I receive my first parking ticket of the year. At least it was after the regular season ended!

Kim changes her flight until Monday to go to tomorrow's ALDS Game 2 with me. She gets to see firsthand the constant logistical nightmares I've been experiencing since March.

Monday, October 3

I am off to Motown with the series tied at one game apiece. Rebecca East is picking me up at the airport. Marcinowski would sure appreciate the ride. I share with her the story of how we wound up on the bus last time. She picks a place for lunch and we sit at the bar. I inform her that I still need a ticket for tonight. With all the excitement last week, I was hoping that the Yankees might reward me with some postseason tickets. They did not.

Shortly after 1 p.m., I post on Facebook that I am looking for a single for tonight's game.

Within three minutes, I get a message from Scott Osborne, my Scottish friend, asking me if I can get to a printer. I'm not sure what he is thinking, but I like the sound of it. A few minutes later, Scott emails a seat in the section behind the Yankees Dugout. "I hope that the seat is good enough," he writes. I can almost hear his accent. I am blown away by his generosity. Sometimes when you know things will work out, you just go with them.

I think back to early May and the wild night with Scott, Marcinowski, Rebecca, Danielle, and Rudy. Thank God Scott survived the trunk incident!

Rebecca drops me off at the Greektown Casino. I'm glad to not be staying at the St. Regis, which brings back bad memories. I forego my daily nap, drop my stuff off, and head for the casino. I am instantly down $100 playing Blackjack.

I move over to the craps table. A tall well-dressed gentleman is throwing the dice. I don't look at him and within minutes I have my $100 back. For superstitious reasons, I never lift my head. I just keep putting up my bets and collecting the money. His roll would last 30 minutes. He is rolling dice like Mariano throws the cutter. When the roller finally throws a seven and craps out, I look up and finally see his face. I thank him as I push my chips to the banker, "Nice roll, buddy." I am up $576, which is enough to pay for my airfare and hotel.

I head out to the game where the Yanks get shut

down by Justin Verlander, and for literally the first time all year I am contemplating what I'll do next. I am one loss away from going home. 165 down, hopefully a lot more to go.

Tuesday, October 4

I sleep in late and do not feel like getting out of bed. I tune into the local radio station, 97.1, The Ticket. It's just past noon and game four is tonight at 7:30. They are talking about the series non-stop. I call in.

> **Steve**: *"Hey, man. I wanted to call in and tell you guys what I'm doing. I have been to all 165 New York Yankees games ..."*
> He cuts me off.
> **97.1**: *"We don't care. Maybe they do in New York, but we don't. Did you want to say something on air?"*
> **Steve**: *"Well, many stations in the away cities have interviewed me. I've been on Good Day New York, CBS Evening News ..."*
> He cuts me off again.
> **97.1**: *"We are not interested. If there is something specific you want to say, fine. Do you?*
> I find him very rude, and my desire to beat the Tigers just grew tremendously. My blood is boiling.
> **Steve**: *"Never mind!"*

I hang up. I must admit that I am pissed. I decide to forget about the media and go downstairs and gamble instead. My phone rings. It's Shawn with the Grand Rapids Fox affiliate, Fox 17. He wants to know if I am available to be interviewed for the evening news.

Game on. I'm back!

Shawn was having lunch at Hockeytown and Rebecca told him about the 162 Tour. He had already read my story a few days before online. She gave him my number and the story stays alive. I go from feeling depressed to feeling alive again. I didn't come all this way to let a rude radio station producer rain on my parade.

I do the interview in front of Tiger Stadium, and make my way into the game. I am very nervous all day as this is the first elimination game of 2011. If the Yanks lose tonight, the season is over. What will I be doing tomorrow? I haven't thought ahead that far. I don't want to jinx anything, so I try not to think about it. We must win.

Thankfully, on this night, the Yankees agree with me as they deliver a punishing blow to the Tigers the entire game and pound out six additional insurance runs in the eighth for a decisive 10-1 victory. Looks like I'm going back to Yankee Stadium.

Thursday, October 6

I am going to this one alone and sitting with the Bleacher Creatures. I go to the Sunrise Mall and get only my third haircut since leaving North Carolina. The stylist keeps talking of her son and how he paints his hair for his high school sporting events.

"Can you make mine Yankee blue?" I ask. I suppose I am trying to live up to being a fanatic. Within ten minutes, I walk out of the Sunrise Mall looking like Marge Simpson.

There is nothing more nerve racking than an elimination game. This is the second time in 167 games that I could be going home early. I drive to the Bronx. If we win, I'm heading to Dallas. I haven't contemplated losing. I try not to think about it.

I keep my streak alive as I pull into an open spot on the Grand Concourse. The bars are way too crowded. I walk by the Media gate looking to tell my story. My 15 minutes of fame is ticking away and I better take advantage of it while I can.

And just as quickly as it began, the entire season came down to a one-run game. As the final out is recorded, the Tigers meet at the mound and commence their celebration. The Tigers are moving on to play the Rangers in the ALCS.

I am stunned, saddened, and feeling a huge sense of loss. I'm not quite in tears, but I'm really close. I walk briskly to my Mustang. My head is spinning.

My thoughts go to my dad. I'll leave New York tomorrow. I am Florida bound.

Friday, October 7

I spend the morning doing laundry and cleaning out my room at Tommy's. I also finish cleaning out Marcinowski's stuff. He has a garbage bag full of clothes. He will be happy to get back his winter jacket.

I call my brother Mike and he is relieved that I'm coming to visit him and my dad.

"I don't know how much longer I can be here by myself," he confides.

As if the disappointment of the end of the season isn't enough, I'm also lost in thought thinking about Kim. We would have celebrated our tenth wedding anniversary today.

I remember reading about the lunar astronauts

and what a letdown it was for them when they returned to Earth. I feel lonely and depressed and wonder if it was all worth it. Even though I know that it was, I'm just indulging in my little pity party.

Melia, Pity Party for one.

Saturday, October 8

My Mustang pulls into my dad's driveway. Mike and my dad both look like they have aged years since I've last seen them. I'm sure they would say the same thing about me.

The next few days consist of a lot of sitting around and waiting. My dad hasn't even had a glass of water since I've been here last. I sit in his recliner as he is drifting in and out of consciousness. He has the AMC Channel on and is watching a Henry Fonda movie. This isn't normally something I would watch, but I know that every moment I spend in that room is precious. He occasionally makes a noise to let me know that he is still watching.

I thank him for fighting to make it the entire season, so I could see him again. He mumbles that I better keep my end of the bargain and finish my book. I tell him that I will keep my promise.

Thursday, October 20

Tommy and Lucy arrive in Florida for Dad's final days. He hasn't eaten in weeks. He stopped drinking coffee and water as well. According to the folks at hospice, he is just about ready. Eileen and Jim have been coming over every day after school as well. We spend most of the time telling stories and playing cards. Once in a while, Dad would call something out that turns out to be mostly a hallucination. He was asking my mom where his watch was.

It is really great to spend time with my brothers and sisters. It's because of my parents' consistency and their 56 years together that we have remained so close.

My dad is down to the end, and although he is down to literally skin and bones, there isn't a place on Earth that I would rather be.

Saturday, October 22
7 a.m.

My brother Mike is making all sorts of noise. I am on the roll-away bed in the spare bedroom. He is even talking to himself. Because I was out late the night before, he probably didn't even know I was home.

As he walks by my room, I call out to him. He is startled. He jumps and blurts out, "Dad's dead."

I had been laying in bed for a while and definitely had that feeling. I sit up. He apologies for being so blunt and reiterates that he thought no one was home.

I slowly move into my father's room to say my final goodbye. My dad had used all of his final strength to sit up in the bed like he was trying to get up. So his final resting position was laying on the width of the bed.

Like he was being called home.

I thank him for being such a great dad and for lasting the entire season. I tell him that I will live up to my end of the promise and write and publish my book and that I will sell a million copies.

We begin to call my brothers and sisters. Tommy and Lucy are the first to arrive. Jim shows up next. Eileen comes after him. Everyone is in the same mood; somber, but happy that Dad isn't in pain anymore.

Just like I did six years prior with mom, I call my sister, Mary, to let her know that Dad is in a better place. I also call Danny and he says that he'll be on the next plane. The hospice folks arrive within 30 minutes as does the coroner. We are in a haze as we make plans for his funeral and wake.

I once read a quote about life. It said that it's not the dates that matter; it's the dash between the dates. The dash is everything you did in your life and the impact you had on people. Over the next few days, I am continually reminded that my dad had quite a dash. He created an amazing family and an indelible legacy that will live on.

Thanks, Dad. I'll always love you.

Daniel F Melia RIP 8/25/1924 - 10/22/2011

EPILOGUE

Thursday, November 17

 I walk into Nutt Street Comedy for the first time since March. I spot Steve Marcinowski across the bar with his circle of comics. It is awkward, but I make my way over and say hello.

 Over the next few months we begin to get along again. His comedy career seems to be in full swing and I learn that Home Depot took him back with a cut in pay. We occasionally bring up a 162 story. I'll always appreciate him and his willingness to drop everything and help me live my dream. I know that he will be one of the funniest comics in America. I hope that we can travel the world together making people laugh someday.

Thursday, April 5, 2012
St. Petersburg, FL

 With my streak still alive at 167 straight games, I attend Opening Day of the 2012 season. Mike and my friend Jennifer Bickford accompany me to "The Trop." Later that night, I do a comedy gig at Treasure Island.

 I watch the Bombers get swept in Tampa and fly to Baltimore for three more with the Bradshaws.

Friday, April 13, 2012
Game 174 - Yankees home opener

I arrive in Da Bronx without a ticket, but very little stress. Scalpers are saying $150 is their cheapest ticket. It takes me a while, but I pick one up for $100. I walk over to The Dugout and it takes me 10 minutes to make it to the bar. I run into a guy looking for a ticket. I tell him that I just got one for $100, but it took some work.

He holds up $150. I can't break my own rules. If I can save or make money easily, take the deal. I do. I'm up $50 for the day.

I work my way back to the stadium and see a couple with a child holding their tickets with a look of confusion.

"You guys need help?"

"We are wondering if our daughter needs a ticket."

She's at least 7.

"She does need one."

I notice that they have a fourth ticket with a $40 face value, which I quickly offer to take off their hands.

I am up $10 and I'm getting into the home opener for free! At least I learned some things last season.

The now retired Jorge Posada is throwing out the first pitch, so I make my way into my 174th consecutive game.

Sunday, April 15
Game 176

Thanks to Danny Hansbury in Customer Service, Tommy, Shane, and I are guests of The New York Yankees. My LegalShield convention begins on Thursday so today will be my last game. The steak ends today. As far as I know, no fan has attended 176 consecutive games. I did the extra nine so someone would really have to go out of their way to break my record.

Thursday, April 19th, 2012

It is 18 years to do the day that Mike and I sat in his 1982 Pontiac. We are at the first annual International Convention with LegalShield. We are at our leadership dinner in OKC. It feels good to be back. Rip Mason has the microphone. I am sitting at the head table with Mike, Kim, President Alan Fearnley, and the partners of Mid-Ocean Advisors.

Rip is announcing his new Executive Advisory Board.

"It is with great pleasure that I introduce the first woman to serve in this capacity with your company. She is also the first Canadian to serve on our board. Ladies and gentlemen, Kim Melia."

With tears in my eyes, I join the 1,000 top leaders in LegalShield in a standing ovation. Kim has come a long way from growing up on welfare in British Columbia. We continue to be best friends. We wanted to be an example that you could stay close with someone that you were once married to. I continue to be her biggest fan.

Thursday, December 20, 2012
Loose Ends

— A few months back, Jeff Olson and I had a falling out of sorts in Fort Lauderdale. Emotions ran high, alcohol was in the mix, and regretful words were said. That was the last time I ever saw him. Because he is such a good friend, I'll always wonder if he purposely didn't try very hard to recruit us because he knew that we were better off staying with LegalShield.

Jeff Olson has had an amazingly positive impact on my life which, in turn, has affected the lives of so many. As I finish this book and reflect, one of the things that I already miss is his friendship, leadership, and big heart. I wish we could have stayed together. I don't blame him for a minute. I'll always cherish our friendship and look forward to the day that we can reconnect.

Although our last night was filled with mean-spirited words, it doesn't change how my family will always be grateful to him. His philosophy and the best-selling *The Slight Edge* are a gift to the universe.

— Derek Jeter and I have yet to become friends.

— My comedy career is moving along. I am now featuring in clubs across North America. In June, 2012, I won my first comedy competition at the Comedy Cabana in Myrtle Beach.

— In 2013, I will tour with the Yankees hitting comedy clubs, promoting *162*, and sharing the LegalShield story. Marcinowski has a standing invitation to join me.

— LegalShield continues to prosper. The Melia Family continues its mission of making equal justice under law a reality.

— The Melia Family continues to promote The Orphan's Hope Project. I am pledging $1,000,000 to our charity through the sale of *162*. I am donating 10 percent of all proceeds from every book in memory of my dad.

Finally, I'm reminded of two profound thoughts: Rush Lyricist Neil Peart once wrote:

> *Some are born to move the world*
> *To live their fantasies*
> *But most of us just dream about*
> *The things we'd like to be*

And American poet Henry David Thoreau reminded us that most people "lead lives of quiet desperation."

Both of those realities make me sad. The truth is, many will go to their graves with a song still in them. The cemeteries are filled with unwritten masterpieces, unfinished paintings, and unrealized dreams.

My path to 162 was paved way before the 2011 season began. It started years earlier when I embarked on the road to personal development. It was nurtured along the way with the people I chose to associate with. And it was fueled by the compounding effect of more good decisions than bad ones.

If anyone is inspired by my story, I hope they'll realize that the human potential, once properly cultivated, is virtually limitless. What's that dream you always had as a kid? What got your heart pumping faster — even if it seemed irrational? For me, it was the crazy idea of attending every single Yankees game in one season. For you, it might be something altogether different.

Stop living some else's life and start living the life you were meant to live. You've only got one shot at this.

Get out there and live your dream!

ACKNOWLEDGMENTS

With A Little Help From My Friends

Mike Melia
Thanks, brother. It has been a fun ride and I couldn't have done it without you. In a world of uncertainty, I've always known that I can count on you and that you've had my back. Thanks for helping me stay true to myself. A special thanks for being there for me and Kim every step of the way. The entire Melia Family will always appreciate the sacrifices you made for Dad.

Kim Melia
Kim, you are one of the most talented and powerful people I know. Thanks for being a huge part of my life and always pushing me to become more. I can't imagine where I'd be without you. I'll always miss what we had and I'll appreciate what we still do have. You are a true giver who makes the world a better place. Thanks for always being so wonderful to Mom and Dad. Thanks for picking up my slack during 162.

Mary Melia and Burger
Thanks, guys, for always being there, no matter what. The two of you have been a huge part of this journey we call life. Thanks for paying my tolls through the entire tour. Mary, thanks for being an incredible friend, sister, and ally. Burger, thanks for being nice to my sister. Thanks for the 162 jersey.

Tom and Lucy Melia
Thanks for a great summer (and late spring and early fall). I'll always fondly remember our daily chats over coffee and the papers. Your generosity and open door sure made the journey easier. I appreciate the daily pep talks, suggestions, and leftovers.

Steve Marcinowski
You are a funny dude! Thanks for having the guts to do something different. I'll always remember you as the 57 Guy, or more formally, Mr. 57. In fact, since you made it through one-third of the season, I am going to give you .33 cents for every book sold. Hopefully this will offset any loss of income you may have experienced with Home Depot. I'll always appreciate and remember fondly our 10 weeks on the road. Please keep telling jokes. You have what it takes to go to the top.

Dan and Maureen Melia, Eileen Melia McElwee, Jim Melia, Matt Dunphy, Shane Melia, Katie Melia, Steve Melia, Dani Melia, Luke and Jeannie, Kim Melia, Jessica Young and the entire family.

Slug and Tina Ferrara, The Breeze, Kurt Thomas, The Dunn Family, Bald Vinny, Tara Cannistraci, Danny, Shawna and Ryder Vulin, and Jim Blakemore.

Chip and Michelle Humphrey, Rob and Charlene Mackenzie, John Busch, and the rest of the LegalShield Family. Thanks to all of you who helped share this experience. Without the support of many of you, this trip couldn't have happened.

Jeff Olson, thank you for your friendship. Our bond goes deeper than any company. Thanks for being there for me and my family.

Evans, Loewenstein, Shimanovsky and Moscardini, LTD and Wagner, Falconer and Judd, LTD.

Timmy Sherrill and Nutt Street Comics and staff, La Jolla Comedy Club, John Tobin and Nick's Comedy Stop, Mark Trinidad.

The New York Yankees players.

Stevie the scalper, Gregory (Section134), Cedric, Danny Hansbury, Alison Njie, Steve Baker, Chantrell Family, Ashley Rice, FDNY, Ben and Lauren Bradshaw (and Nicole and Pablo), Virginia Field, Rich and Rahmi Shulman, Tim Buckley and WWAY staff, Geri Soulierre, Chad Snyder, Scott Osborne, Debbie Terry, Karen St. Sauveur, Brian Capozzi, Jorge and Heidi Tobar, Jay Baker, Ray Last, Mark Hiller, Karen St. Sauvuer, Jen, Kim and Mike Quigley, Bill and Michelle Guyther, Tom and Margaret Marcinowski, Mike and Chris in Toronto, Paul Strazzula, Anne-Marie Hill, Eleanor Hayward, Rauly Williams, Rebecca East, Danielle Cary, Jerry and Sara Wren, Jimmy Koethe, Bob Gold, Julie Eaton, Darryl Campbell, Brian Carruthers, Jose Barros, Karl Bos, Sharla Patrick, Gary Coccaro, Mollie Sherrill, TJ Vranicar, Eric and Laurie Anderson, Tim Boissey, Frank and Theresa Aucoin, Kevin Egan, Julie Stephenson, Sara Ramberg, Michelle Bobo, Al Berger, Nadine Karnowske and Sarah Ptok, Timmer Halligan and Amy Karges, Christine Manchisi, Renee and Amber Olson, Johnny Balestriere,

Michael Wetzel and Corrine Roby, Karen Hewit and Wes Delnea of St. Louis Ribs, Rich Kennedy, Mike Odessa, Mike Fedick, Neil Best, Steve Scott, Mike Feeney, Greg Kelly, Heather Nauert, Louis, Becca and The Dugout gang. Dia Lautenschlager, Steve Maguire, Beth Mountjoy, April Gillespie, Mel Roberson, Mark and Meredith Kopec, Mark and IIvene McDonald, Kevin McDaniels, Julie Hiltsley, Mark Hiller, The Letzter family, Marilyn and Terry Blair, Kim Acosta, Aaron Favs, Brian Mruk, Rachel Wolak, Jill and Laura.

Paul Braoudakis, thanks for pushing me to get this done. I appreciate you pouring your heart and soul into the book! Let's get to one million sold!

Jayce Schmidt for an awesome cover.